Robbing The Grave of Its
Greatness!

8 Steps To Birthing Your Best . .
Right Now!

Dreams

Vision

Change

Purpose

Goals

Potential

Destiny

Time

D0357689

Delatorro L. McNeal II
Foreword by Drs. Randy & Paula White

OTHER EMPOWERING PRODUCTS INCLUDE:

Robbing the Grave of Its Greatness CD
Foreword by Drs. Randy & Paula White
Success Coaching CD Series

From a Hunger to a Craving! Video
LIVE VHS Featuring Les Brown

101 Gems of Greatness Book
Foreword by Les Brown

101 Gems of Greatness CD
Success Coaching Audio Project

Keys to Unlocking Your Greatness CD
Introduction by Willie Jolley
Success Coaching Audio Project

The Five P's of Life
LIVE Audio CD

Does Anybody Have a Heart?
LIVE Christian Audio Project

Verso Page

Robbing the Grave of Its Greatness

Robbing the Grave of Its Greatness

A Noval Idea Publishing Book

A subsidiary of A Noval Idea, Inc.
P.O. Box 27242
Tampa, FL. 33623

ISBN: 0-9721324-5-7
Cover Design: Melanie Steen
Page Design & Typography: Melanie Steen
Editing: N. L. Gill
Photography: David Burgess

PRINTED IN THE UNITED STATES OF AMERICA
SECOND A NOVAL IDEA PUBLISHING: June 2003

This book is available at quantity discounts for bulk purchases. For additional information regarding A Noval Idea, Inc. visit us on the web at
http://www.delmcneal.com or
email us at **info@delmcneal.com,** or
call us at **1-866-GRATNES (1-866-472-8637).**

Dedication Page

*This book is dedicated to the loving memory
of my Great Aunts*

*Sis. Mae Emma Ball - January 18, 2003
&
Sis. Lizzie Mae McCall Wheat - January 19, 2003*

*These two women are no longer with us here on earth,
but are now present with the Lord. Their lives individu-
ally and collectively represent the totality of the spirit
of a Grave Robber. They lived full and died empty!*

*In addition, I would like to dedicate the impact of this
book to the mentors, mates and mentees in my life.*

*Nova T. McNeal
WWIC Family
Olivia B. Fatherly
Michael T. McNeal
Delatorro L. McNeal, Sr.
Donna Hicks Mitchell
Tye Maner
Willie Jolley
Les Brown
The Forbes Family
The Rogers Family
The Bonnett Family
The Rolle Family
The Taylor Family
LaTonya Hicks
Nakreshia Causey*

*Special Thanks to:
Drs. Randy & Paula White
Bishop T.D. Jakes
Dr. Mike Murdock
Dr. Myles Monroe*

Foreword – Drs. Randy and Paula White

In challenging situations, successful leaders help those they lead to accomplish seemingly impossible goals, and incredible levels of productivity. We know first hand how obstacles, struggles, and doubts from others challenged us to overcome, aspire, and passionately pursue our dreams and destinies. It was not so much the pursuit of greatness, but rather the consistent determination to overcome opposition that lead us to a lifestyle of success through a daily routine and principled living that reinforced our foundation in the Word of God.

This life-altering book, Robbing the Grave of Its Greatness, will not only inspire you, challenge you, and give you cutting edge insight, but it will also demonstrate concrete examples that will provoke you to develop a strategic plan for your success. There are a plethora of books about success, but few provide you with tangible, measurable ways to achieve and sustain it. Successful leaders do what unsuccessful leaders fail to do. They risk it all to pay the price to apprehend their dreams. And in so doing, they consistently achieve the impossible. We know what it is to start with nothing but a vision, risk everything, work hard, pray harder, exercise our faith in God and see incredible things happen.

Delatorro is a successful and compelling motivator. In addition, he is a riveting speaker and paradigm-shifting author who will drive you to think beyond the status quo, and dream outside the box. We believe that there are books that have never been written, songs that have never been sung, businesses that have never been established, and relationships that have never been developed. Why? Because some people are not willing to dedicate themselves to the process and risk the threat of failure. Emphatically and unequivocally, we urge you not to be that type of person. Rather, be one who is willing to faith it - until you make it! As you read this powerful book, allow God to rebirth the dreams and desires within you. We recommend that you implement the eight steps to Robbing the Grave of Its Greatness, pursue & apprehend your dreams and, most importantly, NEVER EVER GIVE UP!

Empowered to Prosper and Succeed,

Drs. Randy & Paula White
Senior Pastors of Without Walls International Church
Tampa, FL

Testimonials

"THIS BOOK IS AN ABSOLUTE GOLDMINE! Every page of this book has a nugget of truth and strategy that will equip you for total success. Having spoken for and trained hundreds of thousands of sales and service professionals, **I highly recommend this book to ANY PROFESSIONAL that wants to achieve unlimited levels of greatness. I encourage all meetings planners and conference coordinators to order a copy of this book for each of your attendees.** You will be the star of the conference. Absolutely Amazing!"

Traci Bild – Author of *7 Steps to Successful Selling*
Professional Speaker, Trainer, & Sales Success Coach
Dynamic Performance International Inc.

"Wow! This is an amazing book and I highly recommend that it be read by teenagers and college students. With over 80 separate motivational learning strategies, principles, and paradigms – this book is an **ENCYCLOPEDIA OF EMPOWERMENT** that will lead you toward developing your greatness. Numerous lives will be positively changed because of Delatorro's wisdom and insight shared in this book."

James Malinchak – Author of From *College to the Real World*
Contributing Editor, *Chicken Soup for the College Soul*
Two-time College Speaker of the Year

Testimonials

"**Every person that represents the Body of Christ must get this book!** The wisdom, insight, strategy, quotes, stories, illustrations, life application sections, and paradigms in this book will simply astound you. **As a Pastor, this book empowers me to lead, as a Christian it provides me with the practical "how to" steps that we all need to effectively posses the land that God has already given us.** Delatorro is a Partner to Pastors. He will uplift your congregation and propel them forth to become all that God has already designed them to be. **This book needs to be required reading for your leadership, staff members, congregation, and youth…it is for ours**"

Pastor Dwight Rodgers – Author of *The Not So Silent Thief*
Senior Pastor
Faith Community Worship Center

"Robbing the Grave of Its Greatness has been identified as a **critical high leverage resource tool for any corporate sector** whose goal is to empower its employees through development of one's full potential. **This is a "MUST-HAVE" for every Corporate Training Department in America.** The content of this book will make a **powerful impact on every employee** from the Stock room to the Board room. An invaluable resource indeed!"

Donna Hicks Mitchell - Center Operations Manager
Six-Sigma Black Belt
Ford Financial

Foreword from the Author

Dear Friend,

My purpose in writing this book is very simple. Over the next several chapters and pages, I hope to turn you into a professional thief. I want to empower you with knowledge and ideas that will drive you to commit the most powerful, life-altering positive "crimes" of the century. I want stories to be written about how you were sentenced to success, stoned on significance, hooked on hope, and addicted to achievement. In this book, I want to train you to be a GRAVE ROBBER! I hope to teach you 8 Powerful Steps that, when applied, will surely land you right in the dead center of your destiny. I pray that this book challenges you in ways that you have never been challenged. The material you will find in this book is not regurgitated content from another speaker/author. This material comes straight off the hard drive of my heart - to yours. For years I have been locked up. I am imprisoned by my purpose; which ironically gives me to greatest amount of freedom possible. This page is your warning...MOVE BEYOND IT AT YOUR OWN RISK. Don't start what you can't finish. However, if you don't start nothing, won't be nothing! In this paradigm-shifting book, I hope to give you the tools to snatch back from the grave everything it wants to steal from your life when you die. As Dr. Miles Monroe says, "You should live full and you should die completely empty!" I want to help you do just that. There is more in you, and I want to partner with you to bring it forth!

Delatorro

Certified Professional Grave Robber

Table of Contents

Pay the Toll!
Introduction by Pastor Scott Thomas

Success and *super-achievement* is not an easy or highly sought after path of life. Of course, **many *proclaim* they are striving for the next level, but in reality, few are actually willing to pay the price – *the toll* – to cross "the bridge".** Trapped in a façade-filled world empowered by a self-degrading mindset that elevates income, stock portfolios, and titles over personal growth - these individuals still haven't discovered the greatest investment is that of investing in themselves! *"How does one discover the worth of themselves?"* you ask? Well, this lesson can only be learned if you are willing to **pay the toll** to cross the bridge!

Although possessions and things are wonderful and gratifying, they still don't properly identify the individual who has "crossed the bridge". In fact, true success takes place when one has discovered the hidden treasure lying just beyond their sight. **The difference between *mediocrity* and *greatness*, then, lies in an individual's ability to bridge life's dark abyss of *walking by sight* to now *living by vision*!** There must be a connection of your "present" – *sight* - with your "future" - *vision*. *Sight* makes one man can look at a rundown home and see a trash heap, while *vision* allows another man to see an opportunity for renovation and resale? *Sight* causes one to be stopped by opposition, while *vision* frees another to grow stronger in the opposition! **In other words, many are *blinded* by *sight*, while others are *liberated* by what they *envision*!**

Please understand that crossing this bridge will cost you, because ***everyone must pay the toll!*** Understand that many have started across this bridge, but sadly, failed to see the worth of paying the price of the toll to continue. The path was right, but their ability to envision the worth of "the other side" was limited to what they could and could not see. Yet for others, the mindset is different; "*How can we not continue crossing over?*" The toll is deemed diminutive in comparison with the *vision* that lies ahead. The sacrifice of *not* acquiring what awaits them on the other side will always be greater than the price of the toll. In effect, the toll-price that you are now unwilling to pay to cross over into greatness, is the price that will own you for the rest of your life! **Pay the Toll!**

With all of this in mind, one of the greatest opportunities afforded to you in life is to hear from and walk beside individuals who have already paid the toll and crossed the bridge for themselves, and Del McNeal, II is one of those men. **Armed with a passion for helping others**, Del won't pay the toll for you, but he will empower your vision for the other side, while driving you towards that tollbooth in your life and career! **Del's insight and ability to discover the unrecognized and hidden treasures inside of others has released entombed dreams, fortifying homes and careers that are built to last.** As you glean from the wisdom locked away in this book, be sure to turn the pages slowly because you just may find a nugget of gold that will pay the toll!

Recognize your individual worth; invest in yourself; leave sight and move to vision; cross the bridge; and when the time comes - please **pay the toll!**

One of the greatest gifts an individual can possess is the ability to recognize the undiscovered worth of people, things, and opportunities that exist around them on a daily basis.

One of my Favorite Poems

The Dash by Linda Ellis

I heard of a reverend who stood to speak at the
funeral of a friend.
He referred to the dates on her tombstone
from the beginning…
to the end.

He noted that first came the date of her birth and spoke of the
following date with tears.
But he said what matters most of all
was the dash between those years.

For that dash represents all the time
that she spent alive on earth.
And now only those who loved her know
what that little line is worth.
For it matters not how much you own;
the cars… the house… the cash.
What matters is how we live and love
and how we spend our dash.

So think about this long and hard.
Are there things you'd like to change?
For you never know how much time is left.
You could be at dash mid-range.

If we could just slow down enough
to consider what's true and real
and always try to understand the way other people feel.
And be less quick to anger, and show appreciation more
and love those people in our lives
like we've never loved before.
If we treat each other with respect and
more often wear a smile…
Remembering that this special dash might
only last a little while.

So when your eulogy is being read with
your life's actions to rehash,
Would you be proud with the things they say
About how you spent your dash?

Chapter 1

Creating & Sustaining Positive Change!

Creating & Sustaining Positive Change

Robbing the grave of its goodness is free. However, robbing the grave of its greatness will cost you something. The real question is, *Are you ready to pay the price?* The grave will give you the good of life free, easy, and with little effort. However, if you really want to take possession of the true Greatness that you were divinely granted, that is going to cost you something. And when I say "pay the price", please understand that I am not talking about money. I love the way that astute businessman and Pastor, Bishop T.D. Jakes, puts it, "Money is the easiest thing that life will ever ask you for!"

What does that mean? The reality is my friend, that it's rather easy to write the check, pay the cash, swipe the card, or authorize the transaction to give up a dollar, $5, $10, $20, $100, $500, or even $1000 - if we have the funds in the bank. Money changes hands so quickly in our society that we are used to having money and letting it go, investing it, or spending it. So that process of exchanging money for some product or service or future investment is a normal one, which is easy to accomplish.

"Money is the easiest thing that life will ever ask you for!"

However, the reason I agree with Bishop T.D. Jakes is that I have seen this true not only in my life, but also in the lives of countless successful men and women of today, yesterday, and tomorrow.

Delatorro L. McNeal II

Creating & Sustaining Positive Change

It's easy to put $50 towards a book project. It's much harder to invest early morning time writing the book before you go to work.

It's easy to put $100 towards graphic design services. It's much harder to build your self-esteem to the point where you like yourself.

It's easy to put $500 towards a CD project. It's much harder to search your soul, your failures, and your successes for nuggets of truth that will inspire and motivate people to positive action.

It's easy to put $1000 towards a new laptop. It's much harder getting up the day after you get laid off (going from $50,000 to nothing) and crying your way to the computer (that you don't know how you're going to pay off because now you don't have a job) and mustering up the strength and faith to begin writing your life's story on the prayer that someone will buy it and be changed because of it.

It's easy to pay someone to design a nice website. It's much harder to put 150% of yourself on the line for your dream. My friend, it will cost you something – this thing called greatness. And please understand that when I am talking about greatness, I am not talking about fame. **Because everyone that's famous is not great. And everyone that's great is not famous!** I believe that by the time you finish this book, you will

Creating & Sustaining Positive Change

have earned your Master's Degree in P.G.R.T (Professional Grave Robbing Techniques). You will be armed with knowledge, equipped with skills, and empowered to take consistent daily action to rob your gravesite of the greatness that it wants to hold back from your life.

You deserve the abundant life. I hope that this book is a simple, profound, and paradigm-shifting reminder of just how BAD you really are! Go for it!

Everyone that's famous is not great. And everyone that's great is not famous!

WHAT DO YOU WANT YOUR TOMBSTONE TO SAY?

Michael Patton is a good speaker friend of mine from the Bahamas. He uses an analogy that I really like about the grave. He says, *"Many people's tombstones will read - Here lies Jane Doe, who wished she woulda, shoulda, coulda..."*

After reading this book, and applying its principles, I want you to replace what they were going to write on your tombstone.

Replace it with: "Here lies Jane Doe, who has *BEEN THERE, AND DONE THAT!"*

Delatorro L. McNeal II

Creating & Sustaining Positive Change

Think about your epitaph right now! Here is mine -

Here lies Delatorro L. McNeal, II –
who lived **FULL and died COMPLETELY EMPTY!**

Here lies Delatorro L. McNeal, II –
who has **BEEN THERE and DONE THAT!**

HERE LIES JANE
DOE, WHO HAS
BEEN THERE,
AND DONE
THAT!"

Man of God...Been there, Done that!
Loving Husband...Been there, Done that!
Edifying Father...Been there, Done that!
Victorious Son...Been there, Done that!
Passionate Brother...Been there, Done that!
Best-Selling Author...Been there, Done that!
Life-Changing Speaker...Been there, Done that!
Faithful Church Member...Been there, Done that!
College Graduate...Been there, Done that!
Philanthropist...Been there, Done that!
Millionaire...Been there, Done that!
Humble Servant of Mankind...Been there, Done that!
Dream Builder & Goal Maintainer...
Been there, Done that!
Legacy Leaver...Been there, Done that!

Delatorro L. McNeal II

Creating & Sustaining Positive Change

What about you? How will your tombstone read? Let's create it right now. I showed you mine, now it's your turn!

Here lies _____

who has lived _____ and died_____

Here lies _____who has _____

and_____ .

1. _____…been there, done that!

2. _____…been there, done that!

3. _____…been there, done that!

4. _____…been there, done that!

5 _____…been there, done that!

6. _____…been there, done that!

7. _____…been there, done that!

8. _____…been there, done that!

9 _____…been there, done that!

10. _____…been there, done that!

Delatorro L. McNeal II

Creating & Sustaining Positive Change

Quick Question!

If you were to die today, what goals, dreams, aspirations, visions, and desires would die with you?

1. _____

2. _____

3. _____

4. _____

5 _____

6. _____

7. _____

8. _____

My friend, the things that you listed above are the reasons why I wrote this book. Just for you. Yes, you! I stayed up late, cried, got up early in the morning, sacrificed Friday night movies, prayed, focused, and sowed tremendous seed so that you, yes you, my friend would begin to literally SNATCH YOUR GREATNESS from the grave that is trying daily to hold on to your STUFF!

NOW IS YOUR TIME. Get these things listed above OUT OF YOU and get started TODAY! Keep reading!

Creating & Sustaining Positive Change

LET'S TALK ABOUT CHANGE!

Why do most of us wear shorts and t-shirts in the summer? Why do most of us wear leather jackets, gloves, and heavy clothing in the winter?

Do you wear shorts and t-shirts when it's 10 degrees outside?

Probably not, right? And why? Because you change your clothes based on the weather you are about to encounter.

Well, we must look at **'positive change'** in the same vain. We must learn how to change with the seasons of life. And when it's your season, you better be ready and equipped with the right attire to be successful.

Why let the year change, yet you stay the same?
Why let the times change, yet you stay the same?
Why let the technology change, yet you stay the same?
Why let others around you change, yet you stay the same?

Two reasons!

There are two areas of your personality that require two different responses to change. **I call them liquids and solids.**

Delatorro L. McNeal II

Creating & Sustaining Positive Change

Liquids – These are aspects of your personality that can and should change with the ages and stages of life. These are components of "the self" that can increase or decrease based on your attitude and your decisions in life. Liquids are things like your attitude, your decision-making processes, your manners, your perception of things, your viewpoint on life, your judgments, and your opinions. As you can tell, these are all elements of your personality that can easily be altered based upon life experience, personal trial, organizational affiliation, peer pressure, groupthink, spiritual belief, and a host of other factors. For example, when you are younger in years, you tend to think that you have all the answers to life. After messing up a few good times, you quickly learn that wisdom rests in the counsel of many, so hopefully you develop a Master Mind Group of people who support you and believe in your vision.

Solids – These are aspects of your personality that tend to stay the same regardless of your age, stage, socioeconomic level, or degree of success. These are deeply entrenched components of you that make you special, unique, and memorable. These are the qualities about you that most people learn to appreciate in you over time. Ever run into an old

Maintain your solids and adjust your liquids to the point where you can make lasting positive change a solid in your life.

friend at the mall, grocery store, or gas station? I mean someone you have not seen in years? After your initial reunion, as you talk to them and they talk to you, you realize that even though 5, 10, maybe 15 years have passed by – certain things about that person have not changed. **Yes, my friend, you found a solid!** For some, it might be their amazingly sincere eye contact. For others, it may be their laugh and comical demeanor. While for others, it just may be the compassion of their voice. Whatever that thing is that makes you say, **"That's the same ole "whoever" that I remember!"** – these traits represent a solid in that person's life that never changed.

Solids are very refreshing. They allow you to be confident in someone or something regardless of the vicissitudes of life.

The hurtful thing is when you encounter someone that had a very positive solid, but for some reason they have allowed life, or success, or failure to turn their positive solid into a negative one, or even worse, turn their positive solid into a liquid. For example, you had a friend who was always really sweet, caring, and understanding. In grade school, high school, and even college you all were great friends because of the solids that you latched onto many years back. Well, now, that person has a 6-figure salary in Corporate America and acts like they don't have the time to be bothered with you. You feel crushed because this person

Creating & Sustaining Positive Change

allowed the winds of change that blew positively to negatively impact their personality. This happens all the time, so you must be very careful to select your associates with wisdom.

Name 5 of your solids here:

1. ....

2. ....

3. ....

4. ....

5. _____

Name 5 of your liquids here:

1. ....

2. ....

3. ....

4. ....

5. _____

The goal of this chapter is to get you to identify your solids and liquids. Maintain your solids and adjust your liquids to the point where you can make lasting positive change a solid in your life.

Creating & Sustaining Positive Change

As you are reading this book, you are reading for a specific reason. If we look at it in terms of an automobile and the maintenance needed for its successful upkeep, we can derive the reasons why you are reading this book and the impact that it will most likely have on your life.

If you are reading this book, you will probably fall into one of these six categories:

1. Gasoline Tank Refill – This means that you are already a highly motivated, driven, determined, and passionate person. You already know your purpose and potential in life, and you simply are reading this to get your super octane dose of new motivational techniques that will empower you to continue on your journey. If that's you, I celebrate you and encourage you to keep going and keep changing lives! I know this book will be a tool to help you do just that.

2. Oil Change – This means that you too, are a highly motivated person. However you need some new paradigms, new ideas, and new perspectives that will allow your daily affairs to operate more smoothly. This type of motivation will allow your interactions to be more efficient and your actions to be more effective. The book is loaded with paradigm-shifting concepts and principles to help you in the areas of productivity and proficiency.

Creating & Sustaining Positive Change

3. New Battery – This means that you need a new passion for life. Some areas of your life may be going well. However, without the passion, you find yourself running low on energy, sincerity, creativity, and enthusiasm for what you do. You have lost some of the heart and soul behind what you do, and you want to get that spark back. I celebrate you for taking the step to invest in yourself and I challenge you to allow this material to replace your existing battery. Allow these chapters to give you the jump-start that you need to get back on the road of greatness, and moving with momentum towards your destiny.

4. Engine Treatment – This means that you need a brand new attitude. Your thoughts, your motives, your self-esteem, self-confidence, and self-worth are in question. Once these areas have failed in your life, it's all over. **However, there is great hope today.** As you think, so you are. Therefore if we are really going to change your life, we must change your mind. We have to replace your engine with a new one. By the time you finish this book, you have a V8 Engine powerful enough to launch you into peak performance!

5. Brake Work – This means that there are certain things in your life that you need to break off of your life. For some, it may be breaking away from negative relationships. For others, it may be breaking negative habits that rob you of your most valuable asset – your time. For yet others, it may be breaking

Creating & Sustaining Positive Change

procrastination, or breaking negative thoughts, negative paradigms, or negative spirits that have attached themselves to your life. Whatever it is, I pray that this book will be the catalyst to break these hindering spirits that have been trying to keep you from living your dreams. I celebrate you and I look forward to these chapters breaking many things over your life, and allowing you to soar to new heights.

6. New Automobile – Now if you say that all of the above apply to you, then we may just need to close the book and go look for a brand new vehicle for you! Your entire life needs an overhaul. Your actions, your attitude, your purpose, your potential, your goals, and dreams **are hinged on you doing something different and becoming someone different in the process.** I celebrate you today for taking the first step and I partner with you today for investing in yourself and confronting and identifying that now is your time and season for REAL CHANGE! Let's do it together…don't give up on me, because I **will not** give up on you!

Regardless of your reason for getting this book, and regardless of your age or stage in life right now, the awesome thing is that the common thread among all the reasons why you and I are here on the same page is that you want positive change. I want to help facilitate that process in your life. It requires a six-letter word that most people don't like to experience. However, it is necessary for us to REALLY go to the next level.

Creating & Sustaining Positive Change

Yes, I am referring to C.H.A.N.G.E. I want this book to challenge you to change. Whether in a big way or a small way, positive change must be mandatory in your life.

As the old saying goes, *"If you always do what you always did, you will always get what you always got!"* The definition of insanity is doing the same thing over and over again and expecting a different result. It's time for real CHANGE! Will you spare some? **Goodness is free, but Greatness will cost you! Not nickels and dimes, but paradigms and habits!**

The Story of The Old Howling Dog

There was a woman who was jogging one morning. Off in the distance she noticed a house, on the front porch of the house was an old man rocking in a rocking chair next to a dog that was making a loud howling sound. As she got closer and closer to the house, the howling sound of the dog got louder, even though it did not seem to bother the old man. She jogged up to the house, and passed the house to the continual agonizing sounds of the howling dog. After passing the house by about 25 yards, she stopped in her tracks and turned around to run back to the house to discover why the dog was making all that noise. Sweating, tired, and exhausted she stuttered while asking the old man, "Why is your dog making all of

Creating & Sustaining Positive Change

that noise?" The old man replied, "Well ma'am, you see he is laying down on a nail!" With a perplexed look on her face, she asked, "Well why doesn't the dumb dog just get up and go lay somewhere else?" The old man immediately stopped rocking in his

I want this book to challenge you to change. Whether in a big way or a small way, positive change must be mandatory in your life.

chair, pulled the toothpick out of his mouth, and looked the woman in the eyes and said, **"Well ma'am, it's obvious that it must not hurt him bad enough!"**

And how many of us are in the same boat? We have some thing, some issue, some challenge, some struggle, some problem in our lives that is poking us, **and it hurts us bad enough to complain about it, but it does not hurt us bad enough to CHANGE about it!**

My friend, it's time that you get up! It's time that you get sick and tired of being sick and tired and begin taking small but very assertive steps to removing this challenge from your life. Your goals, dreams, and aspirations are on the line. And the reality is that the very fact that you are facing major obstacles is PROOF of the fact that you have a DREAM worth fighting for - **A DREAM worth some degree of opposition**. It's A DREAM that needs to be challenged, because when it comes to fruition, it will impact countless lives! You are bad to the bone! Your challenges know your future,

Creating & Sustaining Positive Change

and believe in the power of your future.
SO SHOULD YOU!

Allow me to help you understand a few very important things about this thing called CHANGE, the role it plays in your life, and the best techniques that you can utilize to give birth to continual greatness.

TRUE CHANGE TAKES PLACE AT 2 SPEEDS:

Revolutionary – instant, quick, and fast change. It is like microwave speed change.

Evolutionary – slow, gradual, routine/process driven change. It is like conventional oven speed change.

Understanding the speeds of change is very important because it will keep you from getting frustrated with processes that take varying amounts of time based upon which type of change is actually taking place. For example, many people give up on weight loss programs prematurely because they believe that the program will bring them revolutionary results, when in fact, true and consistent weight loss is a rather **evolutionary process.**

Know the end from the beginning and you will stay empowered through the process.

Delatorro L. McNeal II

Creating & Sustaining Positive Change

Once you know which type of change is being made, and the rate at which you can expect it, you become much more powerful and as a result-**less stressed.** Know the end from the beginning and you will stay empowered through the process! Don't forget to continue to tell yourself throughout the process this all-important concept, "IT'S WORTH IT!" You must affirm that everyday!

TRUE CHANGE TAKES PLACE IN 2 WAYS:

Voluntary – American Heritage defines this as *1."Arising from or acting on one's own free will. 2. Acting, serving, or done willingly and without constraint or expectation of reward."* Basically, it's a change that you control. Examples of this are: grooming yourself each morning, the rate of speed at which you drive, the times when you eat, physically getting up and going to the gym, deliberating working on your book, your business, or that proposal. It's doing things because you want or need to. **This change takes place as a clear-cut result of effort.**

Involuntary – American Heritage defines this type of change as *1. "Acting or done without or against one's will. 2. Not subject to control of the volition."* Basically, involuntary changes are things that you have little to no control over; things like the weather, the seasons changing, getting laid off, being in an unexpected

Creating & Sustaining Positive Change

accident, or coming down with an illness out of the blue. But it is also true on the positive. An example of this would be receiving an unexpected phone call for a great opportunity or being in the right place at the right time!

Now once you can predict in which way the change will take place, you know your level of involvement and/or commitment to the effort. If the change that you desire is a voluntary one, then you know that you are the CEO (Chief Executing Officer) of that change. Examples include losing weight, kicking negative people out of your life, getting out of debt, writing a book, being a better parent, empowering your work teams to perform better, starting a business, or getting a degree of distinction from a college or university. All these changes point to you as the primary person in charge of initiating the change that you want.

On the opposite side of the spectrum, you must know that certain things are out of your control and therefore you are dependent on a higher power once your knowledge and action have run out. That's why Scripture reminds us that "Having done all to stand, stand therefore." Once you have performed to the best of your ability, the rest is up to God. **The effort is up to you, and the outcome is up to God.** For example, it's up to you to put your resume together, post it on the Internet, network with the right people, and interview. Now the final decision, which is made

Creating & Sustaining Positive Change

outside of your presence, is up to God. It's like a powerful tag team approach that gives you so much peace because you can rest knowing that you have done your best.

TRUE CHANGE TAKES PLACE IN 2 FORMS:

You've got to understand that at any point in your life you are moving! **You are always going somewhere.** Now some people may teach that you can be going forward, backwards, or standing still. And the reality is that yes, those are three states that a person can find themselves. However, this philosophy has one major flaw in it. You see, we as humans exist in time. **Time is ALWAYS moving FORWARD.** Time is 100% unforgiving, 100% irretrievable, and 100% priceless in terms of its value when placed in the hands of a destined, powerful, and productive person such as yourself.

You've got to understand that at any point in your life you are moving!

With this understanding, let's examine a new paradigm:

· With time moving forward, and you moving forward, the result is that **you're progressing.**

· With time moving forward, and you moving backwards, the result is that **you're digressing.**

Creating & Sustaining Positive Change

· With time moving forward, and you standing still, while time is still moving forward…you guessed it, you, **would be digressing.**

ALWAYS ENGAGE YOURSELF TO GO FORWARD!

· Once you know that each day you have been given 24 hours, 1440 minutes, and 86,200 seconds of time, you must use it to **think** forward, **study** forward, **act** forward, **network** forward, **email** forward, **transact** forward, **play** forward, **forgive** forward, **converse** forward, **prepare** forward, **pray** forward, and **grow** forward.

Progression – If you are doing any of the things mentioned in the last paragraph, then congratulations my friend because you indeed are moving forward. You are progressive, and you are continuing to grow and develop into all that you have already been designed to be. **A positively motivated attempt to get closer to your destiny is progressive, and I believe that your attempt will ultimately be rewarded.**

Digression – This is the purposeful procrastination, delay, or negative focus that goes into moving against your destiny, goals, and dreams to pursue bad habits which will add days, months, and even years to your learning curve, and add more unnecessary pain to your

Delatorro L. McNeal II

Creating & Sustaining Positive Change

process. **Negative folks, negative habits, too many distractions, wasted time, idle activities, too much TV, and not pursuing continual growth through education and mentors,** can all cause seasons of unneeded digression in

Success is not a Seesaw. Others don't have to go down, in order for you to go up.

your life. Even family and close friends who try to keep you standing still in your present season keep you unfocused on using your gifts to pursue greatness. These people are holding you still. This is digression, my friend. On the flip side of that, it takes 2 people to hold 1 person down, so never hold others back because even though you may succeed at keeping that person immobile, **you are also simultaneously keeping yourself immobile.**

Remember, **Success is not a Seesaw.** Others don't have to go down, in order for you to go up.

KNOWLEDGE IS NOT POWER!
APPLIED KNOWLEDGE IS POWER!

I know that for years you might have been taught that knowledge is power, but knowledge by itself is not power my friend. **It's applied knowledge that equals power.** Let me teach you how.

Creating & Sustaining Positive Change

The following is what I call the **Process of Progression.** Now that we have established that we are deciding to move forward in life and progress, let me show you how it really happens.

New Information – Anything you learn comes to you as new information. Information comes to us in many ways; TV, radio, internet, email, websites, mail, newspapers, word-of-mouth, books, CDs, videos, seminars, sermons, billboards, advertisements, and so forth. Now this information comes into our brains and the brain asks the question, "Does this have anything to do with me?" If the answer is no, the brain files it in the "not important" file and tucks away. You will normally see physical proof of this being, junk mail thrown in the trash, emails deleted, and newspapers used as fire wood. If the answer is yes, the information moves to the next step in the process.

New Revelation – Once your brain classifies the new information as important or meaningful to you, it creates new revelation. Once your brain realizes that the information is needed for your success, it manifests itself by actions like you **keeping a flier** for an event – rather than trashing it. You actually **buy the book** instead of leaving it on the shelf. **You save the site** in your favorites because the information is relevant to you. It has created a space in your mind as new revelation.

Delatorro L. McNeal II

Creating & Sustaining Positive Change

New Activation – Once you deem something or someone as relevant to your life, you are then compelled to take an action step to solidify that interest. This could come in the form of placing a phone call, sending an email, scheduling an appointment or lunch date, or reading the book or playing the CD you bought. You take an action in the direction of the new information you received, based on the fact that you deemed it important enough to act on.

New Transformation – Once you have taken action steps towards the new information that is important to you, your action creates reaction. **Your action causes circumstances and people around you to reposition themselves.** This is what creates the real change. The information or knowledge is what started it, but it is your action that will turn your information into power. That's why **the power of voting does not lie in the mind of the voter.** It lies in the physical act of going to the polls and casting your vote for a candidate.

The purpose of this book is not to give you new information alone. The real purpose is to teach you how to make transformations in different areas of your life that will position you for ultimate success.

Creating & Sustaining Positive Change

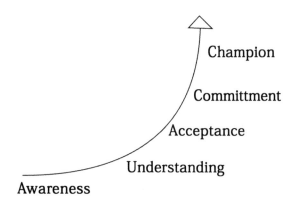

Champion

Committment

Acceptance

Understanding

Awareness

This is a consulting model that I was introduced to when I worked in corporate America. Now, I still use this model in my performance management consulting, as well as in my success coaching sessions with teams and individuals. I call it the **Curve of True Change!**

Let's take a simple example of a residential speed limit to illustrate this point.

Awareness – This is the first level of change that you will encounter. Okay, so you are driving in a new neighborhood, and you see a sign posted that says that you must only go 25 miles per hour in this area. You think to yourself "okay, whatever" and you keep driving at 35mph. Simple awareness does not create true, lasting change.

Understanding – Later that night, you watch a special on ABC about the importance of driving the speed limit. The special gives you statistics, accident rates,

Delatorro L. McNeal II

Creating & Sustaining Positive Change

and vital information that captures your attention. **Now, you turn off the TV with more than an awareness.** You now understand why that 25mph speed limit is important. The next day, you go through that same neighborhood with intentions of going 25mph. But, when see that no one is around, you say "Forget it, I am a good driver!" and you speed up and therefore still don't make the change.

Acceptance – That Sunday in church your pastor tells the congregation to watch their speed because a member of the church was involved in an accident. You feel bad, and now you accept that you, as a driver, must change your driving. You go through the neighborhood for three days straight at the 25mph speed limit and you are very proud of yourself for being obedient to your conviction of driving smart.

On the 4th day, you are late for work, so you regretfully go through at 40mph, explaining it away by saying it will only happen once. Well, that's why this 3rd level of change is good – it does promote change. **However it's not the best because you can accept something one day, and reject it the next.**

Commitment – You go to a Neighborhood Improvement meeting, and they ask for people to sign pledges to the new speed limits and they ask for volunteers to help with the campaign. You sign up, and now you are held accountable for your driving

Creating & Sustaining Positive Change

speed. This keeps you driving within the 25mph for several weeks, and you are happy, and you celebrate for making the change successfully. However no one else knows about your newfound commitment. That leads to our last level of change.

Champion – At the championing level of change, you become an ambassador, an advocate, and a spokesperson for the thing that you have committed to. Now, not only do you stay within the speed limit, you also start telling your friends and family about the importance of it. You even volunteer some time to give presentations about the importance of this policy to other neighborhood programs. You display your passion with the investment of bumper stickers, T-shirts, key chains, and the whole nine yards. You are a Change Champion for this particular effort! I want you to think of something that you are so passionate about that you are willing to climb this ladder of higher resolve to make the ultimate pledge of Champion. There are champions all over the world on every topic imaginable. For example, I am a Change Champion when it comes to Goals, Discovering Your Life's Purpose & Passion, and Maximizing Your Potential & Time. These are things that I am an ambassador of - so much so that I teach these success principles to organizations all over the world.

Creating & Sustaining Positive Change

HOW ABOUT YOU?
WHAT ARE YOU WILLING TO
BE A CHAMPION OF?

Dr. Martin Luther King Jr. said, "If you don't stand for something, you will fall for anything!"

When you are really ready to make a major change in your life, you must make a few positive affirmations that lead you down a path of progress towards your goal. Not only must you believe these things, you must also decree these things. **As you decree these things you must ACT on them. Let's Go!**

IT MUST CHANGE!

There are two words in this phrase that are very important. The word **"IT"**, allows you to identify the thing or things that must change. You see, you cannot change what you do not confront, and you can't confront what you do not identify. **So you must define for yourself what the "IT" is in your life.** The second word that stands out is **"MUST"**. This word puts priority on your change. Far too many of us allow our goals, dreams, and positive changes to be optional,

> *You cannot change what you do not confront, and you can't confront what you do not identify.*

Creating & Sustaining Positive Change

instead of mandatory. As of today, be selfish and place positive changes at the top of your priority list.

I MUST CHANGE IT!

The change you really seek to have must come from you.

The word "I" is the most important word in this phrase. Far too many of us procrastinate on making positive changes in our lives because we are waiting on someone else or some other entity to make the change for us. Once you have identified the thing that must change, you must give the change an owner. **And who is the most qualified? You!** The change you really seek to have must come from you. An old quote says, *"If it is to be, than it's up to me!"* Don't wait for anyone or anything else to create the change that you seek. It's not up to the government, the school system, the corporation, the church, or your family. If it shall come true, then it's up to you. Remember, the effort is up to you; the outcome is up to God!

I CAN CHANGE IT!

Once you have assigned yourself as the owner of the change, you must realize that you possess the power

Delatorro L. McNeal II

Creating & Sustaining Positive Change

to change it. **You can** change your situation, your circumstance, and your scenarios in life. **You can** lose the weight. **You can** be a better a parent. **You can** get into college. **You can** change your friends. **You can** quit smoking or drinking. **You can** start that business. **Yes, you can!** However, my faith in you is not enough. You must *know* this to be true as well. Don't let anyone or anything convince you that it's your destiny to stay in a bad situation your entire life. **You can** do it. You can affect things. **You can** impact this world. You can impact your community. You can rebuild that company. **You can** take that step of faith and live your dreams. **You can** change the government, one policy at a time. **You can. You can. You can!**

I WILL CHANGE IT!

Now, there is a big difference between what you can do and what you will do. So the next thing that you must affirm is that you WILL make the change. I hear many people talk a great game as to what they CAN do. **However, the problem is that "can" is a rather empty term, until you fill it with WILL!** *Can* gives you many options, *will* gives you the chosen option. For example, when you go to a car dealership, there are many deals that the salesperson CAN do for you. However, once they pull your credit report, they quickly narrow those options down to what they WILL do you for. I used to be impressed with what people could

Creating & Sustaining Positive Change

do. Now, the only thing that impresses me is what someone WILL do. You must affirm within yourself that you WILL follow-through on the change that you want for yourself, your environment, and your loved ones. I will change it!

I AM CHANGING IT!

This is normally the most uncelebrated time in a person's life. The process of change is normally very uncomfortable, and therefore we have the tendency to be hard on ourselves because we are constantly reminded that we are not where we want to be. However, I want to encourage you to take a quick look back and not only see, but also <u>appreciate</u> how far you have come. You must affirm to yourself and others that you ARE changing it. You may not be there yet, but keep on working. You are getting closer and closer by the day. Each step you take towards your dreams, God honors by pushing your destiny two steps closer to you. **Begin to celebrate yourself even in the midst of your process. Reward yourself regularly at this stage, because process can be a very lonely place.** For example, hundreds of people show up for the wedding, but few people are there for you during the process of building a successful marriage.

Those who abort the process miss out on the purpose of the blessings in their lives.

Creating & Sustaining Positive Change

Process can be lonely. Thousands show up the day of the big game, but during practice it's just you and the bleachers. **Process can be lonely.** Thousands may buy your books, but few were there when you were writing it. **Process can be lonely. But, process brings provision, protection, and power.** Those who abort the process miss out on the purpose of the blessings in their lives. Don't let anyone get you down. Why? Because YOU ARE CHANGING IT!

I HAVE CHANGED IT!

Finally, you have made it. You started out with something that needed to change, and now you have changed it. CELEBRATE. Don't you dare achieve a goal, without celebrating. And there are several things you need to celebrate.

1. Celebrate **who you have become in the process** of making the change!

2. Celebrate the **change itself.**

3. Celebrate those **who coached you, mentored you, and supported you** during the change process.

4. Celebrate the fact that you **did not give up,** even in spite of the obstacles you encountered.

Creating & Sustaining Positive Change

Don't you dare achieve a goal, without celebrating!

5. Celebrate the fact that you will go into your next change effort **armed with the momentum and wisdom that you gained from this one.** For example, the obstacle that you encounter on Monday, teaches you a skill that you will need to handle the obstacle you will face on Friday. Celebrate the fact that the life lessons you learn from past challenges are now your weapons to fight future struggles.

6. Make sure that you let people know that you have changed. Many should be able to notice, but for those that suffer from **positivity blindness,** let them know that you have made certain significant changes in your life. And now that you have taken a tremendous step forward, don't allow others to pull you back by reminding you of who or what you used to be. For example, I got my braces off in January of 2003. Ever since that time, I have had to wear a retainer at night. Why? To make sure that my teeth do not return to their original state before I had braces. **Once you have made a major change in your life, keep some type of retainer on the thing that changed so that you maintain your change.** So anytime someone tries to remind you of your past, just politely remind him or her, I HAVE CHANGED IT! In the words of a wise grandmother, "I'm not what I should be, but thank God I'm not what I used to be!"

Creating & Sustaining Positive Change

TRUE, LASTING CHANGE STARTS ON THE INSIDE

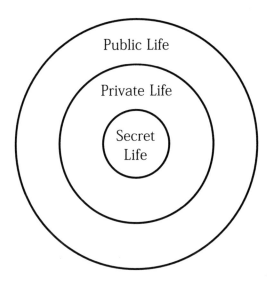

Everyday that you wake up, you live three lives. Dr. Stephen Covey talks a great deal about this. That's right! **Three of you get up each morning.**

Your Public Life – This is the mask that you wear. It's the nice outfit, the uniform, and the façade that we all wear that lets the world know that we are okay. Many times it's the face we put on so that we can keep our personal business from getting out. The public side of you comes out mostly when you are in public settings - where the potential of interacting with other people is very high, you know - work, school, restaurants, running errands, church, etc. This is the front. **There is nothing wrong with this level; however, it is very important that you understand that this is the most shallow aspect of who you are.**

Your Private Life – This side of you is seen by your family, close friends, and loved ones. Your private life includes the more personal details about your life story that make you who you are. Many times we wear things on our person such as rings, necklaces, and other jewelry that represent an aspect of our private life, while we are in public. You tend to let your guard down much more with those who are in your private life because these individuals represent your inner circle. **Many a friendship is lost or gained based on a person's ability to keep information learned in the private life of someone from going public.** The private life reveals your hidden weaknesses and unshared strengths. People in your private life see past your outfit, and see the real you. However, there is still another level of depth.

Your Secret Life – This is where your thoughts lie. This is the innermost part of you. **Your self-esteem, self-confidence, and self-worth lie at this level. Your attitude, your real feelings about things, your fears, your concerns, your deep frustrations, your passions, your real motives, desires, and intentions lie at this level.** This level of your life

Creating & Sustaining Positive Change

must be carefully revealed to others. Most people can't just look at you and ascertain the realities of your secret life. Husband and wife can lie in bed side-by-side and have no earthly clue about the inner-workings of the secret life of the other person. That's why open and **honest communication** is so very important. Your secret life drives you. True lasting change at the private (and ultimately the public level) starts here and then ripples outward.

Empowering Communication Tip:

Always speak from your heart. This allows you to communicate at the deepest level of who you are. Deep calls to deep, and what comes from the heart, reaches the heart. So in dealing with people, always come from a place of truth and sincerity. This creates the shortest and most powerful channel of communication possible. **When you are real with others, it automatically gives license for them to be real with you!** Save the drama for Springer, and just be REAL! It saves time and energy.

What comes from the heart, reaches the heart.

Creating & Sustaining Positive Change

8 QUICK REVIEW POINTS FOR
A NEW BEGINNING IN YOUR QUEST!

1. If you always do what you always did, you will always get what you always got. **If you want something you have never had, you MUST DO SOMETHING you have NEVER DONE.**

2. Knowledge is not Power! **Applied knowledge is POWER!**

3. **GET OFF THE NAIL.** Don't be comfortable with mediocrity. Don't settle for less than the best from life. Decision is a part of change, but not all of change. **You must ACT on your decision to create the change.**

4. Change takes place at different speeds, ways, and forms. **Once you can understand your change, you can withstand your change.**

5. Be the Change Champion for your own life. Move beyond all other levels of change to ultimate ambassadorship of your achievement.

6. Change is a process from "It Must Change" to "I Have Changed It". **Celebrate the process and you will enjoy the final product** – a life you love!

Creating & Sustaining Positive Change

7. Change your secret life first. By doing so you will create a ripple effect that will impact all others of your life.

8. **Don't complain about what you tolerate.** Remember, to tolerate something is to give license to it. If you don't like your life, you can change it. If you don't love your life, you can change it! **Why Settle? You deserve the best of life.**

Notes:

_____

_____

_____

_____

_____

_____

_____

_____

_____

Creating & Sustaining Positive Change

One of my Favorite Poems

The Road Not Taken
by Robert Frost

Two roads diverged in a yellow wood,
And sorry I could not travel both
And be one traveler, long I stood
and looked down one
as far as I could
To where it bent in the undergrowth;

Then took the other, as just as fair,
and having perhaps the better claim, because it was
grassy and wanted wear;
Though as for that, the passing there had
worn them really about the same.

And both that morning equally lay,
in leaves no step had trodden black.
Oh, I kept the first for another day!
Yet knowing how way leads to way,
I doubted if I should ever come back.

I shall be telling this with a sigh
somewhere ages and ages hence:
Two roads diverged in a wood, and I-
I took the one less traveled by,
And that has made all the difference.

Creating & Sustaining Positive Change

REALITY CHECK:
ROBBING THE GRAVE OF WHAT?

My friend, each day that we live and work, we have the wonderful opportunity to rob the grave of:

1. **Sales** Greatness
2. **Academic** Greatness
3. **Ministry** Greatness
4. **Customer Service** Greatness
5. **Emotional** Greatness
7. **Financial** Greatness
8. **Creative** Greatness
9. **Conversational** Greatness
10. **Entrepreneurial** Greatness
11. **Parental** Greatness
12. **Neighborhood** Greatness
13. **Societal** Greatness
14. **Political** Greatness
15. **Governmental** Greatness
16. **Literary** Greatness
17. **Oratorical** Greatness
18. **Philosophical** Greatness
19. **Theological** Greatness
20. **Psychological** Greatness
21. **Collaborative** Greatness
22. **Stewardship** Greatness
23. **Intellectual** Greatness
24. **Economic** Greatness
25. **Environmental** Greatness

Creating & Sustaining Positive Change

26. **Medical** Greatness
27. **Chronological** Greatness
28. **Collegiate** Greatness
29. **Professional** Greatness
30. **Property** Greatness

There is so much that the grave wants to hold onto, and <u>hold back</u> from you. Don't allow that. Each day that you wake up, groom yourself with clothes, smell-goods, a smile, and all of your gifts and talents so that you can be armed and ready to **SNATCH ALL OF YOUR STUFF. It's yours for the taking!**

Notes:

_____

_____

_____

_____

_____

_____

_____

Notes

Chapter 2

Discovering & Mastering Your Life Purpose!

Discovering & Mastering Your Life's Purpose

Let's say you buy a brand new computer. You get it home and open the box, plug in all the cables and start working away. All of a sudden, the computer starts giving you error messages. Then, you get a phone call from a friend who wants to know if you are using certain features of the computer that are really cool. You say no, because you did not know that your computer could do all that fancy stuff. You get off the phone and still see error messages, but now you are even more curious about the many fancy features that your new computer has, that you have yet to take advantage of.

What do you do?

Call the manufacturer or reach for the instruction manual, right? Right. But why? Because you know that the instruction manual is the manufacturer's mind put on paper. You know that if you call, you can get a friendly customer service associate to talk you through your issues. Notice what you did, my friend:

1. You realized that the issues you were dealing with **were too advanced for your own resolution.**
2. You realized that there was **much more that you could do with your computer** – if only you knew how.
3. You admitted that you did not have all the answers, so you consulted someone.

Delatorro L. McNeal II

Discovering & Mastering Your Life's Purpose

4. **The one that you consulted was the one who manufactured your product.**

My friend, the point is very simple. Your life and your purpose in life are just like that new computer. There are certain issues that come up in life that you don't understand. And there are so many fancy things you can do with your life that others do, but it takes special consultation sessions. Just like you would consult Microsoft (the manufacturer of Windows) if you wanted to know the purpose of certain applications, you must consult with the manufacturer and creator of your life to truly understand your purpose.

Make no mistake about it; I am a Man of God. **I believe that the Bible is the most powerful motivational book ever written.** Therefore, in this chapter, don't be surprised to see a few major references to God. Why? Because Jesus Christ is the manufacturer of life and we must know that if we are going to pull nuggets of wisdom and understanding, to ascertain purpose in life.

The second real step in transitioning from goodness to greatness is to discover your life's purpose and walk in it daily.

I'm a Navy Diver. And I'm not just good at it - I was born for it!
Carl Brashier
MEN OF HONOR

Discovering & Mastering Your Life's Purpose

Purpose is the specific reason, intent, cause, explanation or meaning for why a person, place, or thing exists. You were dropped on this earth with tremendous purpose. Nothing in life happens accidental – without cause or reason behind it. All things happen for a reason. All the individuals you meet have purpose behind them. All the books you read have a purpose to serve in your life.

You are a blessed, uniquely special individual with tremendous gifts, talents, abilities, and skills that must be used to change and transform lives in some way. And I believe that the moment that you begin walking towards fulfilling your purpose in life, you transition from existing efficiently, to **living abundantly!**

You see, most people are just out there existing - living from one day to the next, working from one day to the next, driving from one day to the next - but with no real meaning behind why they do what they do. **They are doing a good job at staying alive and paying the bills, but are not living life with a true sense of significance.** The goal of this life-changing chapter is to challenge you to discover and walk in one of the most powerful principles of life.

Discovering & Mastering Your Life's Purpose

POWERFUL POINTS ABOUT PURPOSE

1. Your Purpose is Permanent. When you were dropped on this earth, God deposited within you an assignment - a mission, a reason for your existence. This world should be different before you die, because you walked in your purpose. No matter who you are or what you do, you cannot shake your purpose. It's almost like your race and gender - you can't shake it...Well, nowadays you can, but you get my point. Your purpose is a part of you. It's the thing that gives your life direction and significance.

2. Your Purpose is Individual – There is only one you! Therefore, your purpose is unique to you, your strengths, your weaknesses, your personality, and your life story. **Because your purpose is individual to you, you can stop spending precious time negatively comparing yourself to other people and being frustrated about the giftings that you did not get.** Why? Because if you would have needed someone else's gifting to accomplish your purpose, God would have blessed you with it. Therefore, if you don't have a particular gift, know that you don't need it to be successful or to walk in your purpose. Isn't that refreshing? In other words, if you can't sing worth a lick, don't be jealous of those who can. Just be confident in the fact that your purpose in life will not require that of you. Why is that, Del? Keep reading...

Delatorro L. McNeal II

Discovering & Mastering Your Life's Purpose

3. Your Purpose Births Your Gifts – You see, your **purpose is the womb that travailed all your gifts, talents, abilities, and skills.** In other words, everything that you need in order to complete your assignment on earth has already been given to you in the form of your natural personality, your skills, your makeup, and your divine design. There is a common thread amongst all your gifts, and that common thread is your purpose. Take me, for example. I speak, I write books, I coach people and teams. I consult with major companies and universities, and I produce CD projects and other studio creations. What is the common thread linking all of these things? **Empowering Communication** that educates, equips, and motivates people and organizations to become all that they were designed to be. What about you? What is your mission/purpose? The tree illustration in the coming pages will help you further understand this point.

4. Your Purpose solves a Problem – Every job, every career, every position, every task, every assignment, and every purpose under the sky solves a problem that currently exists. A running back for a football team solves a position problem for a coach that needs more touchdowns. A faculty member at a college solves a problem each day that they lecture. A sales clerk at a department store solves problems for new and existing customers. A car salesman solves a problem for someone with transportation needs. We all are gifted to solve problems for someone or something

Discovering & Mastering Your Life's Purpose

else. **Your purpose, your assignment solves a problem for somebody.** I don't care if you flip hamburgers at a fast food restaurant; your culinary skill might solve a problem for a busy corporate CEO who needs a quick meal before attending a daylong board meeting. **Look at your talents as problem solvers and find someone out there who will pay you to solve problems for them.**

5. Your Purpose is Multidimensional – Your purpose and your assignment grows and expands as you move through different ages and stages of your life. When you are young, your primary purpose is to learn, grow, absorb, and develop into a self-sufficient person. As you get older your purpose shifts from not only learning, but to teaching. Instead of being raised, you start to raise others. If you start a business, your purpose will expand to fit that. If you start a church your purpose will expand to fit that. You get married, you have children, you buy a house; now you have a plethora of other assignments or purposes that your life serves. Being able to switch hats effectively is key once you really begin to walk in the multiplicities of your life's purpose.

6. Your Purpose Precedes Your Plans – I am a huge believer, teacher, and student of goals. However, there are times that in spite of your goal or your plans, life will throw you a curve ball for the sole purpose of moving you into your destiny much faster or more

Discovering & Mastering Your Life's Purpose

My friend, if things had gone my way (according to my plans) you would not be reading this book right now.

aggressively than you would have imagined. For example, my plan was to work for a major corporation for at least 5 years, and then transition into full-time speaking. God had other plans. He knew that you would need this book, so He laid me off of my corporate job, and transitioned me into a speaker, author, consultant, and life coach. **You see, my friend, if things had gone my way (according to my plans) you would not be reading this book right now.** That's why I am so glad that purpose precedes plans. Continue to plan your work, and work your plan. But don't be surprised when purpose comes knocking at your door to transition you into a new season of your life.

7. Your Purpose brings Financial Blessings – Many times in life we are taught to expect our financial blessings to flow out of the reservoir of our educational accomplishments. These yield degrees of distinction - which we exchange for a career that we hope will sustain us and our families. Well, while that may have been true in the past, and while that may be true for some still today, many people are finding out very quickly that the job market is not the greatest source of financial increase. My friend, I am a firm believer that when you really know your purpose in life, and you master your purpose, people will pay you to do what you do. If you will invest the time necessary to begin to operate in your life's purpose and perform your purpose with quality and excellence, **you will see financial prosperity like you have never known it before.**

TRUTHS ABOUT PURPOSE

1. Everything Begins and Ends with Purpose – Put this book down for a moment, and take a good look around. Go ahead, put it down for a moment…Notice the chairs, the tables, the people, the house, the dishes, the carpet, the cars, the traffic, the office, the computers, the airport terminals, the luggage, the classroom, the students, the grass, the trees, the stores, the shoppers, the couples, the singles, the waterfalls, the fountains, the sidewalks, or the playground.

> *EVERYTHING that you can see, and more importantly everything that you cannot see, began and will end with PURPOSE.*

EVERYTHING that you can see, and more importantly everything that you cannot see, began and will end with PURPOSE. Everything that is something today started with a reason for its existence. Think about the light bulb that is shining somewhere to illuminate the pages of this book so that you can read it. The

Discovering & Mastering Your Life's Purpose

purpose of that light bulb began in the mind of the inventor. The purpose of the light bulb ends when it burns out and is thrown away. Why is it thrown away? **Because it has maximized its purpose and potential. Hence, it must be replaced.**

Everything you do in this life should be done with a purpose. The friends you hang with should be chosen on purpose. The clothes you wear should be worn on purpose. The direction you drive to get to and from work should be chosen with purpose in mind. The places you go to eat, watch a movie, and shop should be purpose-driven. The house you build, the car you buy, the money you invest, the phone numbers that you store in your cell phone, the business cards you exchange…all of these things should be done with a overarching meaning, goal, reason, and intended outcome in mind. Why? Because purpose brings clarity. **Where purpose is unknown abuse is inevitable.** You don't want to abuse any of these things in your life. **Once you know the purpose for why you do what you do, you will do what you do better, for the right reasons, and then you expect the right results.**

2. Contentment is Found in the Fulfillment of Purpose – I believe that true joy, significance, and satisfaction of meaning in life only come when we know within ourselves that we are operating on a daily basis within the thing that God originally dropped us on this earth to do. You can earn millions of dollars performing a task well, but never once walk in your purpose, and therefore, miss the entire mission of your life. The goal of life is not for you to earn all the money, buy all the toys, eat all the food, suck up all the air, and drink of all the water you can. **The true goal is to get out of you everything that was deposited in you when you where dropped on this earth.**

Ask Deion Sanders, who has said numerous times in interviews that he had millions of dollars in the bank (even a $10,000 bed) but could get no sleep. He had 300 pair of shoes, but was not going anywhere in life. He had everything money could buy. But he lacked contentment - until he discovered the one true thing that money can't buy. **His divine purpose!** Once he began walking in that, his life became full of contentment, joy, peace, and abundance. My friend, the real happiness that you seek in life is hidden behind the door of your purpose. Use this chapter to help you unlock that door and begin walking boldly in your life's assignment!

3. When Purpose is Unknown, Abuse is Inevitable

Question! Have you ever known a very mischievous child? Well, I was one of those types of children. Many times when I was little, I got in trouble because I messed with (and eventually broke) things that had great value to my parents. Why did I mishandle these precious vases, mirrors, and collectables? Because I

Discovering & Mastering Your Life's Purpose

> *We must stop the cookie cutter approach to life and create our own destiny navigated by the steps towards fulfilling our life's purpose.*

did not understand, discern, or have knowledge of their purpose or significance. Because I was not aware of their value (purpose), I treated them as devalued objects of little importance. Not intentionally, but unknowingly. But trust me, after a few spankings, I learned the value of things really quickly.

The point of that short story is very powerful. We all have gifts, ideas, talents, abilities, and skills that have been given to us to help us facilitate our purpose, call, mission, and assignment in life. When the purpose or value of our life is unknown, we abuse or mistreat our gifts and our life, trying to fit into society and trying to keep up with others. This is a detrimental mistake. Born priceless originals, many of us will die as cheap copies of someone else's purpose. We must stop the cookie cutter approach to life and create our own destiny navigated by the steps towards fulfilling our life's purpose.

4. When Purpose is Known, Greatness is Guaranteed

– Once you know what you are called, assigned, destined, and equipped to do in this life, you are literally unstoppable. There are countless stories of people who discovered their purpose and in spite of lost family members, lost body parts, and lost senses, these people

Discovering & Mastering Your Life's Purpose

have amassed a level of success that is mind boggling - to say the least. Why? **Because purpose is the master key to life. You can do everything else right, but if you did a great job at the wrong thing, the true mission still goes unaccomplished.** However, if you do a good job at the right job, the job goes done with the best level of quality that your life permitted. A little job done is better then a big job talked about.

5. Fulfillment of Purpose Requires Support from Others – You, along with several billion other purpose-packed individuals, have been placed on this planet for a reason - a mission. **Part of your mission is to understand who you need on your team in order to accomplish the mission that you have been assigned.** Always remember the words of my dear friend and fellow speaker Tony McGee. *"You have not been sent to earth on Mission Impossible. Rather, you have been placed here for Mission **I'm Possible**.* Whatever you truly see for yourself in your future, you can have - with smart consistent work and dedication to fulfilling your life's purpose AND the help of those that God has blessed to help you. No man is an island. You can't do it alone, so stop trying. Get the RIGHT people in your corner, and go after your dream as if your life depended on it. Because it does! Smiles!

Discovering & Mastering Your Life's Purpose

Go after your dream as if your life depended on it. Because it does! Smiles!

The goal of your life should be to die completely empty. GIVE YOUR EVERYTHING, because you can't take anything with you when you die. Every day that you are alive, is another opportunity for you to empty out the casket of your life.

YOU MUST BE LIKE A TREE

Your life is symbolic of a tree. A tree has 5 major components. Your life has the same components. Let's parallel the two and learn how we must be like a tree to truly walk in success on a daily basis.

1. Roots – The roots of a tree are symbolic of its foundation. These roots are the building blocks of the tree. The roots pull the nutrients, vitamins, and minerals from the soil to spread life throughout the tree. The only way to kill a tree is to cut its roots. Without roots, a tree cannot live. In fact, when a tree begins to grow - it grows downward (roots) first, then suddenly it beging to sprout up to penetrate the soil. You are much the same. What are you rooted and grounded in? From what source do you pull your nourishment?

2. Trunk – The trunk of a tree is symbolic of a solid mass of possibility. It represents your purpose. Every branch of a tree sprouts forth from the trunk. A tree's height and width are determined by its trunk. Regardless of the season, the trunk of a tree stays the same. It is one of the only aspects of a tree that never changes. Your trunk in life is your purpose and destiny. Your purpose, as you have learned in this chapter, is the one thing in your life that is permanent. **It stabilizes and solidifies your reason for being on this earth.** Your purpose is the fountain out of which everything else comes. What is your tree trunk in life? Not sure? Great! By the time you finish this chapter you will know.

3. Branches – The branches of a tree are the extensions and expansions of the tree. Trees turn into fruit producing agents as a result of the branches that grow from the (trunk) or the purpose of that tree. Your branches represent your gifts, talents, abilities, and

Discovering & Mastering Your Life's Purpose

skills. **Your branches represent the innate talents that you were blessed with in order to bring your destiny to fruition.** If the branches of a tree do not do their job of carrying nutrients from the trunk and roots to the fruit, the fruit will not be produced. What are some of your natural gifts? These are the things that will produce ultimate fruit in your life. And you, my friend, are here on earth to produce much fruit.

4. Fruit – Fruit is the final goal of the seed of a tree. Fruit is the reason why the seed was planted in the first place. An end result - fruit, accomplishments - are the reason why you are planted on this earth. You were built, designed, engineered to produce. Produce what? **Results, goals, visions, dreams, families, communities, degrees, careers, books, CDs, contracts, winning teams, major corporations, businesses, websites, products, services, inventions, laws, policies, training programs, child care programs, churches, scholarships, ministries, and the like.** You were put here to produce something that would leave this world different than it was when you were born. What fruit have you produced? The fruit that you have already produced is a good clue as to what your gifts are and, ultimately, the purpose for your life.

5. Leaves – The leaves of a tree are aspects that make it breathtaking and wonderful to stare at. I like to call them the beautifications of life. Those are the nice

Discovering & Mastering Your Life's Purpose

things about leaves. The bad thing about leaves is that they change colors, they fall off, and most time they end up all over the yard - raked up and discarded. The pretty things of this life are much the same. Nice cars, nice houses, nice clothes, home theatre systems, the jewelry are all leaves. While nice and meaningful to a small degree, these things are the most insignificant part of life. Ever notice how a strong storm or hurricane completely strips trees of their leaves? A major weather change can do it. Leaves come and go - just like nice things. The storms of market downturns, layoffs, downsizing, stock market challenges, church splits, bad investments, crime, home invasions, vandalism, can easily blow the leaves of your nice things right to the ground.

Focus on producing the fruit that you were born to produce and allow the pretty things of life to be byproducts of your greatness.

Well Del, that does not sound very motivational. Actually it is. The point is that you should never spend the majority of your life trying to solely acquire the beautification of life. But, rather, focus on producing the fruit that you were born to produce and allow the pretty things of life to be byproducts of your greatness.

You must be like a tree, rooted in the divine source that created you. The trunk of your purpose is the fountain out of which you allow your branches or gifts

Delatorro L. McNeal II

Discovering & Mastering Your Life's Purpose

to flow. Once you extend your branches, take daily consistent action steps to produce the fruit that you were planted to produce. As a reward for your production, the leaves (nice things) of life will automatically flow towards you.

WHAT TYPE OF PURPOSE PERSON ARE YOU?

Right now, you fall into one of the following 4 categories. And before you take the Purpose Inventory Test, you must understand which area you fall into. Identification is the first step to making any major change in your life. You must identify where you are. Once you know where you are, use this chapter to chart your course towards Discovering and Mastering your Life's Purpose. After coaching, mentoring, counseling, interacting with, and interviewing thousands of people - I have found that most people fit into one of these categories.

1. The Unconsciously Unpurposed
He who knows not, and knows that he knows not, but thinks that he knows!

These are people who don't know about the principle of purpose, and they are not doing anything to walk in their destiny. However, instead of seeking knowledge to bridge the intellectual gap, they act like they have themselves all together. Scripture reminds us that we perish because of a lack (lazy desire) of knowledge. This individual can be very dangerous, and needs many walls and facades torn down before real change will manifest in their life.

2. The Consciously Unpurposed
He who knows, that he knows not!

These are people who are aware of the principle of purpose, but for either one of two reasons they are not walking in it. **First, they may have chosen to be rebellious to the call or plan of destiny on their lives. They could very well be running from it, like Simba did in The Lion King. Second, they could be aware of the principle but have no clue how to really discover their own unique purpose** and begin to take steps towards walking in it.

I believe many people in our society are in this particular stage of purpose! There are many things that feed into this.

We live in an "I wanna be like Mike" generation that says that it's cool and okay to wanna be like someone else. And because we try so hard to be like other people, we focus externally instead of internally. In addition to that, we shun our own innate gifts, in exchange for futile attempts to become "the next" someone else. It's like a cookie cutter approach to life.

Discovering & Mastering Your Life's Purpose

Listen, don't live your life trying to be "the next" anybody. Become the first You. Become the one and only unique, special, blessed, gifted, and talented You. Now there is nothing wrong with admiring someone for their success. However, you should never live your life trying to become them. You will fail miserably. Not that you will fail in your efforts, you may actually do well. But, you will ultimately end up failing yourself.

> *Listen, don't live your life trying to be "the next" anybody. Become the first You.*

My dear friend and mentor Pastor Scott Thomas says, "Don't be easily impressed by people. Because if you can be easily *im*pressed by people, you can be easily *de*pressed by people." A person who can easily impress you or depress you - simply by acting a certain way - has way too much control over your emotions.

What you cannot produce, you will tend to imitate. This is powerful because when we become impressed with people, we start to focus on what they possess, that we don't. This causes many people to want to dress like, sound like, walk like, talk like, and live like someone else. **Every day you spend trying to copy someone else is a day you trade being a cheap copy instead of a priceless original.**

Discovering & Mastering Your Life's Purpose

The Unconsciously Purposed
He who knows not, that he knows!

> *One of biggest and most accepted definitions of success is - doing what you love to do, and finding someone to pay you to do it.*

These are people who by some happenstance in life have actually ended up stumbling into a career, job, position, or opportunity that is almost 100% in alignment with their ultimate purpose and destiny. They have no clue that they are doing what they are naturally and divinely gifted to do. So much so, that it normally takes others to point it out of them. **Usually these individuals enjoy what they do, but don't believe they could make a living doing it.** They do not realize that they possess a very rare and special gift that, if cultivated and marketed correctly, could bring them millions of dollars.

Many times this type of person manifests in the girl who designed her own prom dress because she has a natural flare for fashion, or the gentleman who never goes to the barber because he cuts his own hair and everyone thinks he gets it done by a professional, or the person who details cars on weekends as a hobby, yet doesn't realize they can make a living at it.

One of biggest and most accepted definitions of success is - doing what you love to do, and finding someone to pay you to do it. Think about it. If you

Delatorro L. McNeal II

Discovering & Mastering Your Life's Purpose

needed to hire a maid to clean your house, would you hire someone who enjoys cleaning, or would you hire the person that LOVES to clean? I'd choose the person who wakes up thinking of new ways to clean, daydreams about cleaning, and has a way of making things look nice.

People in this season of Purpose remind me of the elephants, tigers, and other wild animals that you find in major zoos. Ever wonder why a 200lb tiger or a 1000lb elephant can be controlled and directed by a 90lb skinny animal trainer? Is it that the trainer is stronger? NO WAY! The truth is that from birth the tiger and the elephant had been trained, shackled, and disciplined to obey the instructions of the trainer. Therefore, even when it's full-grown it does not know any better. Even though the reality is that the tiger and elephant's true potential far exceeds it present behavior, it does not know any different so it does not perform differently. It was born to win, but has been conditioned to lose! We will talk more about this in Chapter 4.

Imagine how awesome you really are. Imagine how bad to the bone, you really are! Imagine how dangerous (in a positive way) you could be. Imagine the impact that you could make once you realize how blessed, how gifted, how awesome, how powerful, how wonderfully you are made, and how much destiny lies inside you.

Delatorro L. McNeal II

Discovering & Mastering Your Life's Purpose

The Consciously Purposed
He who knows, and knows that he knows!

Imagine how awesome you really are. Imagine how bad to the bone, you really are!

These are people who know the power of walking in purpose, and experience that power on a daily basis, because they are walking in their divine purpose. Once you figure out and fully understand your purpose – baby it's all over. Once you know, and know that you know, you start to walk differently. You start to talk differently. **Your life makes sense.** Your battles and challenges even make sense because you know the gift that your challenges are coming against. **Your victories are sweeter because you understand their significance in the grand scheme of things.** Once you know, and know that you know, you become UNSTOPPABLE! Look out, the leader within will begin to emerge, the power behind your profession will be unleashed.

Purpose gives you access. Would you try to use your car keys to get into your house? No, of course not! Because if you did, you would be using the car keys for the wrong purpose. Doing this too many times, and with too much force, could permanently damage the car keys to the point that they are no longer workable in your car.

Discovering & Mastering Your Life's Purpose

Well, just as you use the right keys for the right locks on doors, you must use your life for the right purpose so that you can unlock the blessings that lie behind the door of divine purpose in your life.

DISCOVERING YOUR PURPOSE INVENTORY

The questions that you are about to answer are 100% self-reflective. They will require you to really soul-search, experience-search, knowledge-search, and any other kind of search you can think of.

You may not be able to answer some of these questions right away. Others, you will be able to whiz right through. This inventory of questions may be something you want to do alone. **In fact, I recommend that your first pass-through be solo. The second time you go through it, get a best friend, spouse, or significant other involved because they will help you see things about yourself** that you may be a little blind to.

The major goal is to try to get you to think systematically about the many aspects of your life and how those aspects relate to your ultimate purpose and destiny.

Don't give up on this inventory. Don't allow yourself to get frustrated, annoyed, or irritated if you can't

Discovering & Mastering Your Life's Purpose

answer all the questions. This inventory is meant to get you excited and motivated by the fact that **everything in your life has been shaping, designing, illustrating, and navigating you towards your purpose and destiny.** By the time you finish this chapter you will have a roadmap for what direction you should be traveling in.

Remember the movie Forrest Gump?

Do you remember the scene when he was playing football in college? Because he loved to just run, many times he would catch the ball and just start running. He had the ball and the opportunity, but he was simply running in the wrong direction. Well my friend, you have won the race for life. You are here on earth, and you have the ball (the blessing of life). Now, I want to show you how to run in the right direction so that you can score touchdowns in the end zone of your destiny all life long!

Repetition is the mother of skill. Pay very close attention to your answers to each question. You will see the same answer come up several times during the inventory. This is a very good sign. This is exactly what should happen. This is confirmation that you are heading in the right direction. You will want to revisit this chapter at least 5 times before it all sinks in and you walk in all that is required of you. **I am excited about the purpose-driven YOU that awaits YOU at the end of this chapter.**

Delatorro L. McNeal II

Discovering & Mastering Your Life's Purpose

Question Cluster

¨*Group 1 – (1 - 6) – **Childlike Reflection***
¨*Group 2 – (7 - 8) – **Life's Signals***
¨*Group 3 – (9 – 17) – **People & Purpose***
¨*Group 4 – (18 – 21) – **Creativity/Flow***
¨*Group 5 – (22 – 25) – **Life, Death, Legacy***
¨*Group 6 – (26 – 28) – **Level Playing Fields***
¨*Group 7 – (28 – 30) – **Reflection & Action***

GROUP ONE – CHILDLIKE REFLECTION

1. What do you Love to do?

When you were designed, God placed inside of you a natural passion for specific things in life. There is a difference between what you like and what you love. The things that you love, you are passionate about. These are the things that you will put your whole heart into because your heart is where your passion and love lie. So in answering this question, focus on what you really love to do.

Your Answer:

Discovering & Mastering Your Life's Purpose

2. When you were a child, what did you Dream of Becoming? Why?

I am convinced that many of us would be much further in life if we had the same vision, imagination, and fearless attitude that we had as children. As younger and older adults we have become too educated about what we CAN'T have. That's a bunch of Garbage!

What did you dream of as a child and why did you want to be that? I wanted to be a member of Boyz II Men. I wanted to have a famous singing group. Why? Because I loved to sing, I love harmony, I love inspiring people, and I love seeing the reaction of people's face when I helped them feel better with my message. I wanted people to be able to buy my products and enjoy them for years to come. I wanted to help people feel happy and empowered.

Although I am not a professional singer (which was my dream), I actually am a professional speaker and author (which is my destiny). God had my message to come primarily from my spoken voice instead of my musical voice. I am so glad that I did not get my dream, because not getting it, yielded my destiny. Also, everything I wanted to accomplish as a singer, I now accomplish all that and more as a professional speaker and author. **Sometimes, not getting your dream is a good thing because is puts your destiny on silver platter in front of you.**

Discovering & Mastering Your Life's Purpose

Your Answer:

Discovering & Mastering Your Life's Purpose

3. What Are Some of Your Favorite Hobbies?

Your hobbies are the things that you enjoy and/or love doing in your "spare time" or in your "leisure time". However, the reality is this - you can turn your play into your profit, your leisure into your labor, and your part-time hobby into your full-time profession once you discover and master the things that you love to do. Like I said before, one of my favorite definitions for success is, "Doing what you love to do, and finding someone to pay you to do it!"

Your Answer:

Discovering & Mastering Your Life's Purpose

4. What are you Naturally Good at?

Do you realize that there is gold on the inside of you?
**Absolute, priceless, rare gold – in the form of your
gifts, talents, ideas, and skills lies inside of YOU.**
*Never forget that! Because the reality is that you will
only pursue in life what you honestly feel you can
apprehend. Know that you can achieve untapped
levels of greatness in your life - that's why God
blessed you with the gifts.*

Your Answer:

_____

_____

_____

_____

_____

_____

_____

_____

_____

_____

Delatorro L. McNeal II

Discovering & Mastering Your Life's Purpose

5. What do your close Family & Friends tell you that you are good at?

Sometimes we need someone on the outside looking in to tell us just how gifted we really are. Pay very close attention to the gifts that others celebrate within you. Family and friends are those who know you best, and they are encouraging your talent for a reason. Discover that thing, and use it.

Your Answer:

_____

_____

_____

_____

_____

_____

_____

_____

_____

Discovering & Mastering Your Life's Purpose

GROUP TWO – LIFE SIGNALING YOU!

6. Looking back over your life, what are some instances that have been signaling you towards your destiny?

I believe that from the time you were born, life has been giving you certain clues and flashing lights as to what your true purpose is. For example, my mom says that when I was little, I would always say, "I can do it!" anytime she tried to help me with something. Well that same positive attitude I had back then has followed me to adulthood because I travel the world showing people that "they can do it!" What are some things that you used to say or do as a child that have carried over into your maturity now? These things are clues to point you in the right direction.

Your Answer:

Discovering & Mastering Your Life's Purpose

7. When you find yourself bored with your "Day Job" what do you dream about doing instead?

Many times our goals and dreams give us sneak previews of what is really to come in our lives. I can remember coming to tears while doing routine work in Corporate America, because my destiny was flashing things upon my mind and heart. I had visions of me speaking to other corporations, colleges, churches, and associations. Your vision is probably just as real for you now, as mine was for me then!

Your Answer:

Delatorro L. McNeal II

Discovering & Mastering Your Life's Purpose

8. What percentage of your true potential do you feel your present job demands of you? How could you increase that number?

This is a POWERFUL question! Most people's regular 9 to 5 only demands a small percentage of their true potential. **And while many people find that very frustrating and upsetting, it is also very educational.** *Let's say that you're a lawyer, but while at work you're only using 20% of your true potential and gifts. What would you need to do at work to make that percentage increase? The answer to this question lets you know what you really should be focusing on. Remember, soar with your strengths! Smiles!*

Your Answer:

Delatorro L. McNeal II

Discovering & Mastering Your Life's Purpose

GROUP THREE – PEOPLE & PURPOSE!

9. What were you doing when you made a major impact on someone else's life? How did it make you feel?

The reality is that we all have a human need for significance. We all want and need to be significant in our own lives and in the lives of those around us. Your purpose will make a significant difference in someone else's life. What have you done that has made significant positive differences in the lives of other people?

Your Answer:

_____

_____

_____

_____

_____

_____

_____

_____

Delatorro L. McNeal II

Discovering & Mastering Your Life's Purpose

10. What were you doing when you were 100% at the top of your Game?

We have all had those times in our lives when we were "In the Zone!" **What were you doing when you felt a rush of energy and excitement so much so that you felt "I was born to do this"?** *Find your zone, and work inside your zone daily. Learn to do what you love to do, and find someone to pay you to do it. Smiles!*

Your Answer:

_____

_____

_____

_____

_____

_____

_____

_____

_____

_____

Discovering & Mastering Your Life's Purpose

11. What is the common thread amongst all your Gifts, Talents, and Abilities?

Amongst the many gifts and talents that you have, there is one common thread. For example, I am a speaker, author, consultant, and success coach. I love to sing and write, and empower people. The common thread among them all is Effective Empowering Communication. What's yours?

Your Answer:

_____

_____

_____

_____

_____

_____

_____

_____

_____

12. What is the thing that people admire most about you?

The things that people admire about you are gifts that are natural to you. Pay close attention to what people are always complimenting you on and encouraging you to do. Even if it's something that you are a little embarrassed about, explore it. That just may be a key towards walking in your divine purpose.

Your Answer:

Discovering & Mastering Your Life's Purpose

13. What gift do you have that negative people are jealous or envious of?

Hate, jealousy, and envy are excellent teachers. They inform you about what your powerful gifts are. If negative people talk about you because of your singing ability, chances are, you can probably sing very well! **Whatever negative people say you shouldn't be doing, is the very thing that positive people will challenge you to continue doing.**

Your Answer:

_____

_____

_____

_____

_____

_____

_____

_____

_____

Delatorro L. McNeal II

Discovering & Mastering Your Life's Purpose

14. What gift do you naturally possess, that other people have to pay money to learn how to do?
This one is HUGE! Do you perform certain tasks so skillfully that the only way that others could compete with your gifting is through taking courses? You have certain skills that God just dropped on you. Other people are paying money and sitting in class to learn how to do what you do naturally. **Be thankful right now for that, and use what you have. It's priceless!**

Your Answer:

15. What problems in others are you good at solving?

*I love this one too. **Begin to pay attention to the things that most people come to you for counsel about.** What are the things that people are asking for your wisdom and input regarding? These are all telltale signs pointing directly towards your purpose. For example, if people are always coming to you asking for relationship advice, that's a really good sign that Relationship Counseling or Coaching may be a target for you!*

Your Answer:

_____

_____

_____

_____

_____

_____

_____

_____

Discovering & Mastering Your Life's Purpose

16. What talent do you execute so well, that people cannot determine whether you are working or playing?

There is something that you do so well that if someone did not know you , they would be confused because they would not be able to tell if you were working hard, or playing hard. What is that for you?

For me, when I speak in front of a group, I am working and playing. I am having a blast doing what I love to do – while doing what I was designed to do. I confuse people who don't know me because I have so much fun living my dream. What is that for you?

Your Answer:

_____

_____

_____

_____

_____

_____

_____

_____

17. What are some things that grieve or frustrate you the most about this life and society?

The problems that aggravate you the most in society are the things that you have been assigned to solve. Don't forget your purpose solves a problem. My greatest frustration is people who live below their potential and privilege. I solve motivational challenges in people. What about you? Could it be the homeless, legislative policy, uneducated children, or abused women? The options are limitless, and your impact could last a lifetime.

Your Answer:

Discovering & Mastering Your Life's Purpose

GROUP FOUR – CREATIVITY & FLOW!

18. When you watch movies and TV programs, what are the types of stories that impact you the most? Why?

The stories that move me the most are those about someone using their gift of speaking, writing, coaching, or counseling to speak a word of encouragement and empowerment to transform a person's life. The relationship between Mr. Miyagi and Daniel in The Karate Kid are great examples. Those types of movies and scenes move me to tears because that's exactly what I do. Well, what about you?

Your Answer:

_____

_____

_____

_____

_____

_____

_____

_____

Delatorro L. McNeal II

Discovering & Mastering Your Life's Purpose

19. If you could star in a Blockbuster movie, what role would you play and why?

Sometimes we can't get a large vision for our own lives, unless we envision it through the eyes of fantasy or movie magic. Most people have a favorite actor or actress that plays roles with a similar passion and conviction that they aim to guide our lives with. Having this understanding, if your life were a movie, what would be the major theme or storyline of it? Why would people want to come see it?

Your Answer:

Delatorro L. McNeal II

Discovering & Mastering Your Life's Purpose

20. What would you do with your life if you knew that you COULD NOT FAIL?

Les Brown says, "Many people allow their fear of failure to outweigh their desire to succeed!" I agree wholeheartedly. Failure is a natural part of the equation! You must fail; it is required for success. My challenge to you is to feel the fear, and do it anyhow!

Your Answer:

_____

_____

_____

_____

_____

_____

_____

_____

_____

_____

Discovering & Mastering Your Life's Purpose

21. If God were to grant you 3 wishes, what 3 wishes would you like granted?

The opportunities that you really want reveal the talents that you want to showcase. These talents will align with many of the gifts that you have already listed about yourself.

Your Answer:

Discovering & Mastering Your Life's Purpose

GROUP FIVE – LIFE, DEATH, AND LEGACY!

22. If you had 3 days to live, what would you do and why?

This is a critical question. This question really allows you to skip past the drama, and focus on the things that mean the most to you and yours. The things that you would do in these 3 days represent the things that are most important, most pressing, most related to your legacy, and most related to your destiny. That's the focus!

Your Answer:

Discovering & Mastering Your Life's Purpose

23. If you had 10 minutes to address the world, what would you talk about, and why?

Scripture reminds us that out of the abundance or overflow of our heart, the mouth speaks. If you had the world's ear, what would you say? **What you would say is in direct relationship to the strongest passions and desires of your heart.** *This question forces you to focus on making a meaningful impact in the lives of people universally.*

Your Answer:

Delatorro L. McNeal II

Discovering & Mastering Your Life's Purpose

24. At Your Funeral, what 2 sentences would you want people to be able to truthfully & sincerely speak of you?

In January of 2003, my family went through a tremendous time because we lost 2 very special members of our family. In addition, our family's local church lost 5 members of their congregation within 1 month. Each weekend, we were attending funerals of key people within the church who all died unexpectedly. My friend, I ask you this question because at your funeral there should be certain positive things that everyone at your funeral says truthfully about you. Whatever they say is how your life will be summed up. Whatever people say about you represents the amount of greatness that you robbed from the grave. Remember, your entire life is summed up in that little dash.

Your Answer:

Discovering & Mastering Your Life's Purpose

25. What have you done to make this world different from the way you found it?

When you showed up on this earth, you were blessed with gifts that were installed into your life, through your purpose, so that you could change this world. Therefore, the things that you have done to make this world different, are the things that are connected to your life's mission. **You are here on a mission - to rob the grave of its greatness - and to change this world, one person, one smile, one day, and one goal at a time.**

Your Answer:

Delatorro L. McNeal II

Discovering & Mastering Your Life's Purpose

GROUP SIX – LEVEL PLAYING FIELD

26. If every job in the world paid the same salary, what career would you choose? (*If money was not the issue*)
If money had no value or purpose, your desire to work for "money" would not exist. What would you do to be fulfilled every day?

Your Answer:

Discovering & Mastering Your Life's Purpose

27. If you were laid off or fired tomorrow, and your living expenses were covered for 3 months, how would you invest your time?

Many times we get stuck in the routine of making a living, and we forget to live our making! Well, if you no longer had the stress, pressure, and strain of making a living and you could design your day from start to finish – doing what you love instead of doing what "pays the bills" - what would your day look like?

Your Answer:

Discovering & Mastering Your Life's Purpose

28. If you had $100,000 cash today to start a business, what type of business would you start and why? Who would be your business Partners? *Did you know that every 10 seconds, a new home-based business is started somewhere in America? Well, now is your time to prepare for the type of business that you want; doing what you love to do, and finding consumers to pay you to do it. Turning your play into your profit is the ultimate goal here. IT'S POSSIBLE! Who are the key players in your life right now who would be your business partners in the venture? Start working on this right now. Remember, you don't have to be great to get started, but you've got to get started to be great!*

Your Answer:

Discovering & Mastering Your Life's Purpose

One of My Favorite Poems

The Master In the Art of Living
- Author Unknown

Below is a Powerful Poem that a good friend and business colleague of mine, Manuel Lopez, gave me one day after a long conversation about purpose and passion in life. Copy it and post it somewhere special.

The Master in the Art of Living

makes little distinction between,

his **work** and his **play**,

his **labor** and his **leisure**,

his **mind** and his **body**,

his **education** and his **religion**.

He hardly knows which is which.

He simply pursues **his vision of excellence**

in whatever he does,

Leaving others to decide whether

he is working or playing........Why?

Because TO HIM, HE IS ALWAYS DOING BOTH!

Delatorro L. McNeal II

Discovering & Mastering Your Life's Purpose

29. What are some common answers that continued to show up on your worksheet? What in this life is worth you procrastinating? Now is your time to walk in your Purpose!

*Now it's time for you to conduct a self-analysis of what the real answers to all your questions really mean. In order to do this, you need to start back from the beginning of this inventory **and circle all of your common answers.** The answers that continued to come up over and over again, are flashing green lights to let you know that you have discovered a key component of your purpose and destiny in life. What came up for you?*

Your Answer:

_____

_____

_____

_____

_____

_____

Discovering & Mastering Your Life's Purpose

Writing?
Dancing?
Fitness Training?
Singing?
Speaking?
Operating?
Counseling?
Driving?
Advertising?
Banking?
Selling?
Litigating?
Merchandising?
Retailing?
Wholesaling?
Fashion Designing?
Constructing?
Home Building?
Landscaping?
Movie Writing?
Preaching?
Pastoring?
Real Estate Investing?
Teaching?
Mentoring?
Training?
Event Planning?
Photography?

None of these?

Delatorro L. McNeal II

Discovering & Mastering Your Life's Purpose

Well, what repeatedly came up for you?

Next question: **Who in this world is worth putting your goals and dreams on hold? Let me help you....NOBODY!** *Nobody and nothing is worth you waiting another moment to go after your dream. You are here to make a tremendous difference. Don't allow the grave to rob you of your time each day with things like procrastination, the paralysis of analysis, fear, doubt, or distraction. GO FOR IT!*

30. What 7 specific action steps can you implement RIGHT NOW that will allow you to begin walking in your divine Purpose & Passion in life?

I found that most people hide behind the excuse of task-complexity or a feeling of being overwhelmed as a way of getting out of taking action on their dreams. **I want you to list (yes, physically write in this book right now) seven simple action steps that you can begin to take today that will allow you to start walking in alignment with your purpose and destiny in life.** *If you are already taking these steps, what can you do to take it to the next level? How can you penetrate the proverbial "glass ceiling"? What seven steps can you take right now? List them here, and begin each one with an action verb!*

Discovering & Mastering Your Life's Purpose

Here are a few examples:
1. Call a close friend and tell them my goals/action steps so they can keep me accountable.

2. Meet with my mentor to have them sharpen my list.

3. Arise 30 minutes earlier each day to devote towards my own future.

4. Visit a professional in the area of my dream and ask them to help me.

5. Conduct online research about how to break into the field of my choice.

6. Complete this Purpose Inventory with someone I love and respect. Their opinion will empower me.

7. Read the next chapter of this book! Smiles!

Your Answer:

_____

_____

_____

_____

_____

Delatorro L. McNeal II

Discovering & Mastering Your Life's Purpose

12 THINGS YOU SHOULD DO - ON PURPOSE

In order to really rob the grave of its greatness, you and I must decide to live life on purpose - not by accident. We must make a concrete decision that the actions we take will be wrapped with wisdom and insight; that everything we do will align itself in some way with where we are going. In order to live like this, **I believe that there are many things we must do purposefully.** Every action has a motive anyway, so why not make a conscious decision to act on purpose? Here are 12 examples of what I mean:

1. **Choose your Associates & MMGs - on Purpose**. Please my friend, have a reason for why you surround yourself with the people that you do. **Each person in your life either adds to your life, or subtracts from it.** They either multiply your efforts or they divide them. You have invested too much of yourself into your dream to allow someone (i.e. friend, family, church member, business colleague, school friend, roommate, or otherwise) to delay your date with destiny. Choose your associates and your MMG (Master Mind Group) intentionally. You should have a concrete reason for why each person you know and respect is in your life. **Every person in your Master Mind Group should be pushing you, developing you, empowering you, stretching you towards greatness, towards financial excellence, and towards your destiny.** Each person in your life needs to be a grave

Discovering & Mastering Your Life's Purpose

robber in their own right!
Either you are developing
them, or they are developing
you, **but some type of
development needs to be
going on! Smiles.**

*Remember, the
people with whom
you network,
ultimately determine
your net worth.*

2. **Network and Meet New People
- on Purpose.** Zig Ziglar says, "Everyone is a
prospect"! Which means that we must purposefully
network and meet new individuals constantly. You
can't get to greatness without other people. Positive
people are your bridge to get you to the other side.
**Live your life based on the premise that 50% of
the people who will be responsible for helping make
your dream come true, you have not met yet.**
Purposefully put yourself in the right place to meet
the right people. Make it a goal to meet someone new
each day. You never know who that person may know.
Remember, the people with whom you network,
ultimately determine your net worth.

3. **Give & Sow Into Others' Lives - on Purpose**. To
whom much is given, much is required. In order to
receive much, you must first give much! He who sows
little, will get little. But he who gives a lot, gets a lot.
Many millionaires are philanthropists. They are givers,
tithers, and seed sowers. They invest in the visions
and dreams of other people. We must do the same
thing. Pour into someone else. How have I developed

such strong relationships with key people of influence? I served them and invested in what they were doing, and in turn, I began to get what I needed.

4. **Educate Yourself on Your Topic - on Purpose**. Dr. Mike Murdock says, "Pursuit is proof of passion"! I can tell how bad you want something – not by how much you talk about it – but rather, by how much work you invest into it. You must educate yourself in your selected field of interest. You must know where the industry is headed and where your specific gifts fit into the big picture of the industry. You must research, join associations, attend conferences, and get weekly updates on the happenings with your industry. You will be amazed at how much knowledge there is out there. **You can always learn more about your talents. This will keep you sharp and craving for continuous improvement.**

5. **Master Your Gifting - on Purpose.** Sound similar to #4? Well it might, but in truth they are very different. I know many people who read books, listen to tapes, and attend conferences, but they still never walk in their destiny. **Their gift goes unmaximized because they do not put that knowledge into consistent practice.** Let's take football for example. It's great to watch films of games, study playbooks, and research statistics, but nothing beats good old-fashioned PRACTICE. You must practice your talent, regardless of how good you are. You must rehearse it and refine

it or you will be quickly outdated - then others will be getting the opportunities that could be yours.

6. **Seek Mentors & Mentees to Develop You - on Purpose.** You need someone who is more advanced than you in your life. You want to learn from them, glean from them, and be sharpened by their influence and wisdom. **You need multiple mentors in different areas of your life (I.e. Financial, Spiritual, Professional, etc.)** Submit yourself to the advice, correction, and training of a mentor – someone who has been there and done that! Also find someone to pour your life lessons into. **Find someone who wants to be where you are right now, and potentially even further than you.** Show them how to get where you are, while learning from your mistakes so that they don't have to endure all of what you did. **In other words, find someone who can help you cut your learning curve, and find someone whose learning curve you can cut.**

7. **Plan Your Life one Year at a Time, but Live your Life one Day at a Time - on Purpose!** This is critical. I believe that we all have the power to create our destiny. What we do today, literally shapes what we experience tomorrow. We don't have to dial 1-900 numbers to learn about what our future holds; **because the truth is that the future holds what you deposit into it today.** If you invest nothing in tomorrow today, you will have nothing tomorrow.

Discovering & Mastering Your Life's Purpose

Find someone who can help you cut your learning curve, and find someone whose learning curve you can cut.

However, if you invest time today working on your dream, it will ripple into your tomorrow and bless your socks off. So plan your life for the year. You should know in January how you want December to close out. We will talk a lot more about this in Chapter 6. Once you have a vision for your year, **wake up each morning and put your 100% best into that day – allowing it to get you a little closer to your year-long goals.**

8. **Select Your Jobs & Dreams - on Purpose!** Pick jobs and careers that are in-line with your purpose. Select each job not necessarily based on how much money you will earn, but on how closely it aligns with your destiny – knowing that it is only a stepping-stone to get you higher and closer to your manifestation of greatness. **Know what your dream is.** Have a clear picture of it in your mind, and up on your walls. You will learn much more about this in Chapter 5 – Caught between a Dream and a Job!

9. **Take Consistent Daily Action - on Purpose.** Wake up each morning and envision a clean piece of paper (life) on which you have a few preprinted items, (I.e. traffic, school, work, getting dressed, eating, and etc.). Now beyond the basics of day-to-day living you have **the creative power to add to your day certain**

Discovering & Mastering Your Life's Purpose

consistent action steps that will get you much closer to your dream - much faster. Decide that you are going to be a consistent person and your life will change radically. Pick an action step or steps and be like a stamp, STICK TO IT until delivery is complete.

10. Share your gift with this World - on Purpose! Make up in your mind that the world needs the gift that you have. Why would you be placed on this earth, if you were not meant to benefit this earth with your presence? Don't wait to be perfect - that will never

Greatness is going to cost you. What? Taking a step of faith!

happen. Don't wait for 100% support from everyone you know - that will never happen. Don't wait for all the money to be in the bank - that will never happen. Why. Because Greatness is going to cost you. What? Taking a step of faith! It will cost you believing enough in the dream that you will go after it with all you have, in spite of the circumstances. Don't spend your life tuning your instrument - start making music now. Trust me, someone needs the gift that you have. Been rejected in spite of your best effort? Their loss! Pick up your pieces and move on.

11. Be Thankful to the Creator for your Purpose - on Purpose! Be thankful that God dropped each of us here for a unique, special, individual, and powerful

reason. There is purpose behind every victory, every failure, every mountaintop, every valley low, every success, and every storm. All the things that happen to us are trying to teach us something significant about life. So be thankful each day that your daily steps are aligned with a greater purpose and plan.

12. **Play with the Cards that you were Issued - on Purpose!** You were dealt a deck of playing cards called gifts, talents, ideas, abilities, and skills when you were dropped on this earth. Unfortunately, most of us don't play the game of life effectively because we are so focused on the cards that everyone else was dealt. Many people get jealous, envious, and hold grudges because of someone else's blessing. Well, my friend, we must understand that the more time we spend looking at someone else's cards, the less time we spend strategizing, planning, and preparing for our own success. **Play with the cards that YOU were dealt.** Stop feeling cheated or jipped in life. You've got the best hand that was made for you. Use your cards and play this game. **And by the way, PLAY TO WIN!**

Discovering & Mastering Your Life's Purpose

8 QUICK REVIEW POINTS
FOR A NEW BEGINNING IN YOUR QUEST!

1. You were strategically placed here on earth for a special Mission! You are no mistake, no accident, and no mishap. **You are 100% destined for something special.** No one was dropped on earth with the exact same gifting that you possess.

2. **The moment you start walking in your purpose is the moment you shift from existing efficiently, to living abundantly.** The abundant life (financially, spiritually, professional, intellectually) you desire is hidden behind the door of your purpose.

3. You are perfectly equipped for the Assignment of your life. If you needed some other gifting, you would have been blessed with that too. **The absence of it is proof that you don't need it to be great!**

4. True contentment is found in the fulfillment of your purpose, your mission, and your calling. Not someone else's. **You won't be comfortable in anything that's not your destiny.**

5. Money is compensation for using your assignment to solve a problem. **Do what you love to do, and you will find people who will pay you to do it!**

6. Decide to be a Consciously Purposed Individual - **One who knows and knows that he knows.**

Discovering & Mastering Your Life's Purpose

7. Use the questions in the chapter to pull out of you everything that was deposited inside you to steer you towards your divine purpose.

8. Do everything, everyday <u>on purpose</u>. **Let the accidentals of life be gravy.** Live life on purpose!

REALITY CHECK:
DON'T LET IT DIE WITH YOU!

My friend, when this dash of life is all over, everything that you did not give birth to, with some form of documentation or communication of the dream or vision, will die with you.

- When you die, it dies!
- When you die, that business idea dies!
- When you die, that book idea dies!
- When you die, that song lyric dies!

When you live your life, make sure that you are continually giving birth to something. Why? Because if you are continually giving birth to something, even when you die, IT LIVES! So as a result of you completing this book and taking the 8 Steps to becoming a Licensed Grave Robber, these things will be true of you:

Discovering & Mastering Your Life's Purpose

- When you die, it lives on!
- When you die, that business idea lives in your family!
- When you die, that song is sung and heard around the world!
- When you die, that dream was birthed and given life!

Sometimes our dreams will not come true within our lifetime, but as long as the dream and the vision are PUT OUT THERE, then we all have something to live up to. For example, many believe that the great civil rights leader Dr. Martin Luther King Jr. died way before his time. Many believe that he died far before he ever saw the reward for his vision for equality, brought to fruition. Well, that may be true. **However, Dr. King was a grave robber because his vision SET THE STANDARD.** His life and his commitment to the cause set the BENCHMARK for a level of excellence that we all must live up to. Therefore, the purpose of his life was to set the bar for national and international greatness, higher. Now we live in a society that strives to attain the bar and surpass it. Goodness is free, but Greatness will cost you. Are you willing to pay the price? Dr. King was!

Notes

Chapter 3

Maximizing Your Human Potential!

Maximizing Your Potential

Now that we have made a commitment to creating Lasting Positive Change in our lives, and we've done some soul-searching to Discover & Master the Purpose of our lives, now we must begin to start physically taking things out of our casket. This requires the maximizing of potential.

My definition of **potential** is simply the gap that exists between where you are, and where you should be.

My definition of **personal potential** is simply the gap that exists between where you are, **and where you really want to be.**

My definition of **divine potential** is simply the gap that exists between where you are, and where **God would have you to be.**

My definition of **professional potential** is simply the gap that exists between where you are and **where your employer envisions you to be.**

We've got to learn how to begin to close the gap. We all have potential. It's just that most people don't take consistent action to MAXIMIZE their potential

For example, what if you went out and bought a brand new laptop computer that was loaded with all the bells and whistles any professional or student would need. Then you typed a 2-page report on the laptop, turned the report in, shut the computer down and never used

Maximizing Your Potential

it again. Let me ask you a few questions?

1. Did you use the computer to create positive change? Yes!

2. Did you use the computer in alignment with its purpose? Yes!

3. Did you maximize the potential of the computer that you purchased? Nowhere close!

That computer had limitless capabilities, functions, and options to utilize. And guess what? So does your life. You are limitless to the ideas, the possibilities, the dreams, and the goals that you can achieve in life. However, many of us go through life on what I like to call, **"Limited Functionality".** We do the same thing day in and day out (work, school, home, TV, church, gym, etc.)

> *You are limitless to the ideas, the possibilities, the dreams, and the goals that you can achieve in life.*

The moment that you were *dropped on this earth*, your potential took off ahead of you. **This entire race of life is about you catching up with yourself.** Not the Joneses. Who are the Joneses anyway? I would love to meet them because they are responsible for most people living in tremendous amounts of debt today.

Maximizing Your Potential

Why? Because most people spend money they don't have, to buy things they don't need, to impress people that they really don't even like. All because, somewhere along the line, they were taught to "try and keep up with the Joneses! No disrespect to those with the last name Jones. Smiles

My Iceberg Theory

In order to maximize our true potential, we must understand that we all are Icebergs. Humans have different shapes, heights, sizes, colors, depths of knowledge and understanding, drifting speeds (traveling through life at different accelerations), and ultimate destinations. Our lives mirror the major characteristics of an iceberg.

Maximizing Your Potential

·   *Insight about Icebergs*
    All Icebergs are derived from much larger masses than themselves.

·   *Insight about You*
    You were derived from a source much greater yourself!

·   *Insight about Icebergs*
    Icebergs are very unstable without a solid foundation.

·   *Insight about You*
    Without a solid foundation, you can be very unstable!

·   *Insight about Icebergs*
    All Icebergs tower above the water level to some degree or another!

·   *Insight about You*
    You are a success! You stand out in your own unique, individual, special, destined way!

·   *Insight about Icebergs*
    70 to 90% of an Iceberg's true mass is hidden below the waterline!

·   *Insight about You*
    70 to 90% of who you are is yet to be seen. It's hidden below the waterline of your potential.

Maximizing Your Potential

What Potential Really Is!

70 to 90% of who you are is yet to be seen. It's hidden below the waterline of your potential.

Untapped Resources - These are people you have not met, or people you have met but have not maximized your connection with them yet. These could be business cards that you collected and have not followed up on. These could be sales leads that have gone uncontacted. These could be resources of financial or intellectual capital that you have not discovered, or really chosen to uncover due to laziness, being understaffed, or just procrastination.

Dr. Mike Murdock is one of the wisest Champions of Success that I have ever met. He has written hundreds of books, but he has one that I love to death. It's called, "The Law of Recognition". In this book, he says that everything we want and need in life is already in our life in some way or another. It's just a problem of recognition. As soon as we recognize who or what it is, and that they or it exists to benefit us, the light goes off and we see an opportunity to seize that moment.

Dormant Abilities – I see this many times. I have also been very guilty of this in my past. **People with dormant abilities can sing, but they don't. They can write, but they won't. They can dance, they can produce, they can design, they can build, they**

can engineer, they can sell, they can administrate, they can account, they can develop, they can teach, they can motivate…. **BUT they don't.** Their abilities lie dormant inside of them. These people are often jealous and critical of others who are expressing their talents – being overly judgmental towards someone who has successfully taken steps towards greatness that they themselves have not taken.

Sometimes we don't pick the books we read, they pick us. Many times at our jobs, we don't complete the work - the work is completing us. Why? Because many times, life hands us different circumstances,

> *The gap between where you are and where you want to be should not be something that makes you comfortable.*

tests, and assessments, to work the potential, the ability, and the talents out of us. Many people don't discover how physically strong they are until they get in a battle. Most of us don't understand how resilient our human spirit is until we have to bounce back from a major setback in life. You have a choice, either you can be hard on yourself, or life will do it for you. Either way, your abilities will be worked out of you - believe that. And in order to be a grave robber of greatness, you must work out of you everything that lies inside of you.

Maximizing Your Potential

Unused Power – I believe we all have power within us.

- Power to Focus.
- Power to Dream.
- Power to Love.
- Power to Create.
- Power to Invest.
- Power to Change.
- Power to Inspire.
- Power to Motivate.
- Power to Follow God.
- Power to Forgive.
- Power to Serve.
- Power for Work.
- Power to Learn.
- Power to Apply what is learned.
- Power to Concentrate.
- Power to Come back.
- Power to Kick Negative Folk out of our Lives.
- Power to Graduate.
- Power to Excel.
- Power to Live Abundantly.

Now, all this power is great, but only if it is used! Most of us don't use our power. **We let life just act on us – making us reactive (instead of us acting on life – making us proactive).** Would you go to the store and buy batteries for a major device you had a home, only to get home leave the batteries on the counter and never use them? You can't complain

Maximizing Your Potential

about your life not being complete without the use of that device. Why? Because you failed to use the power you possessed through purchase of the batteries.

Several years ago, I was working for a Big 5 Consulting Firm. We did a lot of Organizational Development projects for major Utility Clients. Well, during my stint on some of these projects, I learned some really awesome things about power. **I learned that power cannot be stored or contained. I learned that as soon as electrical power is created, it has to immediately be transmitted and distributed throughout the power lines.** Wow! Now let's look at this from the human perspective. Our power to do all the things I listed previously cannot be stored or contained. It must be transmitted or we lose it to the grave. **So we must begin to transmit our creative power into action steps that will turn cognition into creation, thinking into trying, dreaming into doing, and wanting into walking.** If you don't use what you have, it will leave you and be snatched by the hands of the grave. But you are too awesome, too blessed, and too powerful to let that happen to you right? Great!

Unfulfilled Purpose – Have you ever known someone who was walking in their life's purpose, but they were not maximizing the potential of that gifting in their life? I am sure you know of someone like that. They may be closer than you think. Smiles! You see, I believe that in order to really be great, we must maximize the potential of our purpose.

Maximizing Your Potential

Let's take teaching as an example. If teaching is your purpose and you are teaching now that is great. However, are there others that you could teach? Are there additional subjects or topics you could teach? Are there new types of students you could teach? Are there new methodologies that you could apply in your classroom? Could you change your classroom? Make it outdoors? Take more fieldtrips to really create an illustrated message of the learning?

These are just a few examples of how we (regardless of our industry) can maximize the potential of our purpose, and thus leave a lasting impression on the hearts and minds of those we serve.

One final thought on this topic before we move on. I believe that you and I must not look at potential as optional. It is mandatory that potential excites you, motivates you, and compels you to maximize it. **The gap between where you are and where you want to be should not be something that makes you comfortable.** You should be a little irritated by it. This healthy irritation will be exactly what you need to continue to get you up early in the morning, and investing time later in the evening.

I like the way my friend Gary Coxe says it … "In the beginnings of a business, you will have more time than money to invest. So invest it like a madman. Soon you will experience a reversal, where you will have more money than time – that's when you hire someone to complete some of your tasks for you because you need to invest your potential in other places." Wow! Good Stuff.

STEPS TO MAXIMIZING YOUR POTENTIAL

1. Identify where you are! When you are lost driving to a party or important appointment and you call for directions, what is the first question the person on the other line asks you? "Where are you now?" Why do they ask you that question? Because they cannot guide you safely to where you should ultimately be, until they know your starting point - your current state. Pastor Paula White says, **"You can't change what you don't confront, and you can confront what you don't identify."** So we must learn to identify where we are and move from there. Self-analysis, introspection, and reflection are good ways to do this. Have a starting point for yourself, and chart your success from there.

2. Vision where you want to be! Once you have a clear picture of exactly or approximately where you are, you then must look forward into your future and envision where you ultimately want to be. **Vision is the ability to look beyond your current situation, and see yourself based on what time, determination, focus, and smart work will earn you.** Faith is the key ingredient to having a larger vision of yourself. Create the picture of your future

Delatorro L. McNeal II

that you want. **See yourself with more finances, more education, more degrees, more experience, more provision, more opportunities, more notoriety, more responsibilities, and more clients.** Visions grab you and don't let you go until you accomplish them.

3. Systematically set goals that are aligned with your purpose! This is what Chapter 6 – How to SAM Your Goals and Dreams is all about, so I won't say much here besides the fact that you must use your goals as the vehicle to get you from where you are to where you want to be. A life without goals is like football with no end zones, like basketball with no hoops, and baseball with no bases or home plates. We must have goals, and achieve goals on a regular basis to maximize our potential, because after all, **the overall purpose of goals is to stretch you towards your potential.**

4. Take consistent daily action towards the goals you have set. Again, we will cover this more in Chapter 6. However, **one of the biggest components of success that separates the good from the great is the ability to be consistent.** There must be at least one thing that you are willing to practice and prepare for each day. The thing that you are consistent with is the thing you will manifest in your life.

You must use your goals as the vehicle to get you from where you are to where you want to be.

Maximizing Your Potential

5. Surround yourself with a Master Mind Group.
Most times in order to really seize all of our potential, we need to surround ourselves with others who will see our potential and demand that we get our greatness out. We need mentors; people who have been there and done that. Your Master Mind Group needs to be involved in all the major decisions of your life. They need to meet with you at least quarterly to help you plan, strategize, and focus on your next steps. Your Master Mind Group needs to be your own personal roundtable. They should share your vision, know your spirit, encourage your development, and correct you when you are wrong. They should cut on you, empower you, and help you become all that you were designed to be.

Notes:

_____

_____

_____

_____

_____

_____

_____

Delatorro L. McNeal II

Maximizing Your Potential

8 QUICK REVIEW POINTS
FOR A NEW BEGINNING IN YOUR QUEST!

1. Walking in your life's purpose and maximizing your potential are two separate issues. **Purpose is the correct use of your life. Potential is the maximum use of your life.**

2. Potential is the gap that exists between where you are and where you should be.

3. The moment you were dropped on this earth, your potential began running forward towards your destiny. **The entire race of life is about your catching up with yourself...not the Joneses!**

4. Like an Iceberg, 70% - 90% of your true greatness is still to be seen. **It's hidden...Uncover It!**

5. The root word of Potential is Potent, which means, **strong, focused, concentrated POWER! Your power is locked up inside of your maximizing your potential.**

6. Evidence of potential are untapped resources, dormant abilities, unused power, and unfulfilled purpose.

7. Maximizing your potential has a great deal to do with the individuals that surround your life.

8. The purpose of goals and dreams is to **stretch your action towards your potential and destiny.**

Delatorro L. McNeal II

Maximizing Your Potential

One of my favorite Poems
The Man in the Glass Poem
This poem was written by a man who died at the age of 24.

When you get what you
want in your struggle for self,
and the world makes you king for a day.
Just go to the mirror and look at yourself
and see what that man has to say!
For it isn't your father, mother, or wife
whose judgment upon which you must pass.
For the fellow whose verdict counts most in your life
is the one staring back from the glass.

Some people might think you're
a straight-shooting chum
and call you a wonderful guy.
But the man in the glass thinks you're only a bum
if you can't look him straight in the eye.
For he's the one to please never mind all the rest,
for he's with you clear until the end.
And you've passed your most difficult and
dangerous test,
when the man in the glass is your friend.

For you can fool the entire world down your
pathway of life,
and get pats on your back as you pass.
But your final reward will be headaches and tears
if you've cheated the man in the glass!

Notes

Del's Footnote:

My friend, don't cheat yourself
out of your own greatness!
Don't deprive this world of enjoying your greatness!
We need the gifting that you contain,
that's why you are here!

Notes:

_____

_____

_____

_____

_____

_____

_____

_____

_____

_____

_____

Chapter 4

Born to Win, but Conditioned to Lose?

Born to Win, but Conditioned to Lose?

When I was first given this title, I almost fell out of my seat. I love this title because it encapsulates the place where most people are in their cognitive lives. I used to ask the questions - *"Why, God, are so many people who are gifted beyond belief not possessing the land that they desire? Why are they not living the dream that others are?"* Then Zig Ziglar told a story that summed it all up for me. This story has been told with many different nuances, but they all speak to the same point. I tell this story in the majority of my keynotes because it's so powerful. I hope you enjoy it.

The Fleas in the Jar Story

There once was a scientist who performed a study on fleas. He took about 10 fleas and put them into a jar. Then he screwed a lid on top of the jar. Almost immediately, the fleas began to jump up and down, attempting to get out of the jar. Each time they jumped, they hit their heads on the lid, fell down and tried again. Well, after about an hour, the scientist was able to unscrew the lid off of the jar, and never worry about the fleas getting out of the jar. Why? **Because they would never jump high enough again.**

Fleas that once had the potential to jump 36 inches, now can't jump 8 inches. **They were <u>born to win</u>, but they had been <u>conditioned to lose</u>.** Similar conditioning studies have been done on tigers, elephants, monkeys, dogs, rats, and even humans.

Delatorro L. McNeal II

Born to Win, but Conditioned to Lose?

Yes, we all have been born to win, but most of us have been conditioned to lose in some way.

Del, what conditioned the fleas to not jump as high anymore? GREAT QUESTION.

The temporary lid that was screwed onto their environment is what conditioned them. I like to call it **The Lid of Limitation**. And all of us, my friend, have hit our heads on some pretty hard stuff in life that really hurt us and caused us to not jump as high when opportunities presented themselves again. For the fleas, the Lid of Limitation was a jar lid. For the tiger, it was a shock collar. For the monkey, it was an electric cage. **For people, it's things like a bad home life, a poor neighborhood, debt, divorce, bankruptcy, foreclosure, failed businesses, child abuse, past failures, low self-esteem, poor grades, broken trust, spoiled friendships, negative people... and the list goes on and on.**

These things have conditioned us to not try, to not **trust**, to not **believe in our dreams**, to **not make better grades**, to **not open businesses**, to **not try to get out of the ghetto**, to not **remarry**, and to **not get up and try again.**

And the saddest thing about the experiment is that even when the lid or the obstacle or painful situation is removed or in the case of the fleas – unscrewed, we still don't jump as high. Why? **Because we have**

Born to Win, but Conditioned to Lose?

allowed ourselves to be conditioned by a temporary obstacle, and let that ruin our lifetime possibility. My friend, if you have stopped jumping to reach the things that you want in life, the grave is winning and **it is robbing you instead of you robbing it.**

Well, if we can be conditioned to lose, we can be conditioned to WIN.

The fleas lost their vision. If they still had vision, they would have seen that the lid had been removed. But because of their temporary pain, they allowed that lid to force their eyes off of the prize and onto the problem. They lost sight of the possibility of freedom and an abundant life. What about you?

Many people don't know this, but maybe you do. It is a scientific fact that the bumblebee is NOT supposed to be able to fly! Its body is too big and its wings are too small to support its weight. BUT GUESS WHAT! **Nobody ever told the bumblebee - so it flies!** Well, most of us have not been as fortunate as the bumblebee because most of us HAVE BEEN told that our dream is **too big,** while our finances and abilities are **too small.**

Many of us have been conditioned by the negative words of others for years. **Well, if we can be conditioned to lose, we can be conditioned to WIN.** We can be **conditioned to succeed, to prosper, to**

Delatorro L. McNeal II

Born to Win, but Conditioned to Lose?

achieve, to possess the land, to think entrepreneurally, and to surround ourselves with the right people who see greatness within us.

Here is the exciting news about the fleas. If the scientist introduces a new (not previously conditioned) flea into the jar that has no lid, that new flea will go in, **and jump right back out**. Once the other conditioned fleas see it, they jump out too. So as a professional speaker, I jump into audiences full of people who thought that they couldn't write books, open businesses, get degrees, start families, or live their dreams, and I show them how they, too, can JUMP OUT. **I give people their vision, their fight, and their determination back.**

The fleas lost their vision. Have you? In this chapter, I want to help you get your vision back and condition yourself, through your attitude, to rob the grave of its greatness.

Have you lost your vision?

My family has a history of poor eyesight. Whenever the Ball/McNeal families get together, most of the people present - aunts, uncles, cousins, grandparents, nieces, and nephews - wear some form of corrective lenses because of the bloodline of poor eyesight. It's kind of funny to imagine what would happen if someone took all of our glasses off during a buffet

Born to Win, but Conditioned to Lose?

dinner. We would be some messed up people, let me tell you! Out of about 50 family members, probably 3 would be able to see their way out of that crazy situation. Smiles! Why do I tell that story? Great question, my friend. Keep reading.

One ordinary morning, I woke up before my alarm clock sounded. **Before climbing out of bed, I laid there thinking about the day, the appointments, the meetings, the speaking engagements, the training sessions, and the people I would encounter that day.** Now, because I am nearsighted, I have difficulty seeing things clearly that are more than 5 ft. away from me without my glasses or contacts. Well, I got up and immediately, automatically, and almost instinctively reached my right hand over to the dresser to grab my glasses. To my surprise, my glasses were missing!

I couldn't see a thing. I couldn't tell what time it was. I couldn't read the date on the calendar. My goals that are posted all over my bedroom wall, were fuzzy. It was a mess! I began walking all around my bedroom, trying diligently not to awaken The Queen (my wife, Nova) and searching for my vision - with no vision. I looked everywhere. Finally, after about 10 minutes of searching the whole house, I found my glasses lying under the bed. I have no clue how they got there, but that's where they were. Relieved, I went on about my day with correct eyesight and vision, and I was successful. The point of the story you ask? Keep reading…

Born to Win, but Conditioned to Lose?

I always ask for divine insight and wisdom when I go through a challenge or difficult time in my life. In every experience, I ask 3 simple questions of myself and of God.

- What am I supposed to learn from this?
- What could someone else learn from this?
- How does this incident parallel a life principle that all people could benefit from?

Notice that I ask empowering and wisdom-gaining questions - not negative, victimizing questions whose answers further burden my soul. My friend, **to change the answers you get in life, you must first change the questions that you ask of yourself and others!** We will talk more about this in Chapter 7.

Back to the lost eyeglasses. The moral of that true story comes in the form of a question.
Have you lost your vision?

You see, your vision is the way you see things. It's the way your mind processes a person, place, thing, or idea. Without my glasses, I would have worn a mismatched outfit and I might have even tripped and fallen. I would have driven poorly and definitely gotten into an accident. My book writing would have been awful.

To change the answers you get in life, you must first change the questions that you ask of yourself and others!

Born to Win, but Conditioned to Lose?

My reading of the newspaper would have been futile. My emails would have been incomprehensible, and I would have been walking in the wrong direction all day!

Well, my friend, glasses or contacts are a physical symbol for correct vision. Without correct vision,

- goals and dreams are fuzzy and seem unattainable.
- positive people in your life seem like reminders of where you're not.
- direction is unclear and your action steps get fumbled.
- searching and rarely finding seems to be a pastime.
- your drive and passion for life disappears.
- your focus is lost and you are distracted easily.
- you make bad decisions that cost you significant time and energy.

I don't know about you, but I don't have time to live my life without clear vision. Why? Because I know the benefits of having a clear vision. **Notice, I did not attempt any major task until I found my vision.** I did not try to work towards any goal, dream or aspiration until I had my vision. I did not attempt to help any customers, students, family or friends until I had my vision. Why? Because the blind cannot lead the blind! Now, let me go deeper. From a physical standpoint, I did not attempt anything without my vision. However, do you remember what I did before I reached for my glasses?

Born to Win, but Conditioned to Lose?

Yep, I envisioned my day. I had a vision in my mind and I told my day where to go, instead of asking it where it would go! I imagined how each meeting would play out and how each speaking engagement would go - all before I even stepped out of bed. I painted the picture in my mind of what I wanted. I got up, found my physical vision, and began working to create the picture that I had drawn in my mind. In order to rob the grave effectively, you must do the same thing every day!

The Painted Car Story

The other day, while driving down the road, I noticed a unique sports car. This car was different from any other car that I had seen on the road that day. The thing that made this car so unique was the colors of its paint. Most cars are painted one main color. This car's paint color **actually changed** based on the way the sun was hitting it. When the car was in front of me, it was **pink.** When it was beside me, it was **blue.** When it was behind me, it was **purple.** There were three totally different colors on the same car, with the only difference being the angle at which I was looking at it.

Well, my friend, life is a lot like that sports car. Life is painted with a rainbow of different colors, hues, and gradients. Life is decorated with a plethora of different successes, failures, ups, downs, mountaintops, and

Born to Win, but Conditioned to Lose?

valley lows. And based on the way that you are looking at life, it will give off a certain color or appearance. In other words, your perception can be drastically different, depending on where you are in life.

Do you know someone who, regardless of how hard you try, finds something wrong with everything? **Do you know someone who is committed to complaining, focused on finding fault, and impressed with life's imperfections?** These are the people that always see the glass as half-empty.

When life's challenges are in front of you, they look one way. When you are in the middle of them, they look another way. But, when you have overcome them, they look totally different! So it is our attitude that really determines not only how high we go, but how much we enjoy the flight in the process!

Your vision and your attitude are so critical for success. The reason why one person can look at a layoff and see disaster, while another person can look at a layoff as a golden opportunity, is because one person has a larger and clearer vision and more positive attitude than the other. Why is it that one person can look at a slow economy and want to commit suicide, while another person can look at the same economic situation and think entrepreneurally? It's all about their attitudes. Most people take their greatness to the grave because of a poor attitude towards success and opportunity.

Born to Win, but Conditioned to Lose?

Seven "Must Have" Attitudes that will Condition you for Total Success

Life is always trying to teach us something.

1. Learn from Everything! Life is always trying to teach us something. **Every person you meet, every show you watch, every video you rent, every stranger you bless with money or a hot meal, every customer you serve, every student you teach, every business deal that you negotiate, every mile you drive, and every product you sell is teaching you something. Everything that you do in life is going to produce a result.** It may not always get you closer to the goal, but it will produce a result. So if you can begin to say to yourself that you will LEARN FROM EVERYTHING that you encounter (good or bad), you will be in great shape and your attitude will remain one of greatness!

2. This too, Shall Pass! The problems of life always seem the worst when we are right in the middle of them. However, once you overcome the obstacles, you realize that things were not nearly as bad as you thought. **Don't let temporary setbacks cause you to forfeit your dream.**

I was walking along a beautiful beach one day when I learned a valuable life lesson. I noticed that as violently

Born to Win, but Conditioned to Lose?

as the waves were crashing against my bare feet and legs, no matter how fast and how powerful they came, **the water always receded!** Your troubles are much like those hefty waves. They will pass. **You are in one of three phases at all times. You're either in a problem, have just left one, or are heading towards one.** So learning the process of problems and understanding that they are life lessons, will allow you to be like a ball and bounce back from your setbacks!

3. NO RETREAT, NO SURRENDER! At some point you must get to the level of cognition that mandates that you will not back down from a challenge. No matter what comes your way, you will not turn back. You will not retreat to your old self. You will not give in to the maze of mediocrity. You will not bow down to the negative individuals of this world who want to see you fail. **Today, determine in your mind and heart that you will bend, but never break!** You have come too far, and nobody can turn you around! Nobody! You have taken the opponent's best shot. **Now they'd better get ready for yours! You are Bad!** Remember how awesome you are every single day! Don't ever, ever give up!

4. Half-Full / Half-Empty! Have you ever looked at your credentials, degrees, trophies, and awards and admitted within yourself that you are doing pretty well? But then almost within the same thought-process you feel like you've got so far to go with your goals and dreams that you really haven't done much?

Born to Win, but Conditioned to Lose?

Well, this paragraph will be a breath of fresh air for you! THAT'S ACTUALLY A GOOD THING! You are experiencing what I call being **half-full _and_ half-empty. Occupation of your current level allows you to be full, but desire for the next level commands that you be empty.** On the one hand, you are full of gratitude and appreciation for your current level of success. But on the other hand, you are also full of anticipation and expectation for something that you have not attained yet. THAT'S A GOOD THING! I, and many others who I know and study in the area of success, live as half-full and half-empty. You need this type of understanding because it will keep you right where you need to be. **That is happy with today, but excited and persistent about tomorrow.**

5. Together we can do it! Dr. Mike Murdock says, "Positive People are the Bridge to your Dreams"! My friend, the reality is that none of us can make it through this journey of life alone. We need people, connections, relationships, and the power of networking to succeed. With the statistical fact that each of us is only 3 people away from knowing everyone in the world, it is imperative that we understand the power of relationships. I am a networking fool and you should be, too! Les Brown says, "You should live your life as though you have yet to meet 50% of the people responsible for helping you achieve your dream"! Zig Ziglar says, "Everyone you meet is a prospect"! Here's a nice paradigm. **I can't**

Born to Win, but Conditioned to Lose?

do what you can do. And you can't do what I can do. But together, WE can do anything! Keep a team of positive people around you. Keep a band of grave robbers in your life at all times. We will talk about this more in the next chapter.

6. If it is to be, then it's up to me! The only person that can stop your dream dead in its tracks is you! Nobody else is bad enough to stop you! They can try, but they will not succeed. Some may delay you temporarily, but only you can stop yourself permanently. To maintain an attitude of greatness, you must continually remind yourself that nobody owes you anything. Everything you will get in life is a direct result of what you make happen for yourself. **Success and Greatness don't just land softly on your shoulders - they each carry a nice price tag.** Play your rightful role. You are the CEO. You are the Chief Executive Officer of your own life. Live like it, walk like it and talk like it. If it shall come true, my friend, it is up to you! You are your dreams' best friend, or worst enemy! Choose to be your most powerful ally! I believe in you!

The only person that can stop your dream dead in its tracks is you!

7. I can do all things through Him that strengthens me! For me personally, and many other extremely successful people that I know and study, this single attitude is the cornerstone for all others. When you

Born to Win, but Conditioned to Lose?

realize that with God on your side, you are 100% unstoppable, your motivation goes through the roof. Why? Because you know that your steps are divinely orchestrated and that everything you put your hands on must produce at some point in the future. Whatever the task at hand, with your inner spiritual self engaged, you will succeed. You have the Creator on your side.

Simple Ways to Maintain your Greatness Attitude

1. Avoid Folk! People are just like elevators - they either take you up or down! Know that! Stay far away from negative people who want to see you fail. Negative people give off an energy that sucks the life out of your success. Their very presence drains your enthusiasm. Force people in your life that are close to you to guard and protect you from negative drama-creating individuals. They will attempt to kill your dream, if given the chance.

People are just like elevators - they either take you up or down!

Footnote about Negative Individuals and Thoughts
Psychologists say that the average human processes 40,000 to 50,000 individual thoughts per day. That's a lot! The only disturbing thing about this discovery is that for most people, **85% of those thoughts are negative and self-defeating.** The individuals you surround yourself with are critical.

Born to Win, but Conditioned to Lose?

Reason being, if you are the average person, thinking the average thoughts, according to most psychologists you probably process about **36,000 negative thoughts each day.** That's why listening to positive material, attending seminars, church services, classes, and other empowerment events is so vital. These success activities renew your mind with positive data, which allows you to succeed and prosper. Now, let's say you have 5 negative friends who although they mean well, are not healthy for your greatness. If you interact each day with these 5 negative individuals - **your goals and dreams have the potential of being surrounded by over 180,000 negative thoughts, comments, feelings, and suggestions. Don't surround yourself or your dreams with that garbage.** Your dreams and visions are too precious for that.

The cool thing is that you can condition yourself to think positively and convert that 85% from negative to positive. Doing this means that you surround your goals and dreams with 36,000 empowering thoughts each day. With the addition of mentors, mentees, and success soldiers, you have the potential to surround your dreams with **180,000 positive thoughts, comments, feelings, and suggestions each day.** That's a lot of power and positivity, which is exactly what your goals and dreams need in order to flourish! Think about it!

Born to Win, but Conditioned to Lose?

2. Recruit Success Soldiers. Station 7 positive people around your life at all times. There should be at least 7 individuals that you can call when you get good news to celebrate. There should also be at least 7 people that you can call with bad news who will love, support, pray, encourage, and advise you to come back from your setback. Station these positive people around your dreams, goals, and aspirations. **Be open, real, and transparent with these people. Allow them to shape you, protect you, and challenge you for excellence in your life.** Communicate with at least one of your 7 soldiers daily! Communicate with all 7 bi-weekly. Update them monthly on your success.

3. Expand your Mind. Continue to think outside the box! Be radical about the ideas for success that you have. Allow your mind to be open to many possibilities, and use your morals, values, and spiritual believe system to filter out the things that are not consistent with what you know to be right. Incorporate only those things that align with your greatness. There are numerous ways to get to where you want to go. **Invest in wisdom!** Allow people who have been where you're trying to go to **"Cut Your Learning Curve"!** Allow your mind to be like a sponge, soaking up everything! However, be sure to ring out all the stuff you don't need.

4. Always have a heart to help others! The things that you make happen for someone else, will soon happen for you! I believe that we all will reap what

Born to Win, but Conditioned to Lose?

we sow. **So if we are sowing help, we must reap a harvest of help in our near future. That excites me.** Plus, helping others takes the focus off of your issues and concerns and before you know it, your troubles seem small compared to those that you are assisting. Help always has a boomerang affect. It will come back to bless you! Zig Ziglar's mission is to help people get what they want out of life. In doing so, he and his company get what they want!

5. Renew Your Mind Daily. What you listen to the first hour of your day determines your level of productivity throughout the day. **Always guard the first things that enter your mind each day, and the last things that enter your mind each night. What you listen to in the morning determines what you act on.** What you listen to at night determines what you dream on. Choose to renew your mind with positive material, positive thoughts, and positive paradigms each day. What you put into your mind, determines what comes out of your life. So affirm daily that your goals are achievable, maintainable, and significant. **Affirm each day that you are a special, gifted, and uniquely designed individual armed with anticipation and dangerous with determination to rob the grave of every ounce of your stuff!**

6. Embrace Positive Change! Recognize that the only thing that is constant is change. We talked about this in Chapter 1. Continue to be a proactive person, making life react to your positivity. When positive

Born to Win, but Conditioned to Lose?

change occurs, be quick to help in the implementation process. When negative change takes place, be quick to help think of a positive viewpoint. Nothing is as bad as it first seems. Initial shock puts most of us on the run. **Use change as your friend. Embrace the good, negotiate the bad, and create the change that you want for yourself every single day!**

7. Always look to learn. Remember, everything that happens to you in life - good or bad - is trying to teach you something! Look for the lessons in life that are talking to you all day everyday! **If you will try to learn something from everything that happens in your life, you will never fail. You will only experience hardships designed to teach you a life lesson that will catapult you further into your divine destiny!** When your mind is in gear to learn, you are more open to possibilities, innovative ideas, and success strategies.

Apply these simple success strategies and you will not only possess, but also maintain an attitude of greatness!

Born to Win, but Conditioned to Lose?

8 Quick Review Points for a New Beginning in your Quest!

1. **You were born to WIN! Condition yourself to do the same!**

2. Look at your life through the right lenses and your outlook will be much better.

3. Work towards consistency with your attitude. Moodiness can be an excuse and a crutch. **Don't let the word "moody" be an excuse for your vacillating inability to standardize your attitude.**

4. Every action in your life produces a result. It may not get you closer to the goal, but it will produce some result. So if you will make up in your mind that you will learn from everything, **each "failure" in life turns into a life lesson.**

5. Living Half-Full and Half-Empty is OKAY! Occupation of your current level allows you to feel full, but desire for the next level allows you to feel empty (*thirsting for more*).

6. Renew your mind daily with positive materials that will nourish your dreams, goals, and aspirations.

7. Life is a mirror. **Make sure you display the same attitude that you expect others to approach you with.**

8. STAY AWAY FROM NEGATIVE PEOPLE. Run!

Delatorro L. McNeal II

Born to Win, but Conditioned to Lose?

One of my Favorite Poems
IF - by Rudyard Kipling

If you can keep your head when all about you
Are losing theirs and blaming it on you;
If you can trust yourself when all men doubt you,
But make allowance for their doubting too;
If you can wait and not be tired by waiting,
Or, being lied about, don't deal in lies,
Or, being hated, don't give way to hating,
And yet don't look too good, nor talk too wise,

If you can dream - and not make dreams your master;
If you can think - and not make thoughts your aim;
If you can meet with triumph and disaster
And treat these two impostors just the same;
If you can bear to hear the trust you've spoken
Twisted by knaves to make a trap for fools,
Or watch the things you gave your life to, broken,
And stoop down and build 'em up with worn-out tools;

If you can take one heap of all of your winnings
And risk it on one turn of pitch-and-toss,
And lose and start again at your beginnings
And never breathe a word about your loss;
If you can force your heart and nerve and sinew
To serve your turn long after they are gone,
And so hold on when there is nothing in you
Accept "The Will" which says to them "Hold On",

Born to Win, but Conditioned to Lose?

If you can talk with crowds and keep your virtue,
Or walk with kings - nor lose the common touch,
If neither foes nor loving friends can hurt you,
If all men count with you, but none too much,
If you can fill the unforgiving minute
With sixty seconds' worth of distance run,
Yours is the Earth and everything that's in it,
And - which is more - you'll be a Man my son!

Born to Win, but Conditioned to Lose?

Reality Check:
The Benefits of Paying the Price!

- Goodness will change a student. **Greatness will change a University!**
- Goodness will help a family. **Greatness will help the entire Community!**
- Goodness will land you a job. **Greatness will give you a purpose-driven Career!**
- Goodness will shake a boardroom. **Greatness will shake a Corporation!**
- Goodness will create one sale. **Greatness will earn you Repeat Business!**
- Goodness will allow you to dream. **Greatness enables you to make others' Dreams come true!**
- Goodness touches the head. **Greatness changes the heart!**
- Goodness costs you nothing. **Greatness costs you everything!**
- Goodness is low-risk and safe. **Greatness is high-risk and dangerously positive!**
- Goodness buys the ordinary. **Greatness purchases the Extraordinary!**
- Goodness births problems. **Greatness solves problems!**
- The Good come to church. **The Great are the church!**
- The Good fight just to show up. **The Great show up for the fight!**

Delatorro L. McNeal II

Notes

- The Good operate on scarcity. The Great operate on Abundance!
- The Good die full of desires. **The Great die empty of their greatness!**
- The Good have potential. **The Great Maximize their Potential!**

Notes:

_____

_____

_____

_____

_____

_____

_____

_____

_____

_____

_____

_____

_____

Chapter 5

Caught Between a Dream and a Job?

Caught Between A Dream & a Job!

As I travel across the country, coaching people from corporate America to academia, I find that most people are in the same boat. They are experiencing a very common dilemma that is stopping them from *Robbing the Grave of Its Greatness.* **They are caught between a dream and a job. They are trapped between a paycheck and a promise.**

Without fail, whenever I speak, coach, consult, and interact with people, the number one concern that I hear is a feeling of **being trapped.** Many of us have tremendous dreams in our hearts, but we work to pay the bills. We want to step out and pursue the dream, however, the pressure of routine bills, credit debt, student loans, car payments, and mortgages keep us caught between a dream and a job.

The purpose of this chapter is to help those of you who feel like you're trapped. I was divinely blessed with this concept and paradigm while driving to a speaking engagement early in 2002. I asked God, *"Why are so many people trapped? Why are they so afraid to take that step? Why are they so afraid to go for it?"* He answered and said, "Because they are caught between a dream and a job!" I had to pull over and write the title down because it gripped my heart in a special way.

I immediately began to study my own life and analyze the many times when I had felt the same way. I noticed patterns of behavior among myself and other people

Caught Between A Dream & a Job!

who felt this way. **Feelings of frustration, confusion, fear, anxiety, excitement, anticipation, longing, determination, and perplexity were just a few of the** feelings of people who found themselves caught between a dream and a job. I am sure that after Chapter 2 on Discovering and Mastering Your Life's Purpose, possibly even you may feel Caught Between a Dream and a Job! Would you agree that right now, either you or someone close to you is stuck in this place?

CONGRATUATIONS! That's great. I am happy because I knew the answer would be yes. Even as I am writing this chapter, I am caught. I am in the process of transitioning from a great job, to a great dream. I am doing it smart and I am loving each day of my transition because each day is **strategic.** Each day counts, and each day pulls me further from my job and closer to my dream. This chapter is written fresh off of the hard drive of my heart. My goal is to teach you a few things that I learned so that no matter where you are in life (be it high school, college, the military, corporate America, academia, ministry, or any other arena), you can benefit from the things that I (and so many others) have learned.

In order to Rob the Grave, you've got to get yourself uncaught and **unstuck from the cycle of being caught between the thing that pays your bills, and the thing that pays your destiny.** Being caught is a VERY GOOD THING. However, if you really want

Caught Between A Dream & a Job!

> *I believe that you have 100% pure GOLD on the inside of you.*

GREATNESS (which I know you do), then it's going to cost you getting unstuck and working your way from your job into your dream.

Why am I so passionate about this topic? Because, in the challenging and changing times that we live in, it is more imperative than ever to focus internally. We need to take our eyes off of extrinsic motivation, and focus on the only guarantee - **internal motivation. We have to look inside.** I believe that you have 100% pure GOLD on the inside of you. Jobs will only unleash a certain percentage of that gold. **You must work out the rest through your dream!** Now is your time. Now is your season. You are reading this book for a reason. You are reading *on purpose*! Smiles! The statistics that follow should convince you of the importance of beginning your wise transition into the dream you have been envisioning all your life. I am very excited for you.

Startling Statistics

• **1 out of every 100 Americans will be wealthy by age 65.**
Based on a 40-hour workweek, 1% of all Americans will be wealthy by age 65. This is sad because the average American will have 1 million dollars pass

Caught Between A Dream & a Job!

through their hands in a lifetime. Economic experts say that if all the wealth of the US were stored up in a treasury and deposited equally among every American, **each one of us would have 3 million dollars!** Do you know what that means? **Somebody's got your money! Use your dream to get it back!**

• **9 out of 10 families live paycheck-to-paycheck.** 90% of the working families in America are one paycheck away from being evicted. This is sad because things do not have to be this way, my friend. Even in two income households, an instant gratification attitude keeps most people living far beyond their means and barely making ends meet. **You were never meant to survive on one paycheck, that's why multiple income streams are so important.**

• **65% of College Students finish 4-year degrees in 5 years, and most work in fields not related to their major.** Two thirds of college students today are taking an extra year to graduate. But for what? For a degree that most will not even use upon graduation because they will begin working in jobs that are not in their field of study. Additionally, a recent study released by *USATODAY College* stated that the federal government issues 74 billion dollars each year in Student Financial Aid. 58% of those dollars are distributed as loans that must be repaid. This means that over half of the students in college today, getting any type of financial assistance - are getting loans. This also means they are using

Caught Between A Dream & a Job!

someone else's money to pay for a degree that half of them won't even use after graduation. Again, my friend, things don't have to be this way. We have got to begin aligning our degrees and our dollars with our innate gifts and talents. The days of going to school, getting a good education, and writing your own ticket until retirement are over. **You must think a new way, to live a new way.**

• Student Loan Debt stays with the average American family for 25 years.
Over half of graduating students have to deal with the burden of paying back their student loans. According to many financial experts, student loan debt can take up to 25 years to pay off. **Most students get good jobs with good salaries, but with the expenses of buying homes, buying cars, getting married, and having kids, student loans just become a painful addition to the routine bills of everyday life.** This does not have to be this way either. I have friends right now who are in their late 20's, drive $15,000 cars, live in $130,000 homes, make $35,000 a year, and have $1million dollar DREAMS - but they also have $8,000 in credit card debt, and over $40,000 in student loan debt to pay back! OUCH! Tremendous debt is the biggest net that traps people, and keeps them from stepping out and living their dreams. We've got to do something different if we really want something different.

Caught Between A Dream & a Job!

• **85% of Corporate America reports being dissatisfied with their jobs.**
With downsizing, rightsizing, merging, acquiring, relocating, and every other *-ing* that is going on in Corporate America, people's faith in the golden parachute and dream job with a window view and expense account is quickly dwindling. People are tired of organizations assigning worth to them. My friend, there is nothing wrong with most of these organizations, but the reality is this - **YOU DETERMINE YOUR WORTH!** One of the top reasons why so many people are not happy in corporations right now has nothing to do with money, and everything to do with upward movement. According to a study done in Florida Trend magazine, the #1 reason why good people leave good companies is because of the lack of upward advancement opportunities.

Could these Startling Statistics have anything to do with the fact that only 3% of Americans set and strive towards goals on a routine basis?
Yes! The US Census has produced studies that indicate that most Americans don't write their goals down, and don't take consistent daily action towards them. We have got to realize that if we aim at nothing, we will hit it every time. We will be covering much more of this in Chapter 6. However, it bears stating here that the fastest and smartest way to get from goodness to greatness is to become a goal achiever and goal maintainer. True goal achievers and maintainers take

Caught Between A Dream & a Job!

> *By the time you finish reading this sentence, someone somewhere in the US will have started his or her own home-based business.*

purposeful action daily, and do not allow the obstacles of life to turn them around.

BUT LISTEN! THERE IS HOPE!

• **Every 10 seconds, a New Home-based Business is STARTED in America.**
That's right. By the time you finish reading this sentence, someone somewhere in the US will have started his or her own home-based business. Amazing! That means that 6 businesses are started here in America each minute. That's 6 new opportunities for growth, expansion, development, and unlimited wealth. Six people each minute take the step of faith to transition from their job to their dream. Some succeed, some fail. But nothing beats a failure, except a *try*. **You will miss 100% of the shots that you don't take in life.** At some point, my friend, you've got to just GO FOR IT! In this chapter, I will show you how to do it smart!

• **Everyday in America, 64 Self-Made Millionaires are Born!**
This means that when you rolled out of bed this morning and brushed your teeth, 64 other people did the exact same thing somewhere in America; but those 64 other people woke with 1 Million dollars in total net worth to their credit. Wow! What a great morning! Well friend, when I woke up this morning, I was not

Caught Between A Dream & a Job!

one of those 64. But soon, and I do mean soon, it will be my *"great getting up morning"*. One day, I will be one of those 64. What about you? When will it be your turn? Make the decision that your time is coming, and begin to do each day whatever it takes (positive) to possess the financial prosperity that already belongs to you.

My 2 Schools of Thought on Transition

If you ask 10 people how to transition from a job to a dream, you may get 10 different answers. However, each of those pieces of advice will probably fall into either of two schools of thought. These schools of thought have to do with rate and intensity at which you will make this transition in your life. And make no small deal about this. **Transitioning from your job to your dream is probably one of the biggest decisions and action steps you will ever make.** Knowing yourself and knowing your purpose and mission in life will help you determine which school of thought you will subscribe to.

The first theory that I want to discuss with you is what I like to call **"The Leap Frog Theory"**. This theory, as it sounds, subscribes to the notion that you should just leap off the tree, and grow your wings on the way down. Some people believe that as soon as you believe in yourself and your dream enough to jump out on nothing, you will land on something solid. I have seen

Delatorro L. McNeal II

Caught Between A Dream & a Job!

this theory hold true for some, and leave others in the financial hospital of knee-deep debt, foreclosures, and bankruptcy filings. Some people need the emergency of leaping from the tree (job) 100% before they do the only thing they can do - flap their wings (talents) and fly (produce). This is a very aggressive and very risky approach. It occurs when people quit their jobs with no plan, no goals, and no direction. But they know for sure that they don't want to do what they are doing for another second longer. This theory also kicks in when people are laid off or fired. But instead of leaping, they get kicked out of the nest. That is exactly what happened to me. **I went from a $50,000 salary to nothing in ONE DAY!** The next day I got up and made a vow to never let my destiny be determined by someone else again. I got up immediately and started writing my first book and building my speaking business. The rest is history. You know, I believe that sometimes when you are kicked out of the nest by life's situations that you **did not expect**, that's simply God's way of letting you know that you are **ready to fly**, even though you don't know it!

Sometimes it takes extreme hardship and emergency situations to move people. You need to know what it takes to get you moving towards your dream. Let me help you. **Don't wait for life to act on you. You act on life.** You will be much more successful that way. Don't wait for the carpet to be pulled from under you before you begin to build a solid foundation underneath that carpet to hold you up just in case. Begin preparing right now!

Caught Between A Dream & a Job!

The other school of thought, and my personal recommendation, is what I like to call **"The Tarzan Theory"**. **This theory suggests that it's better to hold on to a good thing, until a great thing comes along.** This theory is one of systematic, strategic progression from one stage in your life to the next. This school of thought is slower. The process is much more involved, detailed, and complex. It involves vision, focus, delayed gratification, continual preparation, mentorship, goal achievement, and building your dream line upon line and precept upon precept. This is my own personal recommendation for the best and wisest way to make a smart transition from your job to your dream. I call it the Tarzan Theory because if you've ever watched the cartoon, you notice how Tarzan moves through the jungle. He swings from one vine to the next. He does not let go of one branch until he has a solid grip on the next one. This allows him to move quickly and systematically through the jungle, and get to his destination successfully. You can do the same thing. Let me teach you how!

The rest of this chapter focuses on implementing The Tarzan Theory throughout your transition. **This approach recommends keeping your day job, while building your dream on the side until your dream is self-sustaining enough to support you and your family.** Which reminds me of another point. Your decision between these two schools of thought should be weighted and considered heavily with the following factors of your life in mind.

Caught Between A Dream & a Job!

- **Age** (What season of life development are you in?)
- **Marital Status** (Are there spouses, children, or other family members directly effected by your actions?)
- **Financial Situation** (Do you have large debts that you owe or major financial commitments?)
- **Experience Level** (Do you know enough about your dream industry to launch with no prep time?)
- **Educational Status** (Do you have the credentials needed or personally desired - to attain your dream?)

For example, you may be able to be a little more risky and take the Leap Frog Theory if you are single, have little to no debt, are young enough to re-enter the workforce (in the event of failure), have no major financial goals pending (like buying a house), and have a fair amount of experience. That leap will be much safer than one with the exact opposite scenario in play.

One last point about the Tarzan Theory: Just because it is less aggressive and more systematic and strategic, **does not mean that it will take years and years. You can transition between your job and your dream using the Tarzan Theory in a period of 1 to 5 years.** It all depends on the magnitude of your dream, the magnitude of your variables, and the magnitude of personal time and money you are willing

Caught Between A Dream & a Job!

to put on the line to make it happen for yourself. I have close friends who made a Tarzan Transition within 1 year.

A good transition gets you from Point A (Job) to Point B (Dream):

- on good terms with your past employer.
- with little financial pressure placed on your dream.
- with the education and credentials necessary to facilitate the dream.
- with a strong partial client base or business already booked towards your dream.
- with a business and marketing plan in place to carry your dream to higher heights.
- with solid financial structure for your dream that you and your family can trust.
- with Growth potential, motivation, and drive to LIVE YOUR DREAM daily!

Commercial Break

Now, let me take a commercial break and say that there is nothing at all wrong with having a job. Jobs are excellent, powerful, necessary, and financially stable stepping stones towards greatness. I got my first official tax-paying job at age 14. **I was a Package Executive at a local grocery store.** It was my job to secure the safe transfer of purchased consumer goods from the

Caught Between A Dream & a Job!

store to the client's motor vehicle in such an ergonomic fashion that… In other words, I was a BAG BOY! Smiles. But I was the best Bag Boy they'd ever had!

My friend, jobs are great. Every job has a purpose, and every purpose solves a problem. Therefore every job solves a problem. Even though the person doing the job may not feel like they are solving a problem, in fact they are. Take my first job, for example. The customer came in, put two carts worth of groceries in their cart, and then unloaded the cart at checkout. The cashier scanned the items and pushed them down to the collection area. It wasn't the cashier's job to bag groceries. That was my job. Now, by me asking the proverbial "Paper or Plastic?" question and organizing the items neatly into bags for the customer, I solved a problem for them. Customers who had picked items and paid for the items, but had no way to store and transfer the items, depended on me to perform my JOB!

That was a simple example of the fact that jobs are critical for the world to go around. We need jobs, but we also need our dreams. So let's talk about the differences of them both.

Caught Between A Dream & a Job!

The Power & Purpose of Jobs

• *Jobs provide you with Structure, Discipline, and Exposure.*
One major benefit of a job is that it provides us with structure. We have set days to work, set hours to work, set tasks to complete, and set pay for our services. This structure allows us to frame our lives around the safety, security, and structure that the job provides. The structure that jobs provide mandates that we discipline our daily behavior so that we may **birth**

habits such as effective time management, project management, people management, and resource management. As we utilize these skills, we gain exposure to clients, competition, and the marketplace. We need this exposure to allow our gifts and talents to grow and develop.

• *Jobs provide you with Experience.*
The second major benefit of a job is that it allows us to gain industry specific experience – hands-on working demonstrable knowledge of a skill that has cash value in the marketplace. This experience over time gives us a solid confidence that our talents and gifts will flourish given a variety of client situations. We need these skills for advancement, salary increases, and solid competition within the changing workforce. Experience speaks on your behalf and communicates your ability to handle multiple client situations with professionalism and proficiency.

Delatorro L. McNeal II

Caught Between A Dream & a Job!

• *Jobs teach you the Professional and Interpersonal skills necessary in today's marketplace.*
Every job has an extrinsic task, and an intrinsic character-building equivalent. For example, a grocery store Bag Boy is not just supposed to learn the kinesthetic movements of bagging groceries, but also organizational skills, ergonomic skills, negotiations skills, communication skills, customer service skills, leadership skills, teamwork skills, money-management skills, work-life balancing skills, listening skills, etc. What intrinsic character building skills is your job trying to teach you?

Every job has an extrinsic task, and an intrinsic character-building equivalent.

• *Jobs provide Monetary Compensation for your time and effort.*
We all need money! *Your life will crash if you don't have cash. Life can be mean if you don't have any green!* Get my point? Every day millions and billions of humans exchange talent for money. Jobs allow us to exchange our time, talents, and abilities for money, benefits, experience, and credibility. The stability of a bi-weekly check gives us the consistency needed to maintain our households.

• *Jobs are emotionally Low-Risk opportunities for growth.*
Many people who have not stepped out into their dream full-time would probably disagree with this

Caught Between A Dream & a Job!

statement. However, allow me to explain. Most jobs are emotionally low-risk compared to dreams, because your dream is very personal and interpersonal. You can emotionally distance yourself from your work, and the people with whom you work. However, when it comes to your dream. **That is 100% personal; you invest your entire heart when you go after your dream.** Therefore, rejections and criticisms are taken much harder when they come from the dream, then when they come from the job.

• *Jobs are Building Blocks for greater pursuits.*
Each job you take should build on the previous one. Each job you have teaches you powerful skills that you will need once you pursue your dream fulltime. The dream is coming, but meanwhile, maximize your time and profit potential by allowing your job to put you in the right position to launch you directly into your destiny.

The Power & Purpose for Dreams

• *Dreams provide Purpose, Significance, Meaning, and Excitement in life.* Your dreams help you to understand your assignment on earth; **the reason why you are here and the meaning behind your passions, pains, tears, and joys in life.** Your dreams give you hope that tomorrow can be better than today. Your dreams confirm that your life makes sense. They comfort you when you feel rejected by the world and by your job.

Caught Between A Dream & a Job!

Dreams are the midwife of your greatness that usher in the travailing of the destiny that others will benefit from throughout the totality of your life.

• **_Dreams provide you with hope and expectation._** Many times, while doing their job, people daydream of doing something else with their lives. These interruptions are scheduled by your destiny to be reminders of your true calling in life. They are designed to be constant reminders that your life and your existence have a far greater weight of importance than your present task communicates to you. They are consistent reminders of how bad you are! Smiles.

• **_Dreams provide you with an outlet for your greatness to be born, and allows others to be blessed by your life's mission._** Without your dreams, your potential would go untapped. You would continue to wear the mask of compromise and settle for the present paychecks that you have already outgrown. **Dreams are the midwife of your greatness that usher in the travailing of the destiny that others will benefit from throughout the totality of your life.** Your dreams confirm that your talents are not for you! They are entrusted to you, to be used by you to benefit others.

• **_Dreams solve a problem for someone._** When you flow in your dream, your gifting will solve a significant problem for someone else. Dr. Mike Murdock encourages that we pay close attention to the things

Caught Between A Dream & a Job!

that frustrate us, because these are the things that our gifting is assigned to solve. When you follow your dreams, you service a need for someone you may or may not know. Your highest feelings of contribution to mankind come when you see the manifestation of significance that your gifting has on someone's life.

• *Dreams provide the largest monetary compensation for your time and effort.* Paychecks from your job are nice, but the only true place that your financial blessings are guaranteed is within your dream and destiny. I was blessed to be able to replace the income from my last job twice over when I stepped into my dream full-time. People pursue dreams not for money, but for fulfillment. Because of the passion and excellence with which dreams are pursued, money is a reward for the impact that your dreams make.

• *Dreams require 150% of you.* Make no mistake about it; **your dream is going to cost you everything - all of your energy, creativity, your emotions, your finances, your courage, your faith, your fortitude, and your zeal.** When you pursue your dream, you take everything related to your dream - personal. Why? Because it's yours. It's literally a piece of you. A job you can easily disown, a dream is birthed out of the reservoir of your embodiment. Therefore it's very personal. You will never cry over a job setback like you will a dream setback. You will never celebrate the victory you have at a job, more than you will the victory you experience with your own dream.

Caught Between A Dream & a Job!

• *Dreams are the only things that make sense out of the tenses of your life.* When you consider your past (ups, down, hurts, pains, successes), your present (current challenges, stresses, and discoveries), and your future (goals, plans, and aspirations), **your dreams are the only things that make the totality of your life experience seem WORTH IT!** A job will never give you the lasting feeling that your past, present, and future challenges are worth it. Dreams will prepare you for the manifold manifestation of the totality of your greatness!

Footnote about Pursuing Your Dreams

I am a tremendous movie fan. I always watch movies that have a motivational theme in them. Recently, I rewatched Rudy, Men of Honor, Remember the Titans, and Rocky. After watching these compelling stories of people who succeeded against the odds, I immediately was inspired to write this.

I believe that there are 6 types of people who are always watching you when you are in pursuit of your dream. Whether close to you or far from you, these individuals are watching. Your success means something different to each of them. Live your dream! Why? Because you have an audience, even if you don't know it. Look for each of the following individuals in the grandstands of the SuperBowl of your Success Story.

Caught Between A Dream & a Job!

1. **Those who never believed in you or your dream in the first place.** These are normally family, friends, and folks from your past whose limited vision pours ice water on your dream. Your success will educate them that it's possible!

2. **Those who always believed in you and your dream.** Your success validates and confirms their livelong support.

3. **Those who have been in your life for a brief time, but whose profound words motivated you to keep going when you felt like giving up.** Your success is a testament to the power of divine connections.

4. **Those who are neutral about your dream.** They don't really know you well enough to support you or discourage you, however they are in position to promote, endorse, and accelerate your career dream.

5. **Those who are living their dreams over again, through your experience.** They want to see you capitalize on their mistakes. Your success is proof of the fact that it could have happened for them. In an odd way, when you succeed, they succeed.

6. **Those who are coming behind you who need your success story to blaze a trail of possibility and opportunity for them.**

Caught Between A Dream & a Job!

My Jobs and Your Jobs:
What did we learn that could help
us with our DREAMS?

To further communicate this point, I would like to walk you through the jobs that I have had from the time I was 14 years old until right now. With each job I will tell you briefly about my duties and I will share with you what I learned from that job to help me be the CEO and Founder of my own company today. Most importantly, I will ask you what job you have had that taught you some of the skills that I learned. Please use this section to take notes about your own life.

1st Job – Winn-Dixie Stores: I was a Package Executive (Bag Boy). I worked there for 2 years exactly. I was very popular, and ended up being head Package Executive. I trained and supervised 14 other Package Executives during my 2-year tenure with Winn-Dixie.

Lessons Learned: Responsibility, Organization, Customer Service, Training & Development Skills, Leadership, and Financial Stewardship.

What job taught you these skills?

_____

_____

_____

_____

Caught Between A Dream & a Job!

2nd Job – St. John Progressive Missionary Baptist Church: I was a Custodial Executive (Janitor). I worked there for 2 years with my older brother Michael and my now deceased step-father. I learned the true meaning of working at a church. I performed many very humbling tasks around the church to keep it in top shape for ministry.

Lessons Learned: Teamwork, Order, Respect for Authority, and Quality

What job taught you these skills?

3rd Job – Service Merchandise: I was a Sales Consultant. I worked in the Sight & Sound Department of the store and I sold electronics. I worked there for 2 years while in transition from high school to my early college days. I learned a lot about teamwork, selling with integrity, and the importance of customer relationships.

Lessons Learned: Teamwork, Time Management, Goal Setting, Sales, and Service

Caught Between A Dream & a Job!

What job taught you these skills?

_____

_____

_____

4th Job – Circuit City: I was a Management Intern. I worked as a manager-in-training for 4 months at 2 separate stores. I wore the Red Jacket that managers wore, but had no real power to make major decisions. I worked in stock, inventory, HR, payroll, and direct customer sales.

Lessons Learned: Integrity, Employee Appreciation, Interviewing Skills, and Money Management

What job taught you these skills?

_____

_____

_____

5th Job – FSU Office of Orientation: This was my dream summer job as a college student. I worked alongside 35 other student leaders at FSU to conduct summer orientation for approximately 14,000 students and parents. This was student leadership at its finest. I loved this job.

Caught Between A Dream & a Job!

Lessons Learned: Team Building, Public Speaking, Leadership, Accountability, and Mentorship

What job taught you these skills?

_____

_____

_____

_____

6th Job – FSU College of Communication: This was a great college job for my major. I worked in the Dean's Office for 2 years while I was earning my B.A. degree. As a peer advisor, I worked with freshman and sophomore students who wanted to get into the College of Communication. I served as a Peer Advisor, giving registration advise to students on the best classes to take.

Lessons Learned: Access, Networking, The Power of Recommendation, Gate keeping, Mentorship, Counseling, and Peer Support

What job taught you these skills?

_____

_____

_____

_____

Delatorro L. McNeal II

Caught Between A Dream & a Job!

7th Job – South Gate Campus Center: I was a Resident Assistant. I was in charge of the 5th floor residents. I had this job for 1 year and 1 summer term. I worked with a team of 12 other RA's to maintain the building, and make sure that the residents behaved, and had all their needs met. Free room and board made this job perfect for me!

Lessons Learned: Appreciation for Diversity, Leadership, Teamwork, Conflict Management, Peer Counseling and Advising, and Mentorship

What job taught you these skills?

_____

_____

_____

_____

8th Job – FSU College of Education: Graduate Assistant. I landed this job opportunity my first semester of graduate school at Florida State. I worked in the Dean's office and served in multiple capacities as needed by higher administration in the College of Education.

Lessons Learned: The Power of Relationships, Work Ethic, How to be Mentored, Being Specific about my Future, Vision, Entrepreneurship, and Multitasking

Delatorro L. McNeal II

Caught Between A Dream & a Job!

What job taught you these skills?

_____

_____

_____

_____

9th Job – W.D. Dick & Associates: I was an Instructional Systems Design Intern. I had multiple jobs in grad school so that I could graduate without taking out a student loan. This internship helped to hone my skills in the Instructional Design industry (which is what my Master's is in), while teaching me the business of being an Independent Contractor.

Lessons Learned: Fake it 'Til You Make It, Partnership, Entrepreneurship, Diversity, Client Relationships, Networking, Family Support, Teamwork, and Delayed Gratification

What job taught you these skills?

_____

_____

_____

_____

Caught Between A Dream & a Job!

10th Job – Andersen Consulting: Organization & Human Performance Analyst. This was my big corporate job after grad school. I learned so much about myself and about corporate America during this job. It was my plan to work there for 5 years and then slowly transition into speaking fulltime, but you already know that's not what happened. I was released from this job unexpectedly, and forced out of my comfort zone. **However, you would not be reading this book right now, had I not been let go! Turn your setback into a comeback! I did, and you can do the same!**

Lessons Learned: The High Life, Politics, The Good Old Boy Network, The School of Hard Knocks, Travel, Client Relationship Management, Leadership, Integrity, Consistency, Character, Loneliness, Career vs. Calling, The Power of Networking, and Entrepreneurship

What job taught you these skills?

11th Job – University of South Florida: Instructional Design Consultant. I was hired on at USF four months after I lost my job with Andersen Consulting. This job is responsible for my transition from my jobs to my

Caught Between A Dream & a Job!

dreams. This job was the catalyst for my concept of "Caught Between a Dream and a Job?"

Lessons Learned: Transition, Stability, Creativity, Teamwork, Oneness, Momentum, and The Possibility of a Dream Job

What job taught you these skills?

....

....

....

....

Now take a quick look back over the skills that you have acquired through the many jobs that you have had. **Every job was trying to teach you something; some skill, some ability, some character trait that will be imperative for you to demonstrate once you ultimately walk in your true destiny, calling, purpose, and dream.**

Never look back on a job with negative conclusions, because even the worst of career decisions have taught you something necessary for success in your destiny. *What have your jobs been preparing you for? When you look at the totality of your experiences, what flashing lights do you see indicating that you are now ready to take the steps necessary to walk in your dream?*

Caught Between A Dream & a Job!

In order to rob the grave, you've got to know that even the job you have right now, is preparing you to be a better CEO when you step out onto the dream you feel in your heart.

Okay Del, I have completed my skill assessment of my past jobs. Now how do I transition from my job to my dreams?

GREAT QUESTION. Keep reading, my friend. Keep reading!

The bridge between your JOBS and your DREAMS is.. A DREAM JOB!

My dear friend Jonathan Sprinkles is a dynamic speaker, author, and personal development coach out of Houston, Texas. He has written a book called Why Settle? It's a simple yet profound question that most people can't answer. Don't settle for average. Don't settle for the ordinary things of life. Pursue the extraordinary - it will only cost you a little extra! Get it?

The number one reason why people settle for "regular jobs" instead of going after their dreams is because of **fear**! There is one thing that stops people dead in their tracks and keeps most people working for someone else all their lives – **MONEY!** Remember,

Delatorro L. McNeal II

Caught Between A Dream & a Job!

your job provides steady income, while your dream is something that guarantees financial harvest. But it normally takes some time.Most people are afraid that if they go after their dream, they will not be able to support themselves and their family during (and even sometimes after) the transition.

- · How will I pay my bills?
- · How will tuition get paid?
- · How will I pay off my credit cards?
- · How will I pay my rent?
- · How will I maintain my present lifestyle?

I really want to do **THIS**, but **THAT** is what pays the bills! Most people think that working for someone else is their source of financial blessing! This could not be anymore incorrect. I am a living witness of that, my friend. My company (A Noval Idea, Inc.) replaced the income I was making in my corporate job within ONE YEAR of losing that job! Two years after my corporate release, my own company will more than **TRIPLE the income** I was used to earning in corporate America. **My friend, all I am trying to tell you is that it's 100% POSSIBLE!**

Okay Del, that's a great success story - but how do I do it? What is it about this Dream Job what will get me to where I want to be? GREAT QUESTION! Keep reading!

Caught Between A Dream & a Job!

Here are **8 Facts about The Dream Job** that is waiting for you to discover it.

1. Your Dream Job will require you to use the same skills needed in your Dream. This job will have you using similar skills as the ones that you will need in order to function at full capacity in your dream. This gives you daily practice opportunities to further hone your skills.

2. Your Dream Job will pay you to practice your dream skills. The employer of your Dream Job may not know this, but while they are paying you to solve a problem for their organization, they are also compensating you to practice your skills on them. **This is a Win-Win deal!** This pay will allow you to maintain and slowly eliminate bills so that you can be more financially free as you move into your dream.

3. Your Dream Job provides you with contacts that will help you when you leave. There are people that you will meet while performing within the dream job, that will serve as great customers, clients, contacts, mentors, mentees, and colleagues once you step out into your dream full-time. Network like it's nobody's business while you are working at your dream job.

4. Your Dream Job provides you a degree of scheduled flexibility to begin to focus some time towards your dream. Time is your friend when in transition from your job to your dream. The Dream

Caught Between A Dream & a Job!

Job that awaits you will require your focus and attention. However, it will also give you routine opportunities to focus on your dream. Want an example? On my dream job, I negotiated a 4-day workweek. That was 10-hour days, 4 days a week. This always gave me one day a week OFF, to focus 100% on my dream. It was great!

5. Your Dream Job will provide you with medical benefits to cover you and your family during the transition period. For many people, this is critical. A steady dream job will give you the comfort of a nice benefit package that will protect you and your family while you get paid to practice your dream. You can work day-to-day with the security of knowing that if anything happens, you and your family are covered.

6. Your Dream Job provides a level of employment credibility so that you can accomplish your major financial goals. Listen, this is huge. When you want to buy a home, or a new car, or office space, most lenders look at brand new businesses very harshly. In fact, in order for your new business's income to even count with most lenders, you need at least **2 full years of tax returns.** Your Dream Job provides the steady income, plus the established name recognition needed for you to secure major purchases while in transition to your dream. Remember that your dream, while big, is still a baby in many ways. You want to take as much financial pressure off of yourself and your dream as possible in the beginning. For example, my wife and I

Caught Between A Dream & a Job!

bought cars, paid off all credit card debt, paid for computers cash, and bought a brand new home while still at our dream jobs, then made our transition afterwards. This made life much easier for us.

7. Your Dream Job builds your confidence in your skill set for your dream. For some people, money is not the issue. Lack of skill is the issue. Some people don't feel competent enough to step out on their dream fulltime, and make good money doing it right away. Well, if that's you, you need a season or several seasons of additional preparation. The dream job further assists you with that. Remember, it pays you to practice!

8. Your Dream Job can provide you with lasting business and personal relationships even after your transition. The people that I met and worked with on my dream job are lifers. You know, those people who you just know will always be a part of your life in some way or another throughout the duration of your existence. I met some of the best quality people this world can make at my dream job. Sandy, Manuel, Linda, Debbie, Wendy, Chris, Pat, Gina, Jennifer, Dr. Tennyson Wright, Dr. Townsend, Wanda, Dr. Davis-John, Dr. Sam Wright, and the list goes on and on. Thank you for helping me to impact millions!

Caught Between A Dream & a Job!

Reminders about the Dream Job!

1. **The Dream Job is not permanent.** Its purpose is not for you to be 100% comfortable. Why? Because you will never be 100% comfortable in something that is not your destiny. Don't get comfortable in your dream job. It is temporary. It is a bridge to something bigger and better. Use it for that purpose and that purpose only.

2. **The Dream Job does not birth the dream.** It simply prepares you and your environment for the dream to be born. Don't settle for the comfort that the dream job provides. Go all the way! Keep putting one foot in front of the other, and don't stop until you get to the other side of your bridge.

3. **Maximize your time while in your dream job.** Don't procrastinate! Expect to work 9 to 5, then come home and work an additional 2 to 4 hours on your dream. Again, this dream job is a window of opportunity to build a silent empire, while you are still benefiting from the stability that your job provides.

4. **Keep a Counsel of Wisdom around you** at all times during your transition. Your Wisdom Counsel will help you predict and determine when your season at the dream job is ending. They will help you identify the final steps that need to be completed before your successful launch into your dream full-time.

Caught Between A Dream & a Job!

5. **Never burn your bridges!** Always treat people with respect and with the knowledge that they could bless you in a special way some time in the future.

Expect Major Transition

As you make the transition between your jobs and your dreams, you will face major change in several areas of your life. I would like to take the next few pages to share with you some TIPS on how you can maximize the change process and use it to your benefit. Willie Jolley, one of my mentors and dear friends defines TIPS as Techniques, Ideas, Principles, and Strategies. That's exactly what I am about to share with you. You can exact massive change in 5 major areas of your life:

- Financial Life

- Social Life

- Attitudinal Life

- Chronological Life

- Spiritual/Emotional Life

The pages that follow will give you some of my best insight into how you can negotiate these changes and transitions like the CHAMPION that you are! But wait!

Caught Between A Dream & a Job!

I have something special I want to share with you. Keep reading…

I am very excited for you! If you have made it this far in the book, I am extremely proud of you. Statistics say that most people never read a book cover-to-cover. In fact, most business professionals read the first chapter of a book, then shelf it. Why? Because of a lack of motivation to continue to invest time in pursuing and apprehending greatness. Well, not you. I am very proud of you. In fact, as a way to reward you for getting this far, if you will send me an email right now letting me know what page you are on in the book, and what benefit you are getting out of the book so far, I will give you one complimentary email coaching session. Visit my website, www.delmcneal.com, and email me at info@delmcneal.com. Be sure to include all your proper mailing information. Act now!

Financial TIPS for Success in your Dream Job

1. Use your Dream Job to build a solid financial foundation for your dream. Trust me, you want as little financial pressure resting on your dream as possible. You don't want to quit a job and rely solely on your dream to dig you out of credit card or student loan

Use your Dream Job to build a solid financial foundation for your dream.

Delatorro L. McNeal II

Caught Between A Dream & a Job!

debt. You want to get some or all of that unsecured debt paid off or paid down dramatically **BEFORE** you step out onto your dream. Why? Because in the infancy stages of your dream, you may not be financially secure right away. Statistics say that it takes the average small business 2 to 3 years to turn its first real profit.

2. Use your Dream Job to get out of Credit Card Debt. This is very important. It piggybacks off the last point, because your business or your dream will require some amount of credit extension. Especially in the early stages, you want your personal credit issues already resolved so that your dream can establish credit in its own name without your personal situation complicating things. A fellow speaker and dear friend of mine, Sanyika Boyce, wrote a book called <u>Crack Da Code</u>. The book teaches about knocking out credit debt. Get that book. Invest in financial wisdom now more than ever.

3. Get a Financial Planner as your Financial Success Coach. A good financial planner will conduct a Financial Needs Assessment on you and your business to help you determine your debt freedom date, as well as the types of funds you will need to launch your dreams and sustain them. **My brother, Michael McNeal is a Certified Financial Planner. If you need a CFP call him at (813) 689-3193.** Your CFP will help you determine how long you will need to stay in your dream job in order to be in good enough financial

Caught Between A Dream & a Job!

shape to step out onto your dream. **Trust me, you don't want to step out there on emotion. It will bankrupt you quickly. I have seen it happen to others.** Be smart, use wisdom!

4. Use your Dream Job to finance major purchases! I touched on this earlier, but it's worth repeating. If you know that you want to buy a home, get a car, or make some other major investment, take those steps with the security and backing of your dream job. Most financial institutions would trust the name of an established employer much faster than they would your new business venture. You will have much fewer headaches this way.

5. Establish bank accounts and credit in the name of your dream as soon as possible. Give your dream or your business an identity. Treat it as a person. Take all the official steps necessary to incorporate, obtain tax IDs, and establish credit in the name of your venture so that people and financial institutions will take it seriously. Put all of these things in place for your dream **WHILE** you are in your dream job!

6. Work with a Bookkeeper, Accountant, and Tax Specialist. These professionals will keep you inline with Uncle Sam and also teach you valuable ways to go about operating your business or functioning in your dream so that it is financially beneficial for you. **TRUST ME, the money they will SAVE you far outweighs the fees they charge to work with you.**

Caught Between A Dream & a Job!

Do your homework, find people that have your heartbeat, and make it happen.

7. Use your Dream Job to create a low-stress environment for your DREAM! You want your dream to be able to grow, develop, be creative, evolve, and expand without the financial weeds of massive debt trying to choke the life out of it and keep you depending on someone else to pay you.

One of my mentors, Dr. Mike Murdock teaches that Money is a Reward for Solving a Problem. **If you want to increase your wealth, increase the number of problems you solve, the types of problems you solve, or who you solve the problem for.** Your dream solves a problem for someone. Solve their problem effectively and money will find you. Be a problem solver for someone or something and watch how money flows your way.

"If you do more than you are paid to do, soon the day will come when you are paid more for what you do".
~Zig Ziglar

Zig Ziglar says, **"If you do more than you are paid to do, soon the day will come when you are paid more for what you do".** I am a living witness of that. When I was 14, I made $4.75 per hour as a Package Executive at Winn Dixie. Now, 12 years later at 26, I earn a few thousand dollars **per hour** as a Professional

Caught Between A Dream & a Job!

Speaker and Author. Because I was willing to pay the price to do more than $4.75 required, now I am compensated nicely for solving motivational problems for people. Pay the price for greatness, and you **WILL** reap the rewards!

Social TIPS for Success in your Dream Job

1. SHUT UP! (Don't Tell Everyone) Audiences love this one. You know, sometimes we ARE our own worst enemy because we advertise our plans to the wrong people. The wrong people are those who are incapable of helping us live our dream. These are individuals whose negativity throws cold water on our dream. As you begin to make the transition from your job to your dream, don't market it! Only tell your mentors and close friends. *The **only people** who need to know about your dreams are those who are able and willing to help you get them. The **only people** who need to know about your dreams are those who are able and willing to help you get them. The **only people** who need to know about your dreams are those who are able and willing to help you get them.* **These are not typos!** Repetition is the mother of skill. You must get this point. Don't tell everyone about your plans. **Tell only those whose wisdom and resources will help your journey.**

Caught Between A Dream & a Job!

Focus on your future.

2. Get Business Cards. I got my first business card at 14 years old. It was simple, but it taught me how to present myself professionally and leave an impression on people. **By the way, your new business cards need to advertise your new dream - not your job!** Remember the dream job is a temporary place. Don't over-advertise this either. Advertise your place of permanence. Let people know where you are headed, not where you used to be. Focus on your future.

But, Del, you just told me to Shut Up. Wouldn't business cards tell my business to people? GREAT QUESTION! You need to develop a client base for your dream. This is a listing of potential people who can benefit from your services. **Business cards let people know that you are serious!** It communicates a level of professionalism and pursuit after the dream. They also remind you of the problem that you solve for others. **Sharing a business card is one thing, sharing a business plan is totally different. Be smart!**

3. NETWORK like it's going out of style! You know, Les Brown says that you have not met 50% of the people that are responsible for helping you achieve your dream. That means you need to network! All you need is to be at that right place, at the right time, with the right product or service and it's all over! Once you

Caught Between A Dream & a Job!

get your business cards, (by the way **Vistaprint.com** is an excellent and inexpensive starting point) take them with you at all times. Everyone you meet needs to have a good impression of you left behind so that they can contact you at a future date (when they are ready for you to solve a problem for them).

4. Treat Everyone you meet with Respect. You don't know who the person you just ignored or treated badly knows. You don't know who the person in traffic you just flicked off is. Just because people are dressed casually, or you see them in casual situations, does not mean they are not important. This reminds me of an incident that happened in the grocery store recently. I saw a man walking opposite me down the bread aisle. It was my intention not to speak becuase our eyes did not meet, but he actually spoke first - so I spoke and was friendly. Thank God I was, because I did not remember him, but he remembered me. He was in an audience that I had spoken to over 2 years prior. He approached me in the checkout line and we had a great conversation. Had I treated him like I was a little tempted to at first (just being honest – that was a very challenging day), I would have potentially messed up the strong impression he had of me from the event he had attended. Treat everyone in public and private with the same love and respect you would want. Just your smile alone can Rob the Grave of Its Greatness because it can brighten someone's day.

Caught Between A Dream & a Job!

5. Change Your Friends! Don't use the word "friends" as an all-encompassing term to describe all of the people in your life. Not everyone in your life is there to empower you. I would be willing to bet that a third of the people you call friends may not be your true friends at all. So change your friends. The peers you surround yourself with should be people that add to your life. **You see, there for 4 types of people in this world - those that add, multiply, subtract, or divide. Those who add joy, multiply your opportunities, subtract worry, and divide your enemies, you KEEP. Those that add drama, multiply your past mistakes, subtract your peace, and divide your focus, you REMOVE.** If you want to soar like an eagle, you can't hang out with turkeys!

6. Maintain a Contact Management System. This is critical for success and I am mastering new ways of doing this all of the time. You need a way of managing all the people you meet, the business cards you collect, the contacts you make, and the relationships you build. Use software like Outlook, Lotus Notes, a Palm Pilot, ACT, Goldmine, Card Scan, Franklin Covey Planners, and Daytimers to help you keep the people that enter and exit your life organized.

7. Develop a Master Mind Group. Napoleon Hill talks about this principle in his book, <u>Think and Grow Rich</u>. My friend, one of the best ways to Rob the Grave is to get other Positive Grave Robbers around you. Dr. Mike Murdock says, "There are two ways to get wisdom – Mistakes and Mentors". I have had my share of mistakes, and I prefer mentors. A Master Mind Group will help you cut your learning curve in half. These people will protect you, look out for you, create opportunities for you, advise you, counsel you, invest in you, sharpen you, and build you. **All of your major decisions in life need to be run through your Master Mind Group.** You should meet with them monthly. Consult with members from this group weekly, and always seek to learn from them as they learn from you.

8. Put yourself in the Right Places. I can remember one time when Donna - a member of my Master Mind Group who is also my big sister in many ways – was helping me do this exact thing. I had flown back home to Tampa from Dallas one Tuesday, connecting through Atlanta. I landed in Tampa at 3:30pm, just in time to rush to a 5:00pm speaking engagement. Needless to say, I had gotten no rest between flights and arriving at the engagement. The event was great. At around 8:00 pm, I left ready to go home and sleep after my LONG day. As I was driving home, I received a voicemail on my cell phone. It was Donna, calling me from a major hotel in Tampa. She was letting me know that there were some very important people I should network with at a hotel. I trusted that Donna knew my schedule, and knew how tired I was, but still called anyway. This meant that it was important for me to be there. I made a U-Turn, went to the event, and **within 3 minutes** networked with some key people I

Caught Between A Dream & a Job!

had been trying to meet for over a year. Mentors and Master Mind Groups will help to keep you in the right place at the right time.

Attitudinal TIPS for Success in your Dream Job.

1. Listen to Something Positive Everyday! Change and transition are very uncomfortable. So it is imperative that we be as proactive as possible to keep our environments positive and empowering. **Studies show that if you listen to something positive the first 20 minutes of your day, you will increase your productivity by 35%.** Look at your mind and your heart as the hard drives of your life. If you install bad software, you will get bad performance. If you install positive software, you will get positive performance. Each morning play motivational tapes, CDs, videos, read inspirational literature, or listen to tapes of spiritually empowering services and events. This will shape your attitude early in the morning, and help to set the bar high for your day.

2. Read 1 Book per Month. Do you know that the average American reads one book per year? While the average American is reading one book per year, **the average self-made Millionaire is reading one book per month!** Readers are indeed leaders. Ask your mentors what books they are reading. Ask the people that you admire in your chosen profession what books they have read, so you can begin a personal library.

Caught Between A Dream & a Job!

Always invest in good material. If you are not disciplined enough to sit down and read the books, then buy them on CD/tape so that you can listen to them during your commute. Make sure that you are building a library of wisdom for yourself

Post your written goals in your bathroom on your mirror or at eye level opposite your toilet.

and your family. **If you are spending thousands of dollars yearly on fashion, and $10 a year on knowledge and wisdom, your priorities need an alignment.** Don't do what I used to do, though. I got so caught up in buying new books that I had more books on my shelf than I could read. I would read one chapter, then go to the next book. I knew a little about each book, but not a lot about any of them. Bad move! Focus on reading one book all the way through, then move to the next one. Create a system that allows you to complete them one at a time, then share them with others.

3. Post Your Goals and Read them Daily. We will talk much more about this in Chapter 6: How to S.A.M. Your Goals and Dreams. As a sneak preview to that material, I will challenge you now to post your written goals in your bathroom on your mirror or at eye level opposite your toilet. Why? Because this guarantees that you will see them daily for at least a few minutes. So while you are brushing your teeth, review your goals so that they stay fresh in your mind. As a human, you process 40,000 to 50,000 thoughts per day, so

Caught Between A Dream & a Job!

you need to keep your goals in the forefront of your mind. That way, you will take the necessary action steps to achieve them.

4. Watch Empowering Television & Movies. Do you know that the average American watches 5 hours of television per day? Meanwhile, the average self-made Millionaire watches 1 hour of television per day - and it's usually something educational. **Input really and truly does determine output, my friend.** So the first step is to limit your television watching to a few hours per day. Once you have done this, you will create more time to focus on your dream. Once you cut back on your hours in front of the TV, monitor the types of things you watch when you do turn on the TV. Try to focus on programs and movies that have moral value, teach empowering principles, and inspire your continued growth and development. *Okay, Del are you saying I can't watch my favorite sitcoms?* GREAT QUESTION. **No. The key word here is balance.** TV is very entertaining and informative, but don't allow it to make you negative, bitter, or jealous of the opportunities of others. I suggest limiting it because when you're trying to transition from your job to your dream, each day counts and gets you closer to your dream.

5. Take Your Vitamins Daily. Now, I know that you probably think I am talking about a pill that you pop each day, but actually I am not. These medical/herbal pills are very important, and I recommend that you

Caught Between A Dream & a Job!

do what your doctor recommends to maintain optimal health. However, I am referring to a different vitamin. You see, my friend, I have certain Positive People in my life that I call Mega-Vitamins. Why? Because these people serve multiple roles in my life, and they give me the daily dose of encouragement and support necessary to stay on top of my game. For example, I have a Mega-Vitamin named Mr. Tye Maner. He is a professional speaker, trainer, author, and entrepreneur. He serves multiple roles in my life; mentor, investment property coach, spiritual counselor, fellow speaker, author, technical support (we have similar computers), financial advisor, and just overall friend. I don't need hundreds of people in my life, as long as I have a few that serve multiple roles. Now just as he serves many roles in my life, I serve multiple roles in his life. **To stay healthy during and after your transition from your job to your dream, you've got to take your vitamins daily, and be a vitamin for someone else.**

6. Pour Into Someone Else's Dream. This is one of the most powerful principles you can learn. MAKE IT HAPPEN FOR SOMEONE ELSE. *Why? Don't I have my own problems to worry about? Why deposit my time and energy into someone else's dream?* Because of the Principle of Reciprocity.

> *What you make happen for someone else, I believe God makes that and much greater happen for you.*

Caught Between A Dream & a Job!

What you make happen for someone else, I believe God makes that **and much greater** happen for you. It's like the boomerang theory. What you send forth, will come back to positively impact your life. I met Les Brown because I was a **servant.** I met Willie Jolley because I was a **servant.** I met Bishop T.D. Jakes because I was a **servant.** I met Zig Ziglar because I was a **servant.** Dr. Steven Covey, Fred Hammond, Dr. Mike Murdock, Maya Angelou, and the list goes on and on. I purposely put myself in the position to assist someone else with their goals and dreams, and in the process, my goals were achieved. Serve someone. **Get behind someone else's vision. Push someone else to the next level. It will come back to BLESS your SOCKS off!**

7. Pray, Meditate, and Vision! We as human beings are just like cell phones. At the end of the day, we need to be recharged. You don't just rest your cell phone on the dresser and expect it to function at full capacity the next morning do you? No! Why not? Because you understand that the cell phone needs to be plugged into an electrical source that is far greater and more powerful than it in order to pull from that source and recharge itself. Well, my friend, we are the same way. **We must recharge ourselves and refocus ourselves on our purpose and potential each day. Prayer allows us to do that.** Communicating with God is sharing our thoughts, desires, concerns, and issues. This process frees us from having to shoulder the entire weight of the daily challenges of life. Meditation births focus. Now

Caught Between A Dream & a Job!

I am not talking about some religious ritual. I am referring simply to dedicated quiet time to connect with yourself, your God, and your goals. As you begin to focus on your future, you can't help but to Vision for your tomorrow and realize that tomorrow will be so much better than today.

8. Create a Dream Room in your House. I got this helpful hint from one of my mentors, Dr. Mike Murdock. I have a room in my house that is 100% dedicated to my future, my business, my goals, my dreams, my accomplishments, my ideas, my support, and my pictures of achievement. This room has pictures of me with great mentors that I study under, letters of appreciation from past speaking events, my calendar for the month with goals, copies of past large and small paychecks from events, my degrees, wisdom keys, pictures of great men and women of God in my life, and newspaper articles that I have been featured in. **In that room, all things are POSSIBLE!** This room challenges me to pursue more, and also encourages me that things will continue to get better and better.

Again, these are just 8 simple changes you can begin to implement in your life that will impact your attitude in tremendous ways. As you transition from your job to your dream and continue to Rob the Grave, your attitude is one of the most powerful things you need to guard.

> *Time is the greatest asset that you have. Today is a gift - that's why they call it the present.*

Caught Between A Dream & a Job!

Chronological TIPS for Success in your Dream Job

Time is the greatest asset that you have. Today is a gift - that's why they call it the **present**. Your today creates your tomorrow. Tomorrow can change, based on your action today. You can't get back yesterday. **Your mind performs 3 functions daily.** It replays the past, plays the present, or pre-plays the future. **Replaying the past is called Memory. Playing the present is called Process. Pre-playing the future is called Vision.** We just talked about the power of vision. Here are a few TIPS for mastering your time while transitioning between your job and your dream. Hint: These TIPS are also good for life in general.

1. Purchase a Planner/Organizer. I know that this sounds simple, but you would be absolutely amazed at the number of people who want to manage their time better - yet have no way of keeping track of it. Pastor Scott Thomas, a mentor and dear friend of mine says, "Start telling your time where to go, instead of asking it where it went!" Determine what type of person you are. Do you like to hand write your daily activities, tasks, and appointments? If so, then get a paper planner like a Franklin Covey or a DayTimer. If you are much more technology-oriented, you probably want to invest in a Palm Pilot, Pocket PC, or some other type of PDA (Personal Digital Assistant).

Now, once you get an organizer, make sure you use it.

Caught Between A Dream & a Job!

I know many people who have purchased equipment to help manage their time, but the planners are sitting at home in the same box that they were purchased in. USE YOUR STUFF. Work towards putting all of your appointments, contacts, tasks, and lists in one place. ***Well Del, I would love to do that, but I am afraid that if I lose it I will lose everything. What do I do?*** GREAT QUESTION! If you have this concern, I would recommend leaning more towards the technology-oriented side of organization. Electronic databases like Outlook, ACT, and Goldmine allow you to make master copies of your information on your hard drive while also allowing you to synchronize that same information with your PDA. Invest in order as it pertains to the chronological details of your life.

2. Write a Task List each morning and work from it. This is a habit that I have developed and operated in for many years now. When I get up each morning, I make a simple list of what I want accomplish in the day. This includes people I need to call, email, write, meet, things I need to mail, or purchase, appointments I need to schedule, and presentations I need to prepare. I work from this list and strike through each item as I complete it. Lists allow you to build momentum. In addition to building momentum, they allow you to take inventory of how you are

"The secret of your success is found in your daily routine."
~Dr. Murdock

Caught Between A Dream & a Job!

investing your time and the benefits you can expect from your labor. Trust me, I have not always been this way. When I was younger, I wasted enough time for several people. If you aim at nothing in your day, you will hit it every time. **Focus your time and energy each day, by starting your morning with a Task List.** You will be amazed how many things you will accomplish each day.

3. Develop a Daily Routine. Chapter 6 talks in detail about this, but I can't say enough about this concept. I am still mastering it, but it is already having a profound impact on my personal, professional, spiritual, and family life. Again, Dr. Mike Murdock teaches that, *"The secret of your success is found in your daily routine."* So dissecting your daily routine will reveal the hidden actions or inactions that are pushing you towards success or pulling your towards failure. **Your days will begin to reward you greatly if you create a success routine within them.** Again refer to Chapter 6 for more details on Mastering Your Daily Routine.

4. Invest 2 Lunch Breaks per Week. This is one of the most powerful principles that you can execute while in transition between your job and your dream. People tell me all of the time that the number one thing that keeps them from building their dream while on the job is time – or a lack thereof. I always encourage

Don't spend time worrying about work when you are NOT on the clock. Invest that time in your dream!

Caught Between A Dream & a Job!

people who have busy work schedules to do one simple thing - **maximize your lunch breaks.** Instead of going out with co-workers, eat your lunch at your desk and research on the internet, or take a trip to a store, or visit a mentor, or do something – anything that will feed your dream! It's absolutely critical that you seize the opportunities that your lunch breaks provide you. Whatever your dream is, feed your dream with the time you have each day.

But Del, I have so much to do in order to get to my dream. How can a 30 or 60 minute lunch break get me anywhere? GREAT QUESTION! *My friend, the distance between the first floor and the second floor is great, but the steps in between are very small.* It's little action done consistently that will lead you to your destiny. Two hours invested each week in your dream over one month turns into 8 hours. That's a full workday a month towards your dream. That's great! What would happen if you added some weekends, some nights after work, and some paid days off? I challenge you to seize the time that you are not paid for. Your drive to work is not paid for, your drive home is not paid for. **Don't spend time worrying about work when you are NOT on the clock. Invest that time in your dream!** As my Pastors Drs. Randy and Paula White would say, *"This is good teaching!"*

Caught Between A Dream & a Job!

5. Invest 1 extra hour per day into your dream.
You have 24 hours in a day. That is 8 hours to work, 8 hours to sleep, and 8 hours for yourself. I want you to not only seize your lunch breaks, but also invest 1 of those 8 extra hours that you have into your dream. This hour can be broken out by 30 minutes on the way to work and 30 minutes preparing for your dream instead of watching a sitcom. The only difference between the ordinary and the extraordinary is a **little extra**. So I double-dog-dare you to squeeze an extra hour out of each day that you are blessed to live. **Feed your dream with the entrée of time invested, and watch your dream grow up and bless your socks off.**

6. Get a Mentor NOW! At this stage in your transition, you need someone above you helping you see into your future. A mentor is someone who can give you insight, and help cut your learning curve. I don't care how young or how old you are, get someone in your life who is more advanced than you are in the area that you desire to excel in. If you are a seasoned adult, don't think that you know it all. If you are an unseasoned young person, don't think that you don't know enough. Get the wisdom and counsel of someone who can make your best idea better and your sweetest victory sweeter. Seek out your mentor.

I purposely seek out coaches in all areas of my life so that I can operate in wisdom in all of my decisions and dealings.

Caught Between A Dream & a Job!

Don't just expect them to fall into your lap. They won't. When Daniel Laruso of The Karate Kit was tired of getting beaten up, and ready to get serious about self-defense, he looked for and found Mr. Miyagi. Now, there is a lot about mentorship to cover, but instead of trying to regurgitate someone else's stuff, I would rather tell you to get Dr. Mike Murdock's book - The Law of Recognition. It will teach you worlds about how to recognize mentors in your life. Talk with your mentor at least once a month, about major updates, progress, and setbacks that you have encountered. Many times, these people will be very busy so use their time wisely.

7. Get a Coach NOW! *Del, what's the difference between a mentor and a coach?* GREAT QUESTION. In my opinion, a mentor is someone whose time and wisdom is so valuable that you would be almost disrespecting them by bothering them daily with your issues. A coach, on the other hand, is someone who is down in the trenches with you. They see your pitfalls, valleys, and downtimes, and they are there to coach you through them. They correct you, help discipline you, and encourage you on a weekly basis. Perfect example - Les Brown and Willie Jolley are two of my mentors in the speaking industry. I have all of their contact information and I CAN call them anytime day or night. However, I only communicate with them monthly. Why? Because they are extremely busy people. Hogging their time on a weekly basis would be very rude of me. I have national speaker friends and colleagues that I talk with weekly and sometimes daily and we coach each other. We sharpen each other on products, marketing, websites, and bookings. These are my coaches, and I am their coach. I have a fitness coach, a financial coach, a product development coach, a home-building coach, a real-estate investment coach, a marriage enrichment coach, and the list goes on. I purposely seek out coaches in all areas of my life so that I can operate in wisdom in all of my decisions and dealings.

Does having mentors and coaches exempt you from making mistakes and bad decisions? No. But it does greatly decrease your failures, and increase your successes. Surround yourself with people who have been there and done that, **so that you can go there and do that!**

8. Apply an 80/20 Rule for your Spare Time. Spend 20% of your free time watching someone else live their dream, and spend 80% of your time working to make your own dreams come true. It's a simple principle that speaks for itself. At some point, you've got to turn off the TV, the radio, the XBOX, the playstation, and the computer to focus on YOU! Who will feed your dream if you don't? Who will empty your casket of everything that it possesses? The guy on American Idol? Great Show, but sorry - he will not.

The entire world is run by people who "don't feel like it!"

Caught Between A Dream & a Job!

9. Your time invested is your weapon against the spirit of procrastination that was sent by your grave to rob you silently of your greatness. Don't allow that to happen!

Spiritual & Emotional TIPS for Success in your Dream Job

1. **Don't be Ruled by your Feelings!** Remember this one thing, my friend. **The entire world is run by people who "don't feel like it!"** If you allow your feelings to determine whether or not you will get up each morning and go after your dream, you will starve. **There will be many times when you don't feel like it. Do you think that Oprah always feels like being on camera? Do you think that Bill Gates always feels like talking about technology? Do you think that Denzel Washington always feels like acting or directing?** Do you think that I always feel like speaking? Do you think that each time I came to the laptop to write this book, I was 100% excited about it? Think again! Smiles! This world is run by people who don't feel like it - but they do what needs to be done anyhow. **I may not always feel like speaking, but once I start speaking the gift takes over and greatness is born once again.** Oprah may not always feel like being on camera, but the moment she begins interviewing a guest, her gifting takes over and she creates a great show. My friend, don't allow how you feel to run your life. Command your body to fall in line with your positive mental attitude towards your dream.

Caught Between A Dream & a Job!

2. Get comfortable with being stretched! The purpose of your dream is to stretch you towards your destiny. It should be a constant reminder of how awesome you are, and how much more awesome you can become. When making the transition between your dream and your job, you will be stretched. **This includes your time, your ability to focus, your ability to multi-task, your ability to discern who should be in your life and who should go, your ability to keep quiet about your goals until you have attained them, and so many other things.** Prepare to be challenged! Prepare to be emotionally and spiritually stretched. Prepare to be financially stretched. There will be times when you are moved to sow into the vision and dream of someone else, while yours is still in the infant stage. That's okay! Sow that seed of money, time, or talent. Why? **Because whatever you do to help someone else get their dream, will be made possible for your dream in the future.** Whatever you do to help someone else, does not leave your life. It just enters your future to create an opportunity that you will benefit from later. So get comfortable being in a constant state of change. **Your paradigm will be adjusting with each book that you read, each seminar you attend, and each sermon you listen to.** Your dream will continue to expand as you realize for yourself that "IT'S POSSIBLE!" So instead of looking at change as a one-time thing, look at it as a continual refining process. Did you know that the average plane goes through over 30,000 adjustments while in flight including speed, cabin pressure, altitude, direction, and temperature? As passengers, we don't physically feel all those adjustments, but they are necessary to ensure a safe transformation from where we are to where we want to be. You, too, will experience many adjustments along your journey of transformation. Many won't be easy. Some will be a piece of cake. But all of them, ALL of them, will be working for your good. They will prepare you for greatness!

3. Pour into Yourself Spiritually. I talked with you earlier in this book about how "rechargeable" the human soul is. Our souls and spirits get tired and worn down by life and by transition. We must continue to pour into ourselves. Why? **Because you can't pull anything out of an empty bag!** As a speaker, author, consultant, and success coach, I am always pouring positivity out into others. Whether it's through books, CDs, keynotes, seminars, interviews, coaching sessions, or otherwise, I am constantly pouring. As I pour my greatness onto and into others, I need to continue to be poured *into*. **YOU DO, TOO!** You can't act like you don't need a greater source of strength.

I am so grateful that I have a wonderful relationship with God. He is my strength. He is my all and all. He blessed me with each gift that I have and display. My friend, I am not

> *"Private success will always come before public success"!*
> ~ Dr. Steven Covey

Caught Between A Dream & a Job!

attempting to preach to you. I just want you to understand and admit that like a cell phone, we as humans have to realize that we need to plug into a source far greater than ourselves for strength, rejuvenation, and fulfillment. I pour into myself in multiple ways such as attending church weekly, volunteering with various ministries, praying with my family and with friends, and listening to spiritually empowering tapes, videos, and CDs. When you feel like the world is against you, remember that if you have a relationship with God, "Greater is He that is in you, than he that is in the world."

4. Expect to do much of it ALONE! Goodness is free, but Greatness will cost you! *Cost me what?* **THE LONELY WORK!** I know so many people who started on the road to their dream, but then did a U-turn because they thought that the Highway to Greatness would be packed full of the same type of people that were on the Monorail to Mediocrity. Not so! There will be many times when the dream that you are chasing has you working 100% by yourself. This is not a bad thing! In fact, this is a great thing. Why? Because you get a chance to learn about yourself. **You get a chance to come face-to-face with YOU. You see what you are really made of when you don't have anyone else around you cheering you on.** What you do in your secret, private, and personal time - when focusing on your dream - determines the magnitude of your outward reward. Remember what Dr. Covey says, "Private success will always come

Caught Between A Dream & a Job!

before public success"! Take right now, for example. At this moment I am sitting in my pajamas, listening to some of my favorite praise and worship music (The Binions), and typing away on an old computer that my Dad gave me. No one is around; no kids, no wife, no family, no church friends, no co-workers, no pets. There is nothing but myself, my God, my dream, my destiny, my reasons, my determination, my focus, my greatness, my gifting, my life story, my paradigm, my insight, my foresight, my goals, and my faith. **Come to think of it, I am not that lonely at all.** I have a host of friends around me that believe in my success.

Guess what? **YOU HAVE THE EXACT SAME THING!** Now, once this book is published, thousands will come up to me in excitement to get it signed. But nobody was around when I actually typed it all those late nights. Even though I speak to thousands, when it comes to giving birth to new things for my business, much of it must come from within and come during the lonely hours of preparation for an opportunity that does not even exist yet. Wow! That's why you need to …

5. Celebrate Yourself Often!

Right now, I want you to stop reading this book, go buy some confetti, throw it high in the air in front of you, and walk through your own celebration! Why? That sounds

Nobody is going to celebrate you enough for the amount of hell that you go through in the run of a day.

Caught Between A Dream & a Job!

silly, right? Not really, my friend. You see, nobody is going to celebrate you enough for the amount of hell that you go through in the run of a day. They just won't. That's too much to ask from a teacher, boss, spouse, best friend, or family member. **You have to learn to throw your own party.** Celebrate YOU! You deserve it. Take yourself to dinner sometimes. Buy yourself something nice - because you have worked for it. If you don't have a special person in your life who does these things for you, treat yourself to massages, manicures, pedicures, and things that celebrate your wellness and esteem. With all the changing, working, negotiating, sacrificing, serving, and creating that you will be doing, it is a must that you pour back into yourself with FUN STUFF! **Laugh a lot. Smile as much as you can. Wave at people who don't know you! Why? Because as Tony Robbins says, "Your physiology determines your psychology!"** In other words, what you do with your body and gestures, determines your attitude and mental framework. Celebrate your uniqueness, celebrate your power, celebrate your victories, **celebrate the doors that opened for you, celebrate the doors that were closed for you, and most of all, celebrate how blessed you are to have life. Pay close attention to the first persons you call when you get good news.** This is an indicator of the key celebrators

Don't pursue a mentor for what they have earned. Pursue a mentor for what they have learned.
~Dr. Mike Murdock

Caught Between A Dream & a Job!

in your life. Keep these people close to you. They are your own personal cheerleading section. We all need one.

6. Surround Yourself with the 3Ms (Mentors, Mates, and Mentees). There should be 3 types of people in your life at all times. I teach this all across the country, and every audience really enjoys and benefits from it.

The first type of person should be a mentor. I have talked extensively about mentorship in this chapter, because it's so critical. Most of the self-made millionaires in this county have many things in common. One of those things is that they all had a financial mentor in their lives. **Mentors are learning-curve cutters! They help you get to your goal quicker and with less heartache than they had.** You should always be reaching up to their level. Critical point: **Don't pursue a mentor for what they are earned (degrees, houses, cars, cloths, and the like). Pursue a mentor for what they have learned (wisdom, insight, life lessons, character, and integrity)!** So the first person you should have in your life is someone who is above you.

The second is what I call a Mate. This is like a running mate. This is someone who is at a similar age and stage as you are in life. Why? Because you want someone you can bounce ideas off of. You want someone to experience similar successes and failures with. You will rise up the success ladder together with

Caught Between A Dream & a Job!

this person, and that makes it all the more fun.

The third person you need in your life is a Mentee. This is someone who you are pouring into. This is someone who looks to you as their mentor! Now the tables are turned and you are not focused on getting - you are focused on giving. Mentees are great because they force you to review the totality of your life and squeeze out some nuggets of truth that can help them avoid the many mistakes and pitfalls that you encountered. You need someone into whom you can dump your life lessons so that what you go through will not be in vain; it will have been of some benefit to someone else as well as yourself.

If you will keep these 3 types of people around you and inside your life at all times (Mentors, Mates, and Mentees) you will have a powerful team of people who will help you Rob the Grave on a daily basis.

7. Filter your Stress Often. Determine ways and options that you can use to relieve yourself of stress. Stress, especially yesterday's stress, is a burden and weight that keeps so many people from operating in their full potential. For example, every home as several trash bins in it. You can always tell when trash day is just by driving through a neighborhood. Why?

You must get rid of the waste that takes up valuable space in your secret place.

Caught Between A Dream & a Job!

Because all the neighbors put their trash on the curb to be picked up and discarded. Well, we must do stress and negative thinking the same way. You must get rid of the waste that takes up valuable space in your secret place. People cleanse themselves of stress in different ways. **Some read, some write, some go to the park, some walk the dog, some make love to their spouse, some play a sport, some workout, some rent a movie, some cook, some write in a journal, some go for a swim, some sit in a Jacuzzi, some go to a day spa, some go shopping, some go for a long drive, some take a powernap, and some go on regular weekend vacations.** Whatever method you use, achieve the goal of keeping negative stress at a minimum in your life.

8. Use everything Painful for something Powerful! My friend, please get this point. **There is a purpose behind your pain.** Every hurtful, harmful, painful thing that you go through in life has a major purpose behind it. There is a life lesson that is fueling every painful situation you encounter. We will talk more about this in Chapter 7: Make Lemonade and Sell it for Profit! Meanwhile, let me encourage you by telling you to ask God for one simple gift. **Ask Him to teach you the life lesson behind every painful situation that happens to you. This goes for the big and small stuff.**

For example, I am about to be very transparent by telling you this - but here goes. There was a day when

Caught Between A Dream & a Job!

I checked my online business bank account and it was overdrawn by a small, but significant amount. I was shocked because as a part of my Daily Routine, I check and update all of my online bank accounts. I did not understand what was going on. I balanced my checkbook over again, I called customer service, and I even visited the local bank branch! I had to research back 3 months to find the error. I found a few small miscalculations on my part and deposited the needed amount to clear it up. As I was driving home, I said "God, what was I supposed to learn from that?" He said, *"Well, right now $100 off when you are earning about $100,000 a year seems small. But I want to teach you to be a solid financial steward over your money so that when I bless you to earn $1,000,000, you won't miscalculate thousands of dollars!"* **Wow! God was using something small to teach me an important lesson that I would not want to learn later, because that same lesson learned later would have cost me MUCH more!**

Your spiritual and emotional well-being are two of the most important aspects of your self-development as you walk out the gifting and the mission that has been placed on your life. Use these points above, combined with others that you have learned and will learn from other speakers, teachers, lecturers, mentors, preachers, bosses, and advisors to continue to keep you sharp and focused on fulfilling your destiny and making one of the most powerful transitions you will ever make. *Del, thanks for this*

Delatorro L. McNeal II

Caught Between A Dream & a Job!

great information, but how will I know when I have made the transition from my job to my dream? GREAT QUESTION! You will know when others can't tell whether you are working or playing. Because to you, you're always doing both.

8 Quick Review Points for a New Beginning in your Quest!

1. Being caught between a Dream and a Job is actually a good thing. Have a positive outlook towards this critical transition period in your life. **You will be taking a step that most are not brave enough to take.**

2. Your job will only release a small percentage of your true greatness. In order to unleash all that God has put inside of you, you must pursue your dream with 100% of yourself.

3. If you're going to be a statistic, be an empowering one. Hopefully, one day you will wake up as one of the 64 other self-made millionaires that are born each day here in America.

4. I recommend the Tarzan Theory of transitioning from your job to your dream. It is systematic, methodical, and time-tested.

5. Never burn your bridges! Always keep a positive attitude while using your jobs as stepping-stones towards

Caught Between A Dream & a Job!

your dream. Either you come to a job or you come through a job. I recommend that you come through jobs, picking up as much as you can to build your dream.

6. Dreams are the only thing that will make sense of the tenses of your life.

7. Surround yourself with the 3 types of people you read about (The 3 Ms).

8. Use your job to build a solid financial future for your dream!

Notes:

_____

_____

_____

_____

_____

_____

_____

_____

_____

Caught Between A Dream & a Job!

One of my Favorite Poems
If- Burton Burley

If you want a thing bad enough to go out and fight for it,
To work day and night for it
To give up your time, your sleep, and your peace for it,

If all that you dream and scheme are about it,
And if life seems useless and worthless without it,
And if you'll gladly sweat for it, and fret for it,
and plan for it,
And lose all your terror of the opposition for it,

If you simply go after that thing that you want with all
of your capacity, strength and sagacity, faith, hope,
confidence, and stern pertinacity.

If neither cold, poverty, famine, or gout…sickness and
pain nor body and brain can keep you from the thing
that you want!

If dogged and grim you besiege and beset it, then
with the help of God you'll get it.

Caught Between A Dream & a Job!

Reality Check:
Robbing Made Easy

My friend, I hope and pray that you are enjoying and applying this book so far. Really quickly, I just wanted to interrupt your flow by adding another reality check. These are just a few things to ponder on. I want you to understand the importance of **everything you do each day and the impact that your daily actions have upon the grave.** I believe that most of us are professional grave robbers and we don't even know it. Here are a few examples:

1. Every **encouraging word** you utter robs the grave of a little bit of its greatness!

2. Every **prayer that you pray** robs the grave of a little bit of its greatness!

3. Every **business that you launch** robs the grave of a little bit of its greatness!

4. Every **customer that you satisfy** robs the grave of a little bit of its greatness!

5. Every **song that you sing** robs the grave of a little bit of its greatness!

6. Every **book that you read and apply** robs the grave of a little bit of its greatness!

Caught Between A Dream & a Job!

7. Every **seminar that you attend and maximize** robs the grave of a little bit of its greatness!

8. Every **seed that you sow into someone** or **something** else robs the grave of a little bit of its greatness!

9. Every **person or young child that you mentor** robs the grave of a little bit of its greatness!

10. Every **employee that you reward** robs the grave of a little bit of its greatness!

11. Every **organization that you join to make a difference** robs the grave of a little bit of its greatness!

12. Every **client that you coach** to success robs the grave of a little bit of its greatness!

13. Every **class that you pass** and every **good grade that you earn** robs the grave of a little bit of its greatness!

14. Every **degree that you acquire** and every honor that you earn robs the grave of a little bit of its greatness!

15. Every **political concern that you voice** robs the grave of a little bit of its greatness!

16. Every **vote that you cast** robs the grave of a little bit of its greatness!

Caught Between A Dream & a Job!

17. Every **smile that you share** robs the grave of a little bit of its greatness!

18. Every **hug that you share** with a hurting person robs the grave of a little bit of its greatness!

19. Every **credit card that you pay off** robs the grave of a little bit of its greatness!

20. Every **pound that you lose** towards your health goals robs the grave of a little bit of its greatness!

21. Every day **you stay clean of smoking, drugs, and alcohol** robs the grave of a little bit of its greatness!

22. Every **illness that you fight** robs the grave of a little bit of its greatness!

23. Every **person you forgive** robs the grave of a little bit of its greatness!

24. Every **idea that you act upon** robs the grave of a little bit of its greatness!

25. Every **piece of advice or wise counsel you share** robs the grave of a little bit of its greatness!

26. Every **random act of kindness you bestow** robs the grave of a little bit of its greatness!

Caught Between A Dream & a Job!

27. Every **thoughtful email that you send** robs the grave of a little bit of its greatness!

28. Every **job that you take and every company you bless with your talents** robs the grave of a little bit of its greatness!

29. Every **goal that you achieve** robs the grave of a little bit of its greatness!

30. Every thing **that you become in the process** of reaching the goal, robs the grave of a little bit of its greatness!

SEE HOW WHAT YOU DO DAILY, OVER A PERIOD OF TIME, snatches all of your stuff from the grave? You are an awesome human being, dropped on this earth **to change it.**

Start right now, and never, ever give up!

Notes:

_____

_____

_____

_____

_____

_____

Caught Between A Dream & a Job!

Chapter 6

How to S.A.M. Your Goals & Dreams

How to S.A.M. Your Goals and Dreams

I could hardly wait for you to get to this chapter! I am so excited. *Goals* is one of my favorite topics. The first set of workshops I ever presented was on Goals. Now, it is joined by several other powerful workshops that help people become more successful. However, **I have to admit that my perception of goals, my teaching of goals, and my understanding of goals has changed tremendously over the years.** I am excited about this chapter because it represents what I believe to be the totality of the revelation that I possess about how you can utilize goals to apprehend your destiny.

I used to teach **Goal Setting!** I would show people how, through having a larger vision of themselves, to set the right types of goals and be successful. I learned that the problem most people had was that they were aiming too low in life, and hitting those low targets. I found that many people were settling for mediocrity in life. **They were aiming at low grades, low salaries, low careers, low expectations, low thinking, low dreaming, and low performance, and they were hitting those low targets.** So, my early Goal Setting programs focused on helping people get a larger vision of themselves. These sessions were very successful, and many people's lives were blessed. But, you guessed it! There was a deeper level yet to be uncovered.

After a while, **I began to realize that people who were just Goal Setters were not the most effective**

How to S.A.M. Your Goals and Dreams

people in the world. Why? Because the reality is that you can "set goals" all day long, but without action towards goal accomplishment, your goal setting is in vain. I realized that in my own life, and in the lives of many other great people that I studied, that we all did a lot more than just write down goals. We took additional action steps. So I changed my program from teaching Goal Setting to teaching **Goal Achievement**. Now, I was really getting somewhere. I was getting people to transition:

- from Wanting It…to Walking It!
- from Dreaming It…to Doing It!
- from Thinking It…to Trying It!
- from Cognition…to Creation!
- from Pontification…to Participation!
- from Meditation…to Motivation!

I was teaching people to move beyond decision and into action.

Here is a perfect example of what I mean:

There are three frogs sitting by a still pond.
One decides to jump. How many are left?

Two, right?
Wrong, three are left!

Because one just *decided*!

How to S.A.M. Your Goals and Dreams

Making a decision is not the same as following through on a decision. That is an assumption that most of us make. I know plenty of people (including myself) who have decided to do something, but did not follow through on the decision. I have decided to end relationships with people, but it took me 2 months to really take action on that decision. I have decided to join a gym many times, but it was not until January of 2003 that my wife and I got serious about our fitness. Sometimes it takes me months to get started on a CD project after I have decided to do it. **We have learned that decision is a part of the process - but it is not the entire process.** It's the beginning of the change process.

Prove this point to yourself. List 3 things that you have decided to do, but have not followed through on! Be honest!

1. _____

2. _____

3. _____

I learned through my own life and studying the lives of others, that the achievement of the goal is nowhere close to as important as WHO YOU BECOME in the process of the achievement of the goal. I will say that again to make sure you get it. **The achievement of the goal is nowhere close to as important as WHO**

How to S.A.M. Your Goals and Dreams

YOU BECOME in the process of the achievement of the goal. Your goals are trying to turn and shape you into the right type of person. Many fallen successful people have proven this point. Many people achieve a goal quickly, but neglect to become a better person in the process- so they ultimately end up failing.

Many people's primary goal in life is to have lots of money. The reality is that **money only makes you more of what you already are.** Money only amplifies who you are now. It only magnifies the you that currently exists. In other words, if you are careless with $10 dollars, you will be WORSE with $10,000,000. That's why current statistics teach us that **95% of the people who win the lottery (achieve the goal of financial success) go BANKRUPT in 3 to 5 years.** A once in a lifetime opportunity that creates a lifetime of financial security is lost by 95% of the people who achieve the goal. Why? BECAUSE THEY DID NOT BECOME A WISER PERSON IN THE PROCESS! **Never forget that your goals are trying to turn you into a better person.**

The achievement of the goal is nowhere close to as important as WHO YOU BECOME in the process of the achievement of the goal.

Many people lose weight on diet fads that don't really work. They achieve the goal of losing weight, but within 2 or 3 months, they gain it all back. Why? Because they did not change in the process. They did

How to S.A.M. Your Goals and Dreams

Money only makes you more of what you already are.

not become more disciplined, more focused, more selective, and more committed to habits of fitness. Lottery winners that end up filing for bankruptcy obviously did not become good financial stewards, budgeters, or financial planners over their wealth. Because of this, they lost it. That's why it's so important for us to know and understand what life is trying to teach us about ourselves in the process of the achievement of our goals.

I had to go deeper, because I found a lot of people who achieved goals, but did not maintain the benefits of them. This is what sparked my newfound revelation - **Goal Maintenance.** I learned that there is one final step that we must take in order to really be successful. We must learn how to maintain the goals that we achieve.

You must learn how to **Set, Achieve, and Maintain (S.A.M.)** your goals and dreams in life.

Maintenance is critical. Bank accounts become overdrawn without proper maintenance. Cars break down years before they should without proper maintenance. Houses become rat-infested dumps without proper maintenance. Businesses close their doors without proper maintenance. Computers malfunction with viruses and hard drive issues due to poor maintenance. **So we must focus on maintenance.**

How to S.A.M. Your Goals and Dreams

Most of us assume maintenance is covered when we set a goal and achieve it. **But the maintenance of a goal has its own totally separate set of rules and requirements in order for it to be a success.** Do you remember the old saying, "from rags to riches"? When people say that phrase, they are really talking about Goal Maintenance - not Goal Achievement. Why? **Because I don't know anyone who wants to go from Rags to Riches, and then back to Rags! Smiles.**

What we really want is to go from Rags to Riches and STAY AT RICHES! That means we want to go from poor to wealthy and stay wealthy. If this is what you want, then set a new goal to be wealthier, achieve that through specific and consistent action steps, and maintain it in a similar fashion. It's a cycle.

Goal Maintenance has everything to do with your daily routine, which we will get into in a moment. But first, I had to lay a solid foundation of S.A.M. so that you could understand the 3-step progression that we must work through to create and sustain the success that we desire. Keep reading…it gets better.

Now Is Your Time

In this chapter, I hope to pull some high level motivational concepts down to earth so that you can understand and implement them. I want to expose

How to S.A.M. Your Goals and Dreams

Goal Maintenance has everything to do with your daily routine, some of the secrets of powerful goal setting, goal achieving, and goal maintenance. The purpose of this chapter is to get you from where you are to where you want to be, now that you are committed to making a change in your life. You are well on your way to discovering and walking in your life's purpose. Now that you realize just how much of your true potential is still to be uncovered, you can and must make a transition from your job to your dream. "NOW IT IS TIME!" As Rafiki from The Lion King would say.

Now it is time for you to create the goals that will get you where you want to be. **Now it is time for you to actively participate in a process that only 3% of Americans engage in faithfully.** Now is your opportunity to create your future. **Now is your time** to put yourself miles ahead of the competition. **Now is the time** to paint your dream life on the canvas of time and opportunity with expectation and faith that, with smart work and determination, you will achieve and maintain your ultimate destiny.

Now is the time for you to unleash what is inside of you. **Now is the time** for you to begin or continue to catch up with yourself. **Now is your time** to INK your goals instead of just THINKING them. This chapter

How to S.A.M. Your Goals and Dreams

will help you to get them out of your head and heart and into an Action Plan that will enable you to be successful each and every day.

Let's get started. Let's pretend! Will you pretend with me for a moment? I want you to pretend that because you turned to this particular page in this book, you just acquired a rare disease. This disease mandates three things. **First,** you have exactly one year to live. **Second,** you cannot fail at anything that you attempt within this year. **Third,** any goals you write down on the lines that follow are **miracle goals**. This means that they will come to pass. Based on these parameters, take the next 5 minutes to write down every goal that you can imagine.

Don't edit yourself. If it comes to mind, write it down! Don't try to write what you think I want you to write. Just get your aspirations out of you! Start Now!

1. _____
2. _____
3. _____
4. _____
5. _____
6. _____
7. _____
8. _____
9. _____

How to S.A.M. Your Goals and Dreams

10. _____
11. _____
12. _____
13. _____
14. _____
15. _____
16. _____
17. _____
18. _____
19. _____
20. _____

Great job! Now that you have listed these goals, go back and highlight or circle the ones that **take priority and precedence** over the others. The goals you circled and highlighted are the ones that I want you to keep in mind as we move through this chapter. Okay! I am very excited for your present and your future. Why? Because **it will take your present action to create your future dreams.**

It will take your present action to create your future dreams.

Now, it's important that you take this chapter very seriously because you don't want to be a part of the startling statistics about all of the people who are not taking the needed steps to become

How to S.A.M. Your Goals and Dreams

professional Grave Robbers. I shared some appalling facts with you earlier, but here are just a few more to get you fired up! Why get you fired up? Because it takes people getting mad at something to really make a change. I love the way Willie Jolley says it, *"A success is nothing but a failure that got mad!"* And I want you to use this book as a tool to help you create the change you have always wanted in your life.

Some Startling Statistics
(Sources: USA Today and The Consumer Credit Counseling Centers of America)

When the Average American dies, they will have had **$1 million dollars PASS THROUGH their hands** within their lifetime. Sound good? Not really. Look where most people end up.

·   95% of Americans die without a will. This leaves a weekly surplus to the federal government of $180 million dollars. These funds could have been left for family members of future generations or worthy non-profit organizations.

·   85% of Americans don't have $5,000 in their checking accounts at the time of retirement.

·   87% of Americans retire at poverty level.

·   90% of American families live paycheck-to-paycheck.

How to S.A.M. Your Goals and Dreams

· The average American has $4,500 in credit card debt.

· The Average American Family has $8,500 in credit card debt.

· 67% of Americans abuse credit by using credit cards to finance a lifestyle they knowingly can't afford.

· $74 million dollars per year goes out from the federal government to Colleges and Universities nationwide in the form of Student Financial Aid. 58% of these dollars go out as student loans. Statistics say that the average college student (between the ages of 21 to 35) will change jobs/careers 9 times. Which means that over half of our students attending college today, who receive some form of financial assistance, are borrowing someone else's money to pay for a degree that they have little likelihood of using upon graduation. Now this does not mean that students can't change majors or careers. But what this does mean is that we need to begin to equip and empower our students better so that while they are in college they will make wiser decisions about how they spend their time and money.

COULD THESE STARTLING STATISTICS HAVE ANYTHING TO DO WITH THE FACT THAT **ONLY 3% OF AMERICANS** ARE CREATING WRITTEN GOALS?

Delatorro L. McNeal II

How to S.A.M. Your Goals and Dreams

These stats are proof that if we aim at nothing in life, we will hit it every time. Something has to change, and it starts with you! Yes - you, my friend! So this chapter is dedicated to helping you become a positive statistic, and Robbing the Grave of the financial, personal, professional, and spiritual harvest that awaits you. Let's get to work!

Your Circle of Life

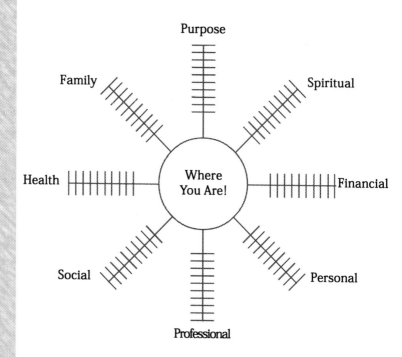

How to S.A.M. Your Goals and Dreams

I call this diagram the Circle of Life. It represents the totality of the 8 different areas of your life. The Circle of Life is made up of the following components: **Your Purpose in Life, Your Personal Life, Your Professional Life, Your Social Life, Your Spiritual Life, Your Financial Life, Your Family Life, and Your Health/Wellness Life.** Yes - all of this is YOU! Your life is comprised of all of these areas. In this exercise, I want you to identify where you are in life. Before I can help you get to where you want to be, I must first help you determine where you are!

For each area of your life, make an honest assessment of where you are. Each little mark on the line represents 1 point. I want you to rate your life on a scale of 1 to 10 in each of these areas with 1 being the lowest and 10 being the highest. So for example, let's say you feel that you are slightly better than average in your social life. You may want to rate yourself a 6 in that area. So, from the center, count outward 6 marks and place a dot there. Do this for each area of your life. Be honest and don't be ashamed. If things could not possibly be better in your life in a certain area, give yourself a 10. But if things couldn't be worse, you might start at a 1 and create a goal to work your way up.

Once you have marked all your dots and done this assessment of yourself, connect the dots. It will make a very interesting picture. **This picture is a picture of your life.**

How to S.A.M. Your Goals and Dreams

The Goal is Balance - a well-rounded circle. You want live a balanced life. True balance encompasses each area of your life equally. Yes, there will be times and seasons when certain areas of your life take precedence over others. But that should be only for a season, and not your entire life. From this, I can help you help yourself because I am sure that there are certain areas of your

life that have dents or dips in them - and that's okay! I want to help you push some of those areas out. Ultimately, you should be working towards positive purpose-driven goals in all areas of your life. This will allow you to build momentum. This is critical. Okay, let's keep going. Pay close attention to your own circle because the severity of the dips will determine how aggressive your goals in those areas need to be. You will work from this graphic again a little later; so don't lose sight of it.

Goals Defined

I have read countless books, attended numerous seminars, and listened to many audiotapes about goals. What I have learned is that each speaker, trainer, and life coach has his or her own definition of goals. Well, so do I. We must define goals if we are ever going to really set them effectively, achieve them efficiently, and maintain them profitably. Therefore, for the purposes of this book, let's use the following definition:

How to S.A.M. Your Goals and Dreams

> *Goals are action items. They require your effort. They require your involvement.*

Goals are deliberate and specific action items that mirror our dreams and aspirations, which are used to create confidence, momentum, and accomplishment in our lives.

Now this definition sounds good, however I would like to break down each major phrase in the definition, so that I can help you create a very clear meaning in your mind and heart. Goals are one the most important components of your life. Therefore, I want to define them properly so that we can reap the maximum benefit from our understanding of them.

Goals are Deliberate and Specific. This is critical. Goals are intentional. You don't just stumble upon them. **You are purposeful in your identification of a goal.** It is a very strategic, well planned out, and methodical process. Goals are determined with wisdom and intelligence. They are specific. That means that they are aimed at a designated target.

Action Items. Goals are not wishes, hopeful dreams, or lofty expectations based on wrong information. **Goals are not mere "to do lists" that you create to solve a temporary "today problem". Goals are action items.** They require your effort. They require your involvement. They require your "elbow grease" in order to live. Goals without action are like starfish

How to S.A.M. Your Goals and Dreams

out of water. They will die quickly. One of the major purposes of a goal is to get you to move. Look at the word. **50% of the word GOAL is GO! The other 50% is AL. So the purpose of a goal is to get ALL of us to GO somewhere in life.** Smiles! I like that one.

Mirroring Your Dreams and Aspirations. Your goals should be little snapshots, little nuggets, and little samplers of your lifetime and long-term aspirations. I should be able to look at your goals of today, and see where you want to be tomorrow. **Similar to a mirror, I should be able to look at your goals and see a reflection of your dreams and aspirations.** The things you want to do, be, and have in the future should be made evident in your present goals.

Used to Create Confidence, Momentum, and Accomplishment in our Lives. This is a huge statement. The purpose of a goal is to help you build and maintain confidence. If your goals don't make you smile and feel good about yourself, you've either got the wrong goals or you are writing them the wrong way. One of the purposes of a goal is to create confidence in your life. You should walk confidently, talk confidently, work confidently, and dream confidently. However, without clearly defined goals, you can't do any of that. You've got to allow yourself to create a relationship with your goals. The root word of confidence is *confide*. To confide means to trust or have a close communicative relationship with. **You**

Delatorro L. McNeal II

How to S.A.M. Your Goals and Dreams

and your goals should have a relationship. You should treat them like a person.

Let's talk about Momentum. THIS IS HUGE! Momentum is simply defined as a driving or propelling force. The root word of momentum is *moment*. In order to create momentum, you must use your goals to learn how to maximize your moments. **Each day, life blesses you with 86,400 small, tiny, powerful, and unforgiving moments to seize.** We call them the seconds. One of the objectives of a goal is to help you take small, consistent, daily action steps that will force you to seize your seconds (or seize your moments) and, therefore, build momentum.

I like to define momentum as two words - "*moment*" and "*um*". This means that when you see a moment, and you seize that moment, your body feels so good it lets out a little utterance like "*um*". And it seizes another moment, and it feels good again so it says "*um*". This cycle repeats itself over and over again, **creating *MOMENTUM*!** We will talk more about this in the last chapter - Chapter 8: Creating and Seizing Opportunity.

Let's talk about Accomplishment! I would like to teach you about this word using a story. There once was a scientist by the name of John Henry Fabrea. He did a study on Processionary Caterpillars. The reason why they have the name of Processionary Caterpillars is because whenever two or more of them gather together, they begin to follow each other around.

How to S.A.M. Your Goals and Dreams

John Henry was very interested in what he had heard about the Processionary Caterpillars, so he decided to put them to the test. He cleaned his desk of everything that was on it, and put a flowerpot in the center of the desk. He then took about 15 of these Processionary Caterpillars and placed them around the flowerpot.

Sure enough, my friend, in a moment's time they had rallied together and began to follow each other in a perfect unending circle around the flowerpot. John Henry was amazed. He wanted to see how committed the caterpillars were to their pattern and routine. He watched for 10 minutes, which turned into 20, then 30, then 45 minutes. Finally, after 1 solid hour of watching these Processionary Caterpillars go around and around in a circle, he got the bright idea to change the study. He took the flowerpot out of the center of the desk. In its place, he put pine needles. **(PAUSE! Educational Point: Pine Needles are the FOOD of the Processionary Caterpillar. PLAY!)** So he put the pine needles in the center of the circle that the caterpillars had made. And, again, they marched around and around, and around, and around. After 3 hours, they all DIED! With food less then 5 inches away, they all died from exhaustion & starvation. WHY?

The purpose of goals is to make you an accomplished person – not an active person.

Delatorro L. McNeal II

How to S.A.M. Your Goals and Dreams

BECAUSE THEY CONFUSED ACTIVITY WITH ACCOMPLISHMENT!

They were busy, active, and moving - but they were not accomplishing anything! And, truth be told, many of us are just like those Processionary Caterpillars. We are busy, busy, busy. We have cell phones, Palm Pilots, planners, Daytimers, and everything else to help us **appear busy.** But, for many of us, we are active without a great deal of accomplishment.

The purpose of goals is to make you an accomplished person – not an active person. You can rock in a rocking chair all day - but not go anywhere. You can worry all day about something, but unless you take action to change it, your worrying does nothing. **Your mind might have been active, but it was not accomplishing much.**

Surfing the internet is activity. **Researching on the internet is accomplishment.** Dating is activity. **Courting someone who you feel has been divinely assigned to be your mate is accomplishment.** Going to college is activity. **Majoring in a specific area on a designated career path is accomplishment.** My goal in this chapter is not to make you more active. My goal is make you more accomplished.

How to S.A.M. Your Goals and Dreams

7 Purposes of Goals

1. To transition you from where you are, to where you want to be.
2. To transform you into all that you were designed to be.
3. To change your personality so that you can maintain what you attain.
4. To force the people in your life to position themselves.
5. To force the enemies of your life to expose themselves.
6. To unleash gifts that you do not realize you possess.
7. To stretch you towards your potential and ultimate power.

Six Characteristics of Goals

So, now that we clearly understand the definition of goals, let's talk about the characteristics of goals. In my effort to better understand Goals, my wife and I sent them an invitation to come over to our home for dinner. We cooked up a really nice meal and then I personally interviewed them. The Queen took notes while I listened intently to what they said. I learned 6 key characteristics of Goals in that short interview. I would like to share them with you now.

1. Goals are not respecters of persons. Goals don't care who owns them. Goals are not racist or sexist.

How to S.A.M. Your Goals and Dreams

They do not favor the rich or the poor. They don't care about your height, your weight, your ethnicity, your religion, your upbringing, or any other those things. Your goals simply do not care. Stop feeling like the victim because of things that you are not. Stop feeling cheated because of your background your race, your ethnicity, your age, or your gender. Why? Because, when it comes to goals, **WE ALL ARE ON A LEVEL PLAYING FIELD.** Goals don't care! Play with your deck of cards and use ALL of who you are - to your advantage! Don't let anything about your divine makeup hold you back from pursuing your greatness - by any positive means necessary.

2. Goals are never 100% independent. Goal achievement in any area of your life is never an isolated success. **Every goal that you achieve will impact another goal somewhere else in your life.** This is why goal achievement is so powerful. When you get into a routine of making things happen in your life, you actually set in motion a domino effect with your goals. When you accomplish one, you actually create an improvement in other areas. For example, let's say you set a goal to get a better job - which is a Professional Goal. You get the job, and your salary doubles. Now your Financial Life just got a big increase. Let's say that you have always been self-conscious about your smile, but you could never afford braces. This new increase in finances allows you to get braces and improve your smile - which is a part of your Health Goals. This improves your self-confidence and self-esteem at the

How to S.A.M. Your Goals and Dreams

same time - which improves your Personal Life. Get the Point? **Goals are never 100% independent; they always bump into other goals in your life.** I believe that this story is a perfect example of this point. Why? Because it was taken from my life.

3. Goals, once achieved, create other goals. This is a really unique truth about goals. Action and accomplishment are the wombs that birth goals. I have found that getting into a routine with goal achievement is a powerful practice. Goals will

Goals have of way of multiplying based on the energy created from the last accomplishment.

regenerate new and exciting goals that challenge you to take new steps. Goals keep you focused on going higher and higher. For example, before I became an author in 2001 with my first book (101 Gems of Greatness), I only had ideas for one book. All I wanted to do was write that one book. Well, my friend, as soon as I began selling that book, I began to get ideas for three other books. Ideas came so strongly that I literally had to shelf two of them so that I could focus on getting this one out. **Goals have of way of multiplying based on the energy created from the last accomplishment. That's a really cool thing about goals.** I love it!

4. Goals are everywhere, and in everything that we do. Think about it. GOALS ARE EVERYWHERE! You set, achieve, and maintain goals all day - every day of your life. **Goals are not just things that you set at**

How to S.A.M. Your Goals and Dreams

seminars, or after listening to tape series. They certainly are not just things you attempt to accomplish at the beginning of each year. What are those called? Oh - New Years Resolutions! Well, as my friend and fellow speaker Tony Powell would say, this book and this chapter on goals is your **New Years Resolution** *SOLUTION*!

Goals are all around you. Think about it. When you reached for this book, you had a goal in mind. When you put it down, another goal will pull you to do something else. What is the purpose of setting your alarm clock every night? **You expect to wake up on time the next morning.** When you turn on the shower, and wait a few minutes before getting in, what is the goal? **You want to let the water get hot!** What is the goal of the green light? **To get traffic to move.** What is the goal of the red light? **To get traffic to stop.** What is the goal of direct deposit? **To get your money to you faster and more conveniently.** These are just a few simple examples of the fact that goals are everywhere and in everything that you do. This chapter is meant to help you focus on, appreciate, and maximize the presence of goals in your life.

EVERYTHING YOU DO IS DRIVEN BY GOALS!

5. **Goals by nature, are abstract. You must make them concrete.** I can remember when my elementary school English teach taught our class about abstract

How to S.A.M. Your Goals and Dreams

and concrete nouns. She said that abstract nouns were things that you could not physically see with the human eye. She gave examples such as character, integrity, determination, and success. She went on to explain that concrete nouns were things that you could see with the human eye. These are things like cars, houses, clothes, office buildings, and stores. Well, if I may, I would like to borrow that same line of thinking to build a case for goals. Goals, by nature, are abstract. You can't see them. They are simply wishes, hopes, and lofty expectations. **You, my friend, must make them concrete. You must take them from high level concepts to reachable, attainable, achievable, buildable, and profitable vehicles to transport you from where you are to where you dream to be.** *Well Del, how do I do that?* GREAT QUESTION. Keep reading. Your answer is coming.

6. Without ACTION towards them, Goals are 100% worthless. If you want something to happen in your life and you are taking NO ACTION towards it, that's not a goal! That is a wish! Your goals are worthless without action towards them. A human is worthless without oxygen. A fish is worthless without water. A bird is worthless without air. A tree is worthless without soil. Why? Because all of these things require the proper grounding and proper

> *If you want something to happen in your life and you are taking NO ACTION towards it, that's not a goal! That is a wish.*

environment in order to function. **Your goals must be grounded in your action, and watered by your faith and positive expectation in order to grow into your destiny.**

The Two Styles of Goals

One thing that can determine how fast your goals are achieved or how quickly they are destroyed is the people with whom you share them. I learned this the hard way. I have trusted certain folks with goals that I never should have, and got burned! I have also seen other great people share their goals with the wrong folks, which caused their dreams to die overnight. So, it is critical that you understand who you share your goals with. In order to understand this you must understand the two styles of goals. Every goal that you set will fall into one of these two styles; it will either be a **Give Up** Goal or a **Go Up Goal.**

The Give Up Goal is typically a negative habit, action, attitude, mindset, methodology, paradigm, or way of doing things that you are trying to give up. You want to start a new way of acting or thinking, but it requires you to drop the old way first. There are many things that can motivate someone to generate a Give Up Goal. Maybe your significant other will not tolerate a smoking, drinking or cursing habit that you have, so you are forced to give it up. Maybe your doctor has informed you of a health condition that can potentially

How to S.A.M. Your Goals and Dreams

have a negative impact on your well-being, so you are forced to stop eating certain foods or drinking certain types of beverages. Maybe you realize that your life is being wasted with negative people and your potential is not being maximized, so you determine to stop playing games, stop lying to people, or stop hanging with certain crowds. Maybe you just come into a deeper level of spirituality, so you give up certain places and things to adopt a new lifestyle.

The reasons can go on and on, but the point is the same. All of these are Give Up Goals. **The nice thing about Give Up Goals is that most people are not directly threatened by you giving up something, so you are pretty safe to tell people about them.**

The only people I would not tell about Give Up Goals are those that simply want to see you fail, and would tempt you while you are trying to get off of the negative habit. Run from these people, and flock to those who support you making the transition.

The Go Up Goal is a totally different motivational monster. The Go Up Goal has some psychology behind it. **The Go Up Goal is a positive advancement that you are trying to make in your life.** It has everything to do with you transitioning your life from good to great. It has

Success is not a seesaw. Others don't have to go down for you to go up. You can go up, and so can they!

How to S.A.M. Your Goals and Dreams

everything to do with you Robbing the Grave of the Greatness it wants to keep. Go Up Goals are things like promotion, establishing a high-paying career, writing a book, graduating from college, penetrating new markets, gaining market share, increasing revenues, starting a business, getting discovered, gaining popularity, winning political office, starting a church, or getting married. There are millions of reasons why you would want to move up, right? **Everyone wants to move up in life, right?**

Right! And that is the problem with Go Up Goals. Now, you are in direct competition with the exact same things that others want. And though it's sad to say, **most people don't look at similar goal paths as collaboration. Most look at similar goal paths as competition.** The sad truth is that many people, once they see you going higher, will do whatever they can to discredit you and pull you down so that they can go higher. Why? Because they think that success is a seesaw. They think that in order for them to go up, you must go down. And vice versa! Garbage! Success is not a seesaw. Others don't have to go down for you to go up. You can go up, and so can they! **Well Del, why do people think this way?** GREAT QUESTION! I have learned that there are two mentalities that most people operate under: either the **Scarcity mentality** or the **Abundance mentality.**

The Scarcity mentality says, "There is one piece of pie. So if you get a big chunk of it, there is LESS for

How to S.A.M. Your Goals and Dreams

me." This mindset breeds competition, division, manipulation, and false friendships. People that operate under this mentality really don't like to hear your good news. Can I be honest with you? **The average person that you tell your great news to will not be happy for you!** They smile and look happy, but deep down they are eating their heart out because they wish it was them. Why? Scarcity Mentality! They see any good news from you as less of an opportunity of good news for them. They see success as a seesaw! Stay far away from Scarcity Mentality People. They will rob you of your joy, peace, and true happiness. They will throw ice water on your dream. The most dangerous person to be around is someone who did not fulfill their dream and who operates on the scarcity mentality!

The Abundance mentality says, **"There is unlimited pie! So if you get a big chunk of it, that just means that mine is on the way!"** That's good news. So when I see my good friend get a promotion, I understand that if I work as hard and smart as they do, mine is coming soon too. It means that, when I see my best friend get blessed with a new house, I know that if I line myself up financially, my house is coming along soon. People who operate on the Abundance mentality view the success stories of others as big navigational signs on the highway of life, letting them know that Success City is just a few miles down the road! **Abundance mentality people are REALLY and TRULY HAPPY FOR YOU when you give them great**

How to S.A.M. Your Goals and Dreams

news about your success. That's why mentors are so important. You want to hang around people who have been there and done that, because they don't mind you going there and doing that. In fact, they will help you!

I covered all that ground to teach you something important. **BE CAREFUL WHO YOU SHARE YOUR GO UP GOALS WITH!** Only share your Go Up Goals with those who can help you do what it says - GO UP! If they are not in a position to pull you up, or push you up from their position in life, don't tell them. By telling them, you are giving ammunition to the enemy. Keep your mouth closed until you have built up so much momentum that their negative response to your success cannot stop the dream one ounce. Protect your Go Up Goals, because they are like little children. **You need to nurture them, and protect them. You don't let just anyone hold newborn babies do you? Then don't let just anyone hold your NEWBORN DREAMS!** Wow!

Secrets of Powerful Goals

Once The Queen (my wife Nova) and I finished the dinner interview with Goals, we took them into the den and served up a household favorite - hot chocolate! It was delicious, and I knew that once the hot chocolate kicked in, Goals would be really relaxed and they would share more liberally some of their top-

How to S.A.M. Your Goals and Dreams

secret information. I was right. After about 10 minutes, they began to talk candidly with me about the secrets that many people know, but few apply. And the fact that those who can make the transition from knowing it to doing it are the

> *Remember when it comes to your goals and dreams, INK THEM, Don't just think them.*
> *~ Dr. Dave Martin*

ones that Rob the Grave and achieve their dreams in life. I was very intrigued, so I began to take notes. This is what I learned:

1. Goals must be written down! I am always amazed at people who don't write down their goals, yet say, "They are in my head!" That is the WORST place to store your goals. Why? Because like I already taught you, psychologists tell us that the average human thinks somewhere between 40,000 and 50,000 separate thoughts per day. In addition, for the average person, 85% of those thoughts are negative. **Leaving your goals in your head means that they get hit each day with potentially 35,000 negative thoughts why you can't achieve them.** Your goals are worth more than that. You don't store fine china in the garage next to the motor oil, do you? No. Why not? Because you know the value of that china, so you would never store it in such a dirty place. Well, what about your goals? Don't your goals, dreams, and aspirations have tremendous value? Yes, they do! So why store them in your head? That thing is a dirty place at times...many times. That's why you must get them

How to S.A.M. Your Goals and Dreams

out of your head and onto paper. **Make me a promise right now. Promise me that as of RIGHT NOW, you will begin to write your goals down.** Everything you really want, you will not just think it - you will Ink It! Write it down! Another reason why you should write your goals down is because writing is a form of secondary reinforcement for your brain. As you write your goals, it further imprints the goal onto your mind so that you don't forget it as easily. **Remember when it comes to your goals and dreams, INK THEM, Don't just think them.**

2. Goals must be Realistic! Now this is a tricky one. There are only two people who can tell you whether your goal is realistic or not - you and your mentor! If the person is not you and they are not your mentor (someone more advanced than you that you trust to speak into your life), then they are not qualified to tell you that your goal is not realistic. **Many times, we let people who are just as messed up as we are, tell us that our goals are not realistic.** The problem is that for many people, we can be our own worst enemy. By this I mean we can talk ourselves out of our own goals. Ever done that? I know I have. But let me teach you something that Bishop Noel Jones taught me. Your Reality is comprised of two things - your Actuality plus your Possibility. In other words,

How to S.A.M. Your Goals and Dreams

Actuality + Possibility = Reality

Your Actuality is comprised of your past and your present. This means that I can take a good look at your past and your present to tell where you **actually are** in life. However, the part that I like is that your **Possibility is comprised of your future.** It takes the addition of both your Actuality and your Possibility to calculate your true Reality. Some people look at your past and present conditions and calculate that your high goals are unrealistic, because they are only looking at your Actuality. PROBLEM! **The problem is that these people are missing the other half of the equation. They judged you based on your yesterday and your today, without taking into account your tomorrow! Mistake!** I want to remind you, my friend, that **the depth of your past and present is nothing but an indication of the height of your future!** Because when the building is going to go really high, builders must dig really low. You may have been dug really low by life, but don't give up because that simply means that the plans for your life are very high. Take your eyes off of your actuality and focus them on your possibility. If you can see it, and are willing to work for it, then it is 150% POSSIBLE FOR YOU! Don't let folks with half the equation label your life with negativity. Allow your mentors to speak life into

If you can see it, and are willing to work for it, then it is 150% POSSIBLE FOR YOU!

How to S.A.M. Your Goals and Dreams

your future, and walk boldly in the fullness of who you are! **Think Big, Start Small, and Scale Quickly**. Dream the big dream, start with a small piece, and scale quickly by taking consistent daily action on that dream and it will manifest itself in its due season. I am excited for you!

3. Goals must be Specific. If you want a specific result, you must set a specific goal and take specific action!

"I want to be a success." That's general!
"I want to write a book." That's general!
"I want someone to love me." That's general!
"I want a career change." That's general!
"I want to go to college." That's general!
"I want to increase profits." That's general!
"I want to lose weight." That's general!
"I want to open a business." That's general!
"I want to date someone." That's general!
"I want a better car." That's general!

The more specific you are upfront, the more detailed and focused your action steps will be and the faster and more powerfully you will achieve the goal.

GET MY POINT? You cannot be general in your goal setting and expect to achieve a specific result. You must be crystal clear about what you want, and that's why you should write it down. Don't say you want to lose weight! Say, *"I want to lose 50lbs of fat from my stomach and thighs, while gaining 10lbs of muscle* *mass in my arms, chest, and legs by December of '03."* That is a specific goal. Now that you created a specific goal, you can work with a personal trainer to help you accomplish it. The more specific you are upfront, the more detailed and focused your action steps will be and the faster and more powerfully you will achieve the goal.

4. Goals must be flexible. Listen, things will not always go your way. Sometimes, I wish that life was more like Burger King, so that I could have it "my way". However, it does not work that way. Because it doesn't, you and I must learn to build flexibility into our goal achievement and goal maintenance programs so that we don't get discouraged when things go wrong. That's why I like what Les Brown says, "When things go wrong, don't go with them!" Be like a tree - where you bend, but don't break! If your goal was to start a business in March, and due to a major financial or family setback you don't get it started til June, don't beat yourself up about it. Just stay focused and, as my dear friend and mentor Willie Jolley would say, "Turn your Setback into your Setup for your Comeback!" Give yourself more credit and take the setbacks as benchmarks that you are closer to your goal than ever before!

5. Goals must be humanized. I challenge you to put a face on your goals. Your mind loves imagery. You will only go after what you see! Think about it. How many times has a pizza commercial motivated you to actually

How to S.A.M. Your Goals and Dreams

I challenge you to put a face on your goals. Your mind loves imagery. You will only go after what you see!

get up and call for a delivery? Why did you do it? Because you want what you see. Think about fashion. How many times has "window shopping" prompted you to buy? Think about cars. People flock to buy the latest car designs because they picture themselves driving them around town – so they buy them!**YOU WILL PURSUE WHAT YOU SEE!** That's how dating begins. That's how people find out about companies that are hiring. They see an ad promoting positions and salaries, causing them to act. **You will pursue what you see.** Your goals function the same way. You must put a picture on your goals. If you want a new house, get a picture of it. If you want a new car, get a picture of you sitting in it at a dealership. **Make your goal as visually realistic as possible.** You will be amazed at how motivated you get about your goals once you have an image of them. For example, during the months of January and February of 2003, I found myself slipping on my book writing goals because I was so busy with speaking engagements. Well, I simply hired my graphic artist to create the cover for the new book and send it to me. I posted it ALL over the house, and within 4 months the book was not only written, but also published. **Why? Because I could see the end product. It became more real to me, so I took a lot more aggressive action to complete it.** Vision is a powerful thing! I can tell you story after story about the many

How to S.A.M. Your Goals and Dreams

goals that I have achieved that started with a picture. Meeting Zig Ziglar started with a picture. Graduating with a 4.0 from Graduate School started with a picture. Purchasing my new luxury SUV started with a picture. The list goes on and on. The same can happen for you. Take pictures of people you admire, all the things you want, and any image that portrays the goals that you desire. Put a picture with it and you will soon be able to manifest it!

6. Goals must be shared! You must share your goals with the right people. I will spend more time on this later in the chapter, because who you announce your goals to, determines the friends and enemies that enter your life. So you need to be very careful about the individuals that are aware of your success moves. **Dr. Mike Murdock says, "When you announce your goals you force your friends to position themselves, and you force your enemies to expose themselves!"** It's true. When I mentioned that I was writing a book, the wrong people exposed themselves by opening their mouths. The right people positioned themselves with their action and support! Once you share your goals with the right people, expect to be blessed! Expect the right doors to open for you.

A goal without a deadline is like football without end zones, baseball without bases, soccer without goal nets, or basketball without hoops.

7. Goals must be measurable! You have to know when you have achieved your goals. You have to have a deadline for its accomplishment, as well was an indicator that you have accomplished it. What does debt reduction mean to you? Does it mean going from $20,000 in credit card debt down to $2,000? Does it mean paying off all credit cards to zero balances? Does it mean paying off your cars? Does it mean paying off your house? **You have to define what your goal is and what measuring stick you will use to ensure that you have reached the goal.** Does debt free mean just getting debt free or STAYING debt free? This illustrates the difference between goal achievement and goal maintenance. A goal without a deadline is like football without end zones, baseball without bases, soccer without goal nets, or basketball without hoops. Make sure you know what success means to you.

8. Goals must be balanced! I want to teach you how to set, achieve, and maintain goals in all 7 areas of your life. Statistically, most men set professional goals. Statistically, most women set family goals. Both are wrong! We need to set goals in ALL 7 areas of our lives. One thing that I feel is critical to mention here is the Benefit of Momentum. People ask me all the time, "How did you get up the next morning after you were laid off, to start writing your first book and building your own business?" I tell them the same thing every time. I was acting on the momentum of the other goals in my life that I was working towards. Just because you have a professional setback that impacts you financially, that does not have to be the end of your

How to S.A.M. Your Goals and Dreams

story. In fact, that's when the real challenge begins. That's when the real test of your fortitude is released! Don't let a setback in one area of your life stop you from maximizing on the benefit of momentum from the other 5 and 6 areas of your life. If you put all your hopes into the goals you have in one area of your life, you are asking for trouble. **Stay balanced! All things exist in a delicate balance. It's called the great Circle of Life!**

9. Goals must be reviewed regularly. Post your goals at eye level in front of your toilet and on your bathroom mirror. I am very serious! Post your goals in these two places and **you are guaranteed to see them and read them daily.** You have to brush your teeth and wash your face. That takes care of the mirror. And you should have a bowel movement daily. That takes care of the toilet location. You may be reading this with your mouth open, but it's TRUE! I have my goals right in front of my toilet so while I am sitting down taking care of business, I am reviewing where I am in life and where I want be. It keeps my goals in front of me. You may laugh at me now, but the laughing stops when people see the goals being achieved left and right. The same will happen for you! **If you want something you have never had, you must do something you have never done.** When you

Post your goals at eye level in front of your toilet and on your bathroom mirror.

How to S.A.M. Your Goals and Dreams

finish this chapter, post your goals in front of your toilet and on your mirror. YOU WILL PURSUE WHAT YOU SEE!

The Three Types of Goals

There are three types of goals that you must be aware of. Each goal has its own unique power and strength. The purpose of this section is to teach you how to utilize the three types of goals to your maximum benefit as you progress through the stages of your exciting life.

Long-term Goals are great for the "big picture" perspective. They allow you to paint a long-term picture of where you want to be. Long-term goals allow you to be able to DREAM BIG, even though your present circumstances may seem meager. **The long-term goal is what keeps you headed in the right direction, and it also keeps you craving for success when you experience short-term challenges.** Typically, long-term goals don't change that much once they are set. Many times, however, long-term goals are ignored or postponed for a season because of personal or professional challenges that take our eyes off of the long-term vision. Some of the goals that you wrote down a few pages ago are long-term. It is critical to understand where each goal fits into the overall plan of your life. Once you have intelligently, purposefully, and prayerfully considered your ultimate

How to S.A.M. Your Goals and Dreams

long-term goals, they serve as the TRUE NORTH in your life. **They guide your decisions, your actions, your intentions, your direction, your career, and your other goals.**

Short-term Goals are also called intermediate goals. These goals are subsets of your long-term goals. They allow you to break your long-term goals into yearly, semesterly, quarterly, or monthly chunks of different success opportunities. The one challenge that most people complain about with long-term goals is that they seem too far off in the future. They seem very large in comparison to the day-to-day realities of the present. That is the benefit of short-term goals. Think about it. You would not drive from Florida to California in one straight trip, would you? No, of course not. You stop for food, for gas, rest areas, and even hotels. Why? Because you understand the value of breaking large trips into a series of smaller trips. Short-term goals do the exact same thing for your life. They take the massiveness of your long-term goals and break them down into bit-sized pieces, so that you have regular, consistent successes along the way. I always tell college students not to focus on getting an A for the semester. I challenge them to get an A each day. Why? Because that small success each day allows them to focus on their current tasks and complete them with quality and excellence. This practice, repeated all semester, produces an A student. *Well Del, that sounds great. But how do you know?* Because it worked for me!

How to S.A.M. Your Goals and Dreams

Most goal setting programs will stop here. They teach you that there are only two types of goals - long term and short term. However, I personally believe that there is a 3rd type of goal. The missing one is perhaps the most powerful of the three that you will learn. I have applied this 3rd type of goal to my life and it has made a tremendous difference for me.

> *The most important goals are those that help you develop and maintain a daily success routine.*

Right Now Goals are goals that you achieve daily! They are small nugget-sized representations of your short-term and long-term goals. **They are your most significant momentum builders. Right Now Goals give you success opportunities every single day of your life.** Right Now Goals are great for helping you assess where you are having challenges. Right Now Goals help you create your Daily Routine. **THE MOST IMPORTANT GOALS ARE THOSE THAT HELP YOU DEVELOP AND MAINTAIN A DAILY SUCCESS ROUTINE.**

I cannot stress to you enough how important your daily routine is to your short-term and long-term goals. **It is a proven fact that it takes doing something consistently for 30 days to turn it into a habit.** The purpose of Right Now Goals is to help you create a regular customized success routine that mirrors your short-term and long-term goals so that you will achieve them. For example, if your long-term

How to S.A.M. Your Goals and Dreams

goal is to be a great parent and have a long loving relationship with your child, then your short-term goal may be to help your child successfully transition through teen hood. Your Right Now Goal may be to have breakfast chats with your teenager daily. One of my goals is to maintain a solid communicative relationship with all my clients across the country. I do this by returning all calls and emails within 24 hours each day. I make it a part of my daily routine. Below is a sample of my Right Now Goals. You can tell by my daily goals what my short-term and long-term goals are.

Del's Sample Right Now Goals

1. Pray 3 times today!
2. Write 3 pages towards my book today!
3. Check & return all emails and voicemails today!
4. Meet someone new today!
5. Drink 3 glasses of water today!
6. Take my vitamin today!
7. Listen to Wisdom, Motivation, and Empowerment teaching today!
8. Say something that touches someone's heart today!
9. Practice a story, poem, quote, or speaking technique today!
10. Check & balance all financial accounts today!
11. Prospect new business and update existing business today!
12. Spend quality time with the Queen today.

Delatorro L. McNeal II

How to S.A.M. Your Goals and Dreams

Habit creates Character and Character creates Destiny.

So, as you can see, I have a list of things that I do daily. You might say, *"Well Del, that's great. But these items seem really small (and some even a little insignificant) to check off daily. Does this really work in creating a daily success routine?"* GREAT QUESTION! You better believe it works. It's in the small things that greatness is born. It's in small boxes that diamonds are presented. It's in small seeds that big oak trees get their beginnings. Big trucks roll on small tires, big doors swing on little hinges, and great companies are born out of small ideas...acted on! **Dr. Randy White teaches, "A small job done, is better than a BIG job talked about!"** Every task on my Right Now Goal list serves the purpose of keeping me focused on mastering my Daily Routine. **Habit creates Character and Character creates Destiny.** So use this section as a huge reminder about how important your daily routine really is to your overall success.

Tips to Mastering Your Daily Routine!

1. Work towards Order in your Life. As I mentioned earlier, it is important to create order and structure in your life. This means creating an organized place in your home, office, vehicle, computer, purse, or briefcase for everything that you use. **Have a special**

How to S.A.M. Your Goals and Dreams

place for all of your mail, bills, books, CDs, homework, client files, business cards, voicemail, keys, laundry, current projects, completed projects, newspapers, videotapes and DVDs. Work towards creating an environment that empowers you to know where everything is. You will have more respect for what is better organized in your life. You will also Rob the Grave of your time when you begin to get better organized and maintain your organization goals by putting things in their rightful places. Try it for one month consistently each day, and you will be amazed how much time you save. You will feel more in control of your life and you will respect organization and order in your life.

2. **Take Daily Account of your Planner, the Internet, and your checkbook.** Begin to look at your planner, the internet, and your checkbook as independent consultants and contractors that work especially for you. **You are the CEO of Your Own Life, so these consultants are assigned to assist you and make your life easier. By making decisions without them, you fail. However, by making decisions with them in your "boardroom", you can never go wrong!** Each day, consult your planner and calendar and do a quick assessment of **The Power of Today!** Listen, my friend. Today has so much power in it. It's not just Monday…No, it's a bridge to something you want to create in your future. It's a treasure chest of literally thousands of miniature opportunities for you to create your tomorrow.

How to S.A.M. Your Goals and Dreams

So consult your planner to assess your weekly and monthly goals and determine how TODAY fits into those goals. Then, log onto the internet to check all of your pertinent resources online such as the weather, news, email, and financial investment accounts. The internet puts the rich and the poor on the same information superhighway. Use this to your advantage. Lastly, and somewhat a caveat to the last point, take daily inventory of what enters and exits your bank accounts. The fastest way to do this, of course, is online. However, if you don't have access to the internet, call the bank and get your balance information to make sure that you are spending and saving according to the same knowledge that your bank has. Overdrafts are no fun. **It's important to respect your money and know on a daily basis where you are financially to make intelligent monetary decisions.**

3. Work from your To-Do List and Your Right Now Goals! These are fantastic momentum builders in your life. When I ask people if they have a sense of success momentum in their lives, many tell me "Not really!" When I ask them if they have a list of Right Now Goals or a To-Do List for each day, they tell me "no". Well, no wonder! My friend, I can't tell you how critical it is for you to live your life on a system each day. **Certain aspects of your life should be left to opportunity, destiny, and God's divine hand. But everything else needs to be strategically set up by you for maximum return on the investment of your time.**

How to S.A.M. Your Goals and Dreams

Get up each morning and speak to your day and tell it where to go, instead of asking it where it went.

Tell the phone to ring, speak to your email account and command a response from someone whom you have already communicated with. GET IN THE DRIVER SEAT. You know the first track on my CD Project called <u>Keys to Unlocking Your Greatness</u> is called "Create a Fantastic Day!" Why? Because I don't believe in just "Having a Nice Day!" That is Reactive. "Having a Nice Day" can be contingent on hundreds of factors that may be within or outside of your control. However, "Creating a Fantastic Day" determines that regardless of what happens TO me, I will control what happens IN me. I will chose to be positive and walk in my blessings daily, knowing that whatever happens to me, will ultimately work for my benefit.

As you complete each small task on your To-Do List, strike through it. Also, as you achieve each small goal on your Right Now Goal list, strike through it also. You will feel good. You will feel the momentum building in your day. You will feel productive and empowered to continue your success throughout the day. All you are doing is working from a plan, but you will be amazed at how much better your day goes. **Studies show that, 10 minutes of planning creates an additional 4 hours of productivity in your day.**

Studies show that, 10 minutes of planning creates an additional 4 hours of productivity in your day.

Delatorro L. McNeal II

How to S.A.M. Your Goals and Dreams

4. Listen to something positive the first 20 minutes of each day. This has been a lifesaver for me and so many other successful people that I know. In addition, studies have proven that professionals and students who listened to something positive the first 20 minutes of their day increased their personal productivity by up to 35%. That is Awesome! The point that this study proves is that **input really does determine output.** Each morning, I pour into myself with praise & worship music, nature music, soft jazz, and motivational songs that have positive lyrics. Why? Because I am feeding my spirit. I am always pouring my positive, motivated, and enthusiastic spirit out onto audiences of all sizes; therefore I must be full in order to give out my best. The same is true for you. You can't pull anything out of an empty bag. We must guard and protect the first thing that we listen to each day and the last thing that we listen to each night.

CREATE YOUR WORLD, AND ENJOY IT. Who says you have to listen to the radio all day every day? You create your world. Whatever you want to put into it that's positive and keeps you smiling and working intelligently – go for it! **Listen to positive material, positive radio, positive television, and positive conversations, and you will create positive** days. *Del, this sounds great. But you don't understand. My*

Listen to positive material, positive radio, positive television, and positive conversations, and you will create positive days.

How to S.A.M. Your Goals and Dreams

world is so negative. How can I apply this stuff to my world? GREAT QUESTION! If your world is so negative that you can't listen to positive material, you can't take advantage of lunch breaks to feed your dream, and you can't create the type of environment that allows your goals and dreams to flourish, then **YOU NEED A NEW WORLD.** You need a job/career change. You need a change of environment. Why? **Because there is a place where your goals, dreams, your personality, and giftings will flourish and be celebrated - not just tolerated. Find that place!** Do whatever you must to create and sustain a positive environment. This leads to my next point.

5. Have Small Success Breaks Daily. I have worked in a variety of settings both corporate and academic, and I speak at a wide variety of professional facilities. It never ceases to amaze me how people with negative "health-depleting" habits take more breaks throughout the workday than those who don't. And I am not trying to be judgmental, but hear my point. The number of smoke-breaks that smokers take in a workday amazes me. At one client site, I saw the same group of employees take at least five, 10-minute smoke breaks throughout that day. I saw other employees with more positive habits only take one lunch break during the whole day. **So, in my opinion, if people can take smoke breaks to destroy their lungs, then positive people can take success breaks to enhance their lives.**

How to S.A.M. Your Goals and Dreams

Success breaks are just extended bathroom trips, chats by the company pond, or brief walks to get fresh air. Some people sing a favorite song, pray, or just to call a significant other to say "I love you!" Listen, I am not encouraging you to skip time at work or loaf around doing nothing. I am simply saying to enjoy your walk back from lunch, enjoy the trip to the copy machine, and enjoy your time between classes. Maximize your downtime with positive energy.

Accountability can be a great friend to you, and it can keep you focused on success strategies that will allow you to rob the grave.

6. Have a Mentor/Coach hold you Accountable.

Accountability is crucial for success. I encourage you to have lunch with one of your mentors or coaches and share with them some of the things you are learning in this book. Ask them to hold you accountable by checking up on you weekly or bi-weekly as it relates to your progress in these areas. If you have a good friend who is also a co-worker, ask them to hold you accountable daily for your success routine. It's important for you to have people in your life that believe in you, support you, and want to see you grow and develop. A quick footnote about accountability: Some people don't like being held responsible by someone or something else. **Well, accountability happens all day everyday.** You just may not recognize it. For example, your alarm clock goes off each morning to hold you accountable for getting to work or school on time. Speed limit signs are meant to keep traffic accountable for the rate at which vehicles travel. The "fasten seatbelt" sign that lights up when you turn on your car is meant to hold you accountable for buckling up. The police officer that is parked on the side of the road with a radar gun is meant to keep you accountable for safe driving practices. The little envelope icon that appears on some cell phones is there to hold you accountable for checking your voicemail for messages. And the list goes on and on. **Accountability can be a great friend to you, and it can keep you focused on success strategies that will allow you to continue to Rob the Grave of your stuff!** Again, ensure that you station positive people around you to hold you accountable for total success in your life.

7. Post and Review Your Goals Daily! This produces vision. Looking at your goals daily builds your faith that they will come true. **It builds your vision that something you do today, will create something you want tomorrow.** Your goals are not there to make you feel like a failure. Rather, they remind you how successful you can and should expect to be. Not only should you look at your goals daily, but also jot down a few notes on your goals so that you can see the progress you are making towards them. For example, when my wife and I were getting out of credit card debt **we had a list of exactly how much we owed each creditor. Then we wrote what pay dates we would make final payments on those credit cards - so that we could**

How to S.A.M. Your Goals and Dreams

Make "Mastering Your Daily Routine" a part of your DNA - your Daily Natural Action!

see how (within 3, 6 or 9 months) all of our debts would be paid. Our goals reminded us how far we had come, and they reminded us there was a light at the end of that tunnel. Use our goals as encouragement. Remember, goals are meant to help you build confidence, momentum, and accomplishment in your life.

My Personal Challenge to You!

Create a daily success routine. Include morning, work, traffic, prayer, family, friends, lunch, dinner, internet, music, laughter, reading, listening, giving good advice to people, etc. Follow your success routine consistently for 30 days, and it will birth your success habit. And that's the real fun, because your habit will become your character, and your character will become your destiny! Get a friend in this with you, and **make "Mastering Your Daily Routine" a part of your DNA - your Daily Natural Action!**

The 7 Categories of Goals in Your Life

The following is a list of the seven different areas of your life where you should have goals established.

How to S.A.M. Your Goals and Dreams

Reflect back on your Circle of Life diagram. These areas, with the exception of purpose, make up the shape that you drew in the beginning of this chapter. Before I have you create your goals for this year, I want you to review these 7 areas and look at some examples of what I feel are good goals in each category. Note that the examples are written in first person so that they seem more personal.

1. Spiritual Goals – Relationship with God, Reading the Word, Prayer, Giving, Ministry, Serving, Tithing
Example: I will read the entire Life Application Bible through this year by reading 5 chapters per day, 6 days and skipping Sundays.

2. Social Goals – Communication Skills, Listening Skills, Manners, Public Speaking Skills, Networking
Example: I will create a 30-second commercial that I can use to introduce myself in public settings. This will teach me to present myself better and maximize the power of networking to build my business.

3. Financial Goals – Debt, Investments, Savings, Checking, House, Car, Mutual Funds, 401K
Example: I will invest $75 per paycheck into my savings account so I can purchase a new laptop computer with cash by the end of this year. This saving plan will yield me $1970, which is enough for the laptop, a 3-year warranty, a computer bag, and 2 back-up batteries.

How to S.A.M. Your Goals and Dreams

4. Family Goals – Relationships, Forgiveness, Support, Children, Vacations, Lifestyle
Example: I will call my mother-in-law bi-weekly and talk with her for at least 10 minutes to maintain communication. We will have breakfast together once a month at her favorite restaurant.

5. Personal Goals – Attitude, Goals, Romantic & Platonic Relationships, Education, Motives,
Example: I will enroll in the MBA program at Florida State University to begin in the Fall of 2003. I plan to attain this degree in 4.5 years with a 4.0 GPA.

6. Professional Goals – Jobs, Careers, Promotion, Salary, Title
Example: I will earn $100,000 during the fiscal year of 2003 by establishing 10 new clients, and with $30,000 in repeat business from my existing clients.

7. Health Goals – Weight, Vision, Dental, Exercise, Diet, Check-ups **Example:** I will lose 20lbs of fat from my midsection and thighs, while gaining 10lbs. of muscle mass in my arms, chest, and shoulders. I will accomplish this with the assistance of a personal trainer on a 3-day per week program.

Now it's your turn. I want you to create at least 3 specific, measurable, achievable goals for yourself that you want to accomplish this year.

How to S.A.M. Your Goals and Dreams

(Your Name)
Goals for 2003/2004

Spiritual Goals:

1. _____
2. _____
3. _____

Social Goals:

1. _____
2. _____
3. _____

Financial Goals:

1. _____
2. _____
3. _____

Family Goals:

1. _____
2. _____
3. _____

How to S.A.M. Your Goals and Dreams

Personal Goals:

1.
2.
3.

Professional Goals:

1.
2.
3.

Health Goals:

1.
2.
3.

My Right Now Goals for 2003/2004

1.
2.
3.
4.
5.
6.
7.
8.

How to S.A.M. Your Goals and Dreams

GREAT JOB! Now I want you to finish this chapter. After that, come back to these goals, revise them as needed, type them out and post them. Do you remember where? Exactly! Post them on your bathroom mirror and right in front of the toilet. Remember, your mind will go after whatever it sees.

9 Steps to Achieving and Maintaining Your Goals

Now that you have set your goals for this year, I want to challenge you even further. I want to make sure that you achieve, maintain, and ultimately surpass the goals you set. But for now, let's focus on what you have. I want to share with you a methodology that I go through when I am about to undertake a major goal. **I say "major" because some goals that you set will not be as hard to accomplish as others. So, for the more difficult, labor-intensive, and time-intensive goals that you have, it's Mission Critical that you walk yourself through this methodology.** This will ensure that you not only achieve the goal, but also become a better person in the process. As I share this framework with you, I will give you an example for each step in the process. For this methodology, I will use the goal of writing my second book.

How to S.A.M. Your Goals and Dreams

1. Identify the Goal. This is the first step. Write down a purpose-driven goal that you have set for yourself. Make sure that you are aiming high, and not just aiming low to give yourself a false sense of accomplishment. Aim high! Be clear, specific, and meaningful when you create the goal.

Example: I will write my second book. The title will be Robbing the Grave of Its Greatness. This book will have 8 chapters, and will be a self-published product of A Noval Idea Publishing. I want the book to be extremely easy to read, a page-turner, and a life-changing reference tool for people across the country. It will be a best-seller within 2 years.

2. List the Reasons for the Goal. (Why?) Shortly after you embark on a major worthwhile goal, you will encounter some hardship. As soon as this occurs, the first question your brain is going to ask you is, *WHY?* It wants you to explain to it, *why* you are subjecting yourself to such discipline, sacrifice, routine, and structure. When this happens, you'd better have some compelling reasons why you are doing what you are doing. Otherwise, your brain will talk you out of it.

For example, I believe that the #1 reason why people quit going to the gym to work out is not because they are lazy. Rather, they have not come up with

How to S.A.M. Your Goals and Dreams

compelling enough reasons to work out. So, they start out going to the gym all excited, but after a few days it

wears off because lactic acid settles into their muscles and they get very achy to the point where they can barely move. As soon as this happens, the brain asks them the question, "Why are we going through all of this pain?" And if they don't have a compelling reason, they won't be able to answer back. Their brain convinces them that it's not worth it.

But why is this, Del? GREAT QUESTION. I like the way that Tony Robbins discusses this in <u>Personal Power II</u>. **He talks about how the human mind will do anything it can to avoid pain and gain pleasure.** So, if the gym equals pain to your brain, it will do all it can to avoid it. In the same manner, if the couch equals pleasure, your brain will gravitate you towards that. Amazing stuff, right? Well, that's why you have to change the neuro-association that your mind makes with exercise. Because your mind has "linked" or "associated" working out with pain, you have to recondition it to associate working out with pleasure.

How do you do that? Combine the unpleasant task with something you enjoy doing. For instance, work out with someone you absolutely LOVE spending time with. Or, work out in an environment that you absolutely love. **I know many people who would never go to a gym to use a treadmill, but at their favorite park, they will jog all day long.** Why? Because by changing their environment, they changed their association. For more on this powerful concept get <u>Personal Power II</u>. It is amazing. Make sure that

you list some compelling reasons why you want to achieve your goal.

Example: My reason for writing this book is to unleash everything that has been divinely deposited in me over the last 26 years of my life. Another reason for writing this book is to allow my motivational material to live on for years and years after I die. I am also writing this book to show people that it's possible, and to serve as a living, breathing example of the fact that dreams can and do come true.

3. List the Benefits of the Goal. You might say, *Del aren't reasons and benefits the same thing?* GREAT QUESTION! In my opinion, reasons and benefits are very different. The benefits of your goals often run far deeper than your reasons for your goals. Many times the reason is internal, but the benefit is external. For example, a person my quit smoking because it's getting too expensive. But the benefits of that person not smoking are not only personal health benefits to the person, but also for the hundreds of other people who will not catch lung cancer because of second hand smoke. Make sure that the benefits are clearly understood in your mind and heart because they will be fuel to your dream. They, along with

> *Many times the reason is internal, but the benefit is external.*

How to S.A.M. Your Goals and Dreams

your reasons, will be what wakes you up early in the morning, or keeps you up late at night.

Example: There are multiple benefits for writing this book. One benefit is that it provides a practical, hands-on solution for people who want to be more successful in life. Another benefit is that someone's life will be so changed by this book that they will impact someone else's life with their success. So, my impact will be never-ending. Another benefit is that it creates additional revenue streams for myself and my family. So, there will be a financial reward for producing this book. A portion of those financial rewards will be sown back into my church, where they will be used to fund ministry efforts across the globe. Children will be feed, clothed, and given a good Christmas because I wrote this book. One more child will get school supplies because I wrote this book. One more family will have a blessed Thanksgiving with food, clothes, and prayers because I wrote this book. **So, as you can see, the benefits of me writing this book far outweigh my reasons. But both are important.**

4. Set a Deadline for Accomplishment. Your deadline is your touchdown. It's your hoop, it's your goal, it's your hole, it's your checkered flag, it's your finish line, and it's your home plate. Your deadline is a date in time when the project, task, or goal must be complete. Once you set a deadline, then you can backdate from there to determine how aggressive you must be with your action in order to accomplish the goal. **My friend**

How to S.A.M. Your Goals and Dreams

and mentor Pastor Scott Thomas says, "As it relates to your goals, you will take as long as you give

My friend and mentor Pastor Scott Thomas says, "As it relates to your goals, you will take as long as you give yourself!"

yourself!" He and his family write out their goals for the year, but they give themselves until June to accomplish them. And the amazing thing is that he and his family have been tremendously successful in accomplishing their divinely inspired goals. So your deadline is up to you. But I like to be practically assertive with my goals because I am not promised tomorrow. In my field, I honestly believe that the type of material that I am inspired to create – changes lives. Therefore, I don't like procrastinating on someone else's breakthrough.

Example: I told myself in December of 2002 that I wanted to release my second book on my 26th birthday, which was June 29th 2003. In order to accomplish this goal, the book needed to be at the printer by the 9th of June. I knew that my Graphic Artist would need at least a month to typeset the book and lay it out. That backed me up to the beginning of May. My Editor would need at least 2 weeks to finish editing my material, so that made my final content deadline for the book April 16th of 2003. Deadlines help to guide your progress towards your goals. They keep you focused, and they keep you working until you accomplish the goal.

How to S.A.M. Your Goals and Dreams

5. Identify any Obstacles to Overcome. I like to think ahead. I am not a huge fan of last minute surprises

and out-of-the-blue monkey wrenches that attempt to mess up a major goal that I am working towards. For this reason, I am very proactive in identifying and preparing for any obstacles that may come against me in the process of achieving my goals. I believe that you should think of yourself as a professional hurdler.

You see professional hurdlers study obstacles. They see them, but they also see through them to the finish line. **And they practice and plan to systematically and strategically overcome each hurdle as it comes in their way to the finish line.** You must be the same way. Think in advance of the negative people with negative attitudes that you will need to avoid. Think in advance of financial hardships that may come as a surprise. Think in advance of the problems you may run into and have a back-up plan, just in case.

Example: In writing this book, I had to think in advance of how much money it would cost me to hire my graphic artist, my editor, my marketing person, and my printing company to help me finish this project. I had to plan financially for this project so that money, or the lack thereof, would not be an obstacle in getting this project completed. I had to think about who to tell, and who not to tell. I had to think of people who could meet my deadlines, and those who would not be able to run at my speed. I was and continue to be proactive about identifying obstacles. Will some things

How to S.A.M. Your Goals and Dreams

still come out of the blue? Yes! But that's why you have step number six.

6. Set a Basic Acceptable Bottom (BAB). A BAB is a safety net of sorts. It gives your deadline a cushion just in case a few things go wrong along the way. For example, you may want to lose 50lbs by the end of this year. Your BAB says that if you lose 45lbs. you will be happy! Why? Because you still got pretty close to the goal and that should be commended and celebrated. BABs allow your goals and deadlines to be flexible to the point where you bend but you don't break. For some goals, you can't afford a BAB. The deadline is the deadline. But for the ones that will allow for such a cushion, it's a great way to take some of the pressure off and still achieve your goals without going crazy.

Example: For this book, I built in BABs along the way instead of at the end. I was not willing to extend the deadline because I, without negotiation, wanted my second book to be released on my 26th birthday. However, I did build in a few days here and there, to give me the BAB flexibility during the process to be successful with the book project overall. And as you can see, it worked! Thank God!

7. Identify the Master Mind Group you will need to achieve your Goal. This is one of the best and most powerful tips I can give you. My friend, you will not be able to accomplish your goals 100% on your own. You will need a small team of people who believe

How to S.A.M. Your Goals and Dreams

in you and who support you. Select a small Master Mind Group. **This group should consist of mentors,**

coaches, and people with the professional expertise to help you accomplish your goals. These should be skilled people with vision and insight. These cannot be folk that are jealous or envious of you in any way. **They must be dependable, professional, reliable, confidential, and supportive people who demand excellence from you.** These people won't let you quit. They won't allow you to procrastinate, and they will help you reach your goal 10 times faster. CEOs have board members, Pastors have church staffs, and you have a Master Mind Group.

Example: When I began my book, I enlisted the help of my mentors, three friends with a literary eye, my graphic artist, three marketing specialists, my editor, several fellow speaker friends, and my close family. I pulled on the skills of these people at different stages of the project and they all played a major role in helping me go from the cognition to the creation of this book.

8. **Implement Your Action Plan.** Now that you have created the goal, listed reasons, benefits, deadlines, obstacles, your BAB, and your Master Mind Group, it is time to take some specific and targeted action steps towards the achievement of the goal. **These action steps should be broken down into monthly, weekly, and daily tasks based on the overall deadline for your project.** While implementing your action plan with

How to S.A.M. Your Goals and Dreams

various members of your Master Mind Group, do whatever it takes to positively accomplish your mission. When writing your action plan, I recommend that you use statements that start with action verbs. Remember, the purpose of this stage is to actually make it happen.

Example: My action plan for the book went a little like this:

    a. Create an outline of chapters
    b. Organize chapters in logical order
    c. Request Foreword and Introduction from contributors
    d. Create cover text and get it edited
    e. Hire graphic artist to design cover
    f. Write 3 to 5 pages per day over lunch and in the evenings
    g. Contract with my Editor to get goals and revision cycles
    h. Call the Book Printers to give advance notice of pending order

As you can see, there is a great deal that goes into writing a book. But with the help and support of your team, and with clear purpose-driven goals, reasons, and benefits you can make anything that you dream a reality.

> *Do something significant to celebrate how far you have come, your achievement of the goal, and (most of all) – the person you became in the process.*

9. Treat Yourself to a Reward. Congratulations! After you achieve the goal, throw the biggest party

How to S.A.M. Your Goals and Dreams

possible. Call all of your friends, family members, mentors, coaches and staff to

have a ball! You deserve it! Treat yourself to a major reward. Take a vacation. Have a big dinner party. Do something significant to celebrate

You see, when you celebrate, you are not just celebrating the goal. You are really celebrating THE NEW YOU that the goal created.

how far you have come, your achievement of the goal, and (most of all) – the THE PERSON YOU BECAME IN THE PROCESS. Hopefully, you became more **skilled**, more **patient**, more **determined**, more **driven**, more **focused**, more **dedicated**, more **articulate**, more **self-confident**, more **motivated**, more **empowered**, more **resilient**, more **thick-skinned**, more **inspired**, more **anointed**, more **directed**, more **enlightened**, more **special in your own eyes**, more **giving**, more **caring**, more **concerned**, more **engaged**, and the list goes on and on. You see, when you celebrate, you are not just celebrating the goal. You are really celebrating THE NEW YOU that the goal created. Why? Because it's the new you that must now shift from goal achievement mindedness, to goal maintenance mindedness. ***Now what's going to allow me to be able to maintain the goals I achieve?*** GREAT QUESTION! The person that you became in the process will be the one who will be able to maintain and later transcend this goal and take you higher to the next goal above it. Why? Because goals, once achieved, create other goals!

How to S.A.M. Your Goals and Dreams

Example: When I finished this book, my friends, family, church family, mentors, mentees, and colleagues had a HUGE celebration and Book Release party. It was a fantastic and amazing way to bring out the book and ring in my 26th birthday. I started getting emails left and right about the book and its impact on people's lives and I was able to look back over the entire process and say these words - **"IT WAS WORTH IT!"**

<u>Your Jabez Action Plan!</u>

In the space provided below, I want you to create your own sample Action Plan. Use the content on the previous pages as a guide. I am excited about your success!

Write a Goal.

List 2 Reasons for the Goal.

1.
2.

List 2 Benefits of the Goal.

1.
2.

How to S.A.M. Your Goals and Dreams

Set the Deadline for the Goal. ....

Identify 2 Obstacles that may come in the way of the Goal.

1. ....
2. ....

Will your goal allow for a BAB? If so what is it?

_____

_____

_____

Identify 3 people who can help with this goal.

1. ....
2. ....
3. ....

Create an Action Plan with at least 5 steps.

1. ....
2. ....
3. ....
4. ....
5. ....

D e l a t o r r o   L .   M c N e a l   I I

How to S.A.M. Your Goals and Dreams

How do you want to celebrate the achievement of this goal?

_____

_____

_____

What 3 things do you think this goal will help to develop within you?

1. _____

2. _____

3. _____

The Profile of the Procrastinator

One of the biggest enemies of your goals and dreams is Procrastination. My definition of procrastination is:

The intentional delaying or putting off of a task, assignment, decision, or action – out of a spirit of laziness, neglect for time management, and utter disregard for momentum and positive motivation.

Procrastination is the Grave's best friend! He silently robs your time each and every day! He disguises himself using phrases like "There's always tomorrow" and "It's no big deal when I do it, as long as it gets done". The reality is that we all procrastinate at some point about something. The issue is how long we

Delatorro L. McNeal II

How to S.A.M. Your Goals and Dreams

procrastinate and what it costs us in the long run. **Procrastination can kill you.** If you don't believe me, ask the hundreds of thousands of people who die each year of heart disease and cancer simply because they procrastinated about eating a healthy diet and creating a regular exercise routine.

What about finances? Multi millionaire, speaker, real estate guru, and author Robert Allen uses the follow example in his article <u>"The Seven Secrets of Extremely Prosperous People"</u>:

"Suppose you could sock away $200 per month. You set a target to have it grow at 20% per year for the next 20 years. Now, 20% is no small feat...but with some fancy stock picks, some real estate and perhaps a small business on the side, you think you can pull it off. According to my calculator, $200 per month at 20% interest for 20 years grows into $632,000. Not bad!

*Now, suppose, instead of starting now, you wait 1 year to get started. This leaves you only 19 years of growth instead of 20. How much is in your bank account 20 years from today? Only $516,000. That's $116,000 less than what you could have had if you had started on schedule. In other words, **your procrastination cost you $116,000 future dollars! Procrastination is expensive!"***

How to S.A.M. Your Goals and Dreams

Whatever you water, grows in your life. Stop feeding your fears and start focusing your faith.

Get the point? I an effort to expose procrastination, I want to share with you a teaching done by Pastor Scott Thomas on The Profile of the Procrastinator. Below you will find 10 characteristics of a procrastinator. After each characteristic is my own personal one line response.

1. They have good intentions.
Remember, a little job done is better than a big job talked about!

2. They tend to be disorganized in the area of their procrastination.
That garbage will never get cleaned out, unless it gets organized first.

3. They have a bundle of excuses.
As my old Coach Tipton used to say, "Excuses are like dirty gym socks, everyone has them and they all stink!"

4. They have difficulty saying "No".
Whenever you say "yes" to something on someone else's plate you are simultaneously saying "no" to something that is on your plate.

Delatorro L. McNeal II

How to S.A.M. Your Goals and Dreams

5. They focus on the Negative.
Whatever you water grows in your life. Stop feeding your fears and start focusing your faith.

6. They expend much of their energy worrying about what they should be ACTING ON!
Worrying is just like a rocking chair. It gives you something to do, but gets you nowhere!

7. They feel overwhelmed often.
Start saying no to others, and yes to yourself! Others are not responsible for your success!

8. They look for others to rescue them.
Nothing comes to a sleeper, but a Dream. Nothing comes to a doer, but Success!

9. They claim to work better under pressure.
Stress and time-crunch are not the incubators of greatness. Instead they are merely the excuse of those in pursuit of it.

10. They hate being REMINDED!
The remedy for constant reminders is consistent action!

> **Stress and time-crunch are not the incubators of greatness. Instead they are merely the excuse of those in pursuit of it.**

How to S.A.M. Your Goals and Dreams

How to Break Procrastination!

1. Admit that you're a Procrastinator. It's okay to admit that you procrastinate. We all do, but it's the amount that we procrastinate and the amount that it costs us that really creates the challenge. Businesswoman and Evangelist Dr. Paula White says, *"You can't change what you don't confront, and you can't confront what you don't identify."* So we must come face-to-face with the fact that procrastination is a major player in keeping us from possessing the land that we have been promised.

2. Identify what type you are. Now that you admit that you're a procrastinator, you must classify yourself.

¨   Are you a **Habitual Procrastinator** (one who procrastinates as naturally as breathing)?

¨   Are you an **Occasional Procrastinator** (one who depending on the activity or season tends to put things off)?

¨   Are you a **Seldom Procrastinator** (one who takes action most times, and rarely gets stumped into the rut of long-term procrastination)?

It's important to classify which one you are, because this will drive how you counteract this enemy to your goals and dreams.

How to S.A.M. Your Goals and Dreams

3. Get Organized. Like I have said numerous times in this book, it is critical that your life be organized if you want to live an organized life. I don't **mean a boring, ritualistic life, but one that has structure, order, fun, excitement, and momentum.** All of these things come with organization. I really love my life. There are many times when I cry, work hard, sweat, serve, sacrifice, bit my tongue, and get frustrated – but there are more times when I laugh so hard that I feel like falling under the table. There is also time to enjoy intimate time with my wife, intimate time with God, and private time with me. All these things come with organization. Tell your life where to go. Don't ask it where it went. **Be in a constant process of BECOMING! Because the reality is that all of us, ALL of us, are "Under Construction!"**

> *It is critical that your life be organized if you want to live an organized life.*

4. Break all tasks into small pieces. As you will learn in Chapter 7: Make Lemonade and Sell it for Profit (Overcoming Obstacles), **one of the biggest reasons why people procrastinate is because of task-complexity.** The job, task, or action is too big so people just ignore or avoid it in anyway that they can. How sad, when all they had to do was break the task up into small, more manageable pieces. Think about it like this - would you try to eat an entire Filet Mignon in one bite? Of course not! Why not? Firstly, because

How to S.A.M. Your Goals and Dreams

you would choke, and secondly because you would want to savor each bite. Well, the same thing holds true with your goals and dreams. Think BIG, but start small, then scale or progress quickly!

5. Build Momentum with Small Successes. Allow the small successes in your life to help you build up momentum and speed. Think about it like a 18-speed bike. When the chain is on the small crank you can pedal faster and more aggressively, but you don't go as fast. However, that small crank is good to get you started. Once you get the bike moving, you change gears and transition to the larger cranks. As you transition, the pedaling gets more and more challenging, but now your bike is flying! It takes fewer rotations for you to go faster. The same rules apply when it comes to your goals. Start with smaller more achievable, confidence-building goals and then move systematically to larger projects that require more of your energy and drive.

6. Combine difficult tasks with something you love. We talked about this earlier, but it bears repeating. Make sure you combine unpleasant tasks with things that you love to do. For example, I know business people who have heated conversations with their most difficult clients while getting a full body massage. Why? Because they would procrastinate on making the call if they did not have something enjoyable to do in the process. They combine their difficult task with something they enjoy doing. Many times, when I

How to S.A.M. Your Goals and Dreams

am returning hundreds of email and phone calls, I listen to some of my favorite music lightly in the background, so that I am motivated to get the task done.

7. Focus on your goals and review them regularly. Make sure that you post and review your goals. Additionally, I would highly recommend that you give copies of your goals to your mentors and coaches so that they can call you whenever they want to, holding you accountable for your progress. You know the old adage says, "Out of sight, out of mind!" Well, it's hard to ignore something you see daily and it's hard to ignore something that your mentors call you about regularly. Stretch yourself and go for it! The land is yours to possess!

8. Personalize tasks to your energy cycle. This is critical. Determine what type of person you are. **Are you a morning person?** This means you are at your best energy, creativity, motivation, and alertness in the morning. **Are you an afternoon person?** This means you are at your best after 12 noon. **Are you an evening person?** This means your juices really start to get going around 4pm. **Or are you a late night owl?** This means you get your best energy around 9pm. This is important to understand about yourself, because you

Create your best when you are at your best!

Delatorro L. McNeal II

How to S.A.M. Your Goals and Dreams

should customize your day's activities around your energy cycle. Don't try to write your book or your business plan in the morning if you are a night owl. Why? Because even though you have identified a very worthwhile goal, **you are working against your own energy cycle. In other words create your best when you are at your best!** Customize your "To Do" lists so that your difficult tasks are done when you are fresh and alert.

9. JUST DO IT! – Take Action! Sometimes you don't need a big fancy step. Sometimes you just need get up off the couch, bed, rocking chair, play station, television, or computer and DO what you need to do to GET YOUR STUFF BACK. Take consistent action on the things that you want and need in life, and life will reward you greatly. **Be like Nike and JUST DO IT!**

10. Get Psychological / Spiritual Help. If all of these steps have failed you, then you may need to seek some professional help from someone far more advanced than me to assist you. Whatever you determine, make the decision that you don't have to live with procrastination at your door. You can kick it out of your neighborhood by allowing faith, determination, and persistence to move in. Why? Because the entrance of one, means the automatic exodus of the other! I LIKE THAT! I am excited for you my friend!

How to S.A.M. Your Goals and Dreams

<u>Give Yourself a Raise!</u>

Do you realize that you can actually give yourself a raise by investing your spare time into your own goals and dreams? Yes, you don't have to wait for your yearly 3% raise from your company. You can give yourself a pay raise by investing your spare time into your dream. I know from personal experience that this works because in 2002, I gave myself and my family a raise of an extra $41,000 in income because of the way that I invested my time. In 2003, I will give myself and my family a raise of an extra $110,000 in additional income. **Please don't be impressed by this. I'm not. But I am inspired and motivated to keep increasing the numbers.** The only difference between the *haves* and the *have-nots* is the investment of time, talents, and treasures.

So let's look at an example of this principle.

If your job pays you **$30,000** a year, each hour of your time is worth **$15.37.** If you invested only 1 extra hour per day per month into your own business or your own profit-generating ideas over the course of one month you could **virtually give yourself a raise of $312.50**. That may not sound like a lot but if you think about it, that's a car payment. That could go towards wiping out credit card debt. That extra $312.50 per month could be invested into a money market account or some other investment. Now, take that same amount of effort each day and multiply it

How to S.A.M. Your Goals and Dreams

out over a year. **By the end of one year, you could give yourself a raise of at least $3,750.00.** That is a nice down payment on a house, an investment property, or a new car. That's tuition paid for a full year at many colleges! GET MY POINT? Don't wait for others to give you your raises and increases. Do you deserve them? Yes! Have you worked hard for them? Probably! But in today's economy it's the entrepreneurs that are possessing the land and making the real impact. It's the people that learn about a simple concept called, "Multiple Income Streams" that really create and sustain wealth.

Notes:

_____

_____

_____

_____

_____

_____

_____

_____

_____

How to S.A.M. Your Goals and Dreams

<u>8 Quick Review Points for a New Beginning in your Quest!</u>

1. Once you set a goal, make sure that you achieve it. Once you achieve your goal, make sure that you maintain it. **Remember, no one wants to go from Rags to Riches and back to Rags.** Each success step should take you higher and higher.

2. It's not so much the achievement of the goal, **but WHO YOU BECOME IN THE PROCESS, that really counts.** Always be in the process of BECOMING!

3. LIVE A BALANCED LIFE. Marriages fail and families are torn apart because of unbalanced lives. Companies split and go bankrupt because of unbalanced lives. Become a Balance-aholic! **There is a time and a place for everything under the sun.**

4. Don't confuse activity with ACCOMPLISHMENT. Use **your goals to shift you from being a busy person to being an accomplished person.**

5. Be careful who you share your GO UP Goals with. Don't trust your baby to everyone. Only share it with those who can help you achieve it.

6. **Your Actuality + Your Possibility = Your Reality.** Never let others who have no vision educate you about how realistic your goals are. 99% of the time, they will be missing a critical piece of the equation.

Delatorro L. McNeal II

How to S.A.M. Your Goals and Dreams

7. Use your Right Now Goals to help you create and maintain your Daily Success Routine. Remember, the secret to your success or failure is found in what you do daily.

8. ACTION is FREE. PROCRASTINATION will cost you! Don't PAY THAT PRICE! JUST DO IT! Make it Happen!

Notes

Notes

$\mathscr{C}$hapter 7

Make Lemonade and Sell it for Profit!

Make Lemonade and Sell it for Profit!

My friend, I know that you have probably read many great books and attended many great seminars about overcoming failure and tragedy in life. I know that you have heard countless pastors preach on how you can overcome obstacles. Maybe you have heard several top-level executives and CEOs talk about how their companies came back from the challenging economic times in the world. Since I know that you have heard many of these things before, the purpose of this chapter is not to regurgitate all of that information that you already know. Why? Because we are in partnership with our pain.

If you can understand a challenge, you can withstand it so that you can grow and develop into all that you were designed to be.

Every human being on earth has at least one story of tremendous hardship that they have experienced in life. We all deal with challenges, issues, and storms everyday. So pain, hardships, challenges, and obstacles are nothing new to most of us. **In fact, many of us have grown so accustomed to adversity that when something good finally does happen to us, we have a hard time receiving it because we feel like at any point, it could be taken away from us and it's "Probably too good to be true!" Right?** Well, I am glad that you made it to this chapter. My goal in this chapter is to expose some truths about the obstacles that you and I encounter on a daily basis, and also to show you how you can better understand trouble.

Make Lemonade and Sell it for Profit!

If you can understand a challenge, you can withstand it so that you can grow and develop into all that you were designed to be.

Obstacles manifest themselves in many ways. In fact, for every category of goals that you want to achieve, there is a corresponding set of obstacles that can (and often do) arise to challenge your success. Below, I have listed these areas and given a few examples of them so that you can identify the type of obstacle you are facing when it comes.

· **Financial Setbacks** – Debt, Bad Investments, Bills, Bankruptcy, IRS Issues, Foreclosure, Stock Market Plunges

· **Personal Setbacks** – Dissolved Friendships, Quitting College, Stress, Depression, Low Self Esteem

· **Professional Setbacks** – Downsizing, Layoffs, Demotions, Relocations, Corporate Scandals

· **Spiritual Setbacks** – Backsliding, Running from God, Lack of Intimate Time, Missing God

· **Relationship Setbacks** – Breakups, Divorce, Death in the Family, Infidelity, Abuse, Neglect

· **Health Setbacks** – Illness, Diseases, Psychotic Episodes, Surgery, STDs, Medicines

Make Lemonade and Sell it for Profit!

· **Logistical Setbacks** – Auto Trouble, Missed Flights, Losing Files, Hard Drive Crash, Sound Problems, Electrical Failure

So, as you can see, there are a plethora of obstacles that can come our way. **But in all of these things, we remain joyful, knowing that although they do not feel good, they are all working for our good.** They are shaping us into better people so that we can ultimately be successful.

Here is one quick point about obstacles. They will always be with us. Obstacles are not once-in-a-lifetime things. I heard one speaker say, "Either you're in a storm, you've just left one, or you're heading towards one!" So that means we must be prepared to deal with hardship when it arises. But also, the goal is to learn not to jump off the deep end over small stuff either. The things listed above are not small things. But, you get my point. **All obstacles are for a reason, and all obstacles are for a season.** There is a purpose behind everything that you go through.

Never just go through obstacles - always GROW through obstacles. Become better in the process.

Additionally, **never just go through obstacles - always GROW through obstacles. Become better in the process.** Become wiser in the process. Become a better judge of character in the process. Don't let life beat you

Make Lemonade and Sell it for Profit!

up for no reason - GET SOMETHING OUT OF THAT OBSTACLE. And that, my friend, is the purpose of this chapter - to show you how to get something positive and profitable out of your adversity.

As I mentioned earlier, each obstacle has a season. For example, my father was wounded in the Vietnam War. He survived, helped create me, got remarried, and now serves as a National Director of the same organization that got him started on the road to recovery after his injury. The bullets that my father endured caused him to be paralyzed from the waist, down. **However, without the proper use of his legs, he has done more with his life than most people, with full use of their upper and lower extremities.** So even though the obstacle knocked my father down, it did not knock him OUT! Why? It couldn't have. Because even when my father (who was alive) was placed in a room full of dead soldiers, he crawled his way out because he was carrying the seed of me. I believe that God knew that I would be born and that I would overcome my own obstacles to write this book that you are now reading. I know that I am here to create positive change all across the world. The impact of the obstacle may be life long for my dad in terms of the physical use of his legs, but the effects of that were short-lived. **My father took the hardship that he had been dealt, and turned it around to be the thing that fueled his passion to help others.**

Make Lemonade and Sell it for Profit!

The Paralyzed Veterans Association (PVA) hired my father as the National Director in 2002. He serves the veterans of this country faithfully every single day. Prior to that, he served as the Regional Director. He took the thing that tried to take him out, and used it to help millions of fellow Americans get back up from their hardships.

Well Del, are you talking about merchandising pain? GREAT QUESTION! **Of course I am!** I believe there is profit to be found in pain. I believe that people pay money (good money) to see, hear, read about, and watch people endure pain and come back to be successful. I remember listening to J. Ricc Rollins, speak to a group of college students one day at USF. He told them all about his troubles in life, and how he still went on to be successful. One line in his speech changed my life forever. He said, *"You must learn how to take life's lemons, make some lemonade, and sell it for profit!"*

> *"You must learn how to take life's lemons, make some lemonade, and sell it for profit!"*

Lemonade is a very interesting drink. People love it because it has a hint of bitterness, but it's very sweet. When you make lemonade, you have to add sugar! **Sugar added to lemons and water is the same as success and victory added to obstacles and failure.** Success makes your failures sweeter! In this chapter, I

Make Lemonade and Sell it for Profit!

want to show you how you, can take the bitter moments of life, add success to them, sell your own brand of lemonade, and make a little cash doing it. Still a little confused? Think about it!

· **Every book you buy** is someone's lemonade that they are selling for profit.
· **Every CD you buy** is someone's lemonade that they are selling for profit.
· **Every movie you watch** is someone's imaginary or real life lemonade that they are selling for profit.
· **Every sitcom or TV special** is someone's lemonade that is being sold for profit.
· **Every Reality TV show** is someone's lemonade that is being sold for profit.
· **Every speech or seminar** is someone's lemonade that is being sold for profit.

Get the point? Now in all fairness, profit is not the only motive for many of these industries. But, we cannot deny that profit is a byproduct of pain. Think about this book. Either you bought this book, or you were given this book by someone who bought it. Either way, this book is full of my personal failures and successes. In other words, this book is one of the many types of lemonade that I sell for a profit. I pay one price to create the book, and you pay another price to buy it. **However, you are buying what took me 26 years to learn. And now, in one handsome package, you have my best advice (and the advice of others that I quote) to help guide your**

Make Lemonade and Sell it for Profit!

life. Whatever you paid was a small investment compared to the potential impact this book can have on your life and the lives of those you share it with.

The Fear Factor

One thing that stops people from Robbing the Grave of Its Greatness and living their dreams is a little word called **FEAR!** But, fear of what?

On this page of the book, I want you to be honest with me. It's just you and I. No one else is around, and if so, then move! Smiles… But seriously, get alone to answer a few questions for me.

1. What are you afraid of when it comes to pursuing your goals and dreams 100%?

_____

_____

_____

2. Who taught you to be afraid of these things?

_____

_____

_____

3.What do you have faith in? What things are you willing to take a step of faith on to just see what will happen as a result of your step?

Delatorro L. McNeal II

Make Lemonade and Sell it for Profit!

----

4. Who taught you how to have faith in yourself and your dreams?

Here is a quick Biological Point about You as a Human Being!

You were only born with 2 fears. There are only two fears that were credited to your account when you were deposited onto this earth. Want to know what they are? I'm sure you do!

> *There are only two fears that were credited to your account when you were deposited onto this earth.*

1. The Fear of Falling.
2. The Fear of a Loud Sound.

Every other fear, including all the ones you listed above, is "learned behavior"! Which means that every other fear that you have, was taught to you somewhere along your journey of life. My friend, my point is simple. **If you can learn fear, you can learn faith.**

Make Lemonade and Sell it for Profit!

Because, as Bishop T.D. Jakes says, "Sometimes you have to faith your fears to death!"

Fear Exposed!

Let's take a few pages to explore some of the most common fears people suffer from and how to break them.

1. Fear of Making the Wrong Decision. Many people suffer from this fear needlessly. The reality is that **you will** make wrong decisions. You will mess up. You have got to stop attempting to have painless success. As you pursue greatness in all areas of your life, trust me, it will cost you. **It's gonna cost you making some wrong choices.** I know that I have, but that's why I am so thankful that I can get up after my mistakes and say, "I learned something from that, and I will be 10 times wiser the next time around!" If you want to operate in more wisdom in your decision-making, get a counsel of mentors around you.

Scripture teaches that wisdom rests in the counsel of many. A man who has himself as a teacher is a fool. We need wise people around us; people who have been there and done that. As Dr. Mike Murdock so simply states, "There are two ways to get wisdom - Mistakes and Mentors!" **And any wise person will tell you to learn from the mistakes of others because you will never live long enough to make them all**

Make Lemonade and Sell it for Profit!

yourself. Instead of being afraid of making the wrong choice, fear the consequences of inaction. Have the faith to put wisdom around you. Then, step out there! Faith your fear to death, and GO FOR IT!

2. Fear of Finishing. I've found that students and professional consultants suffer from this one in a big way. Students suffer because they must transition into the new world of adulthood. While, on the one hand it's great to be independent, on the other hand, it is very scary because of the amount of personal responsibility and accountability that comes along with independence.

High school students have a fear of finishing. They don't want to go on to college and beyond because that represents change.

Many college students have a fear of finishing because, by the time they graduate, many of them have little real clue what their career will be. Also, most have high credit card and student loan debt that will soon come up for repayment. Bills, apartments, an insecure job market, and the pressures of taking care of themselves with little to no solid financial game plan, scares most students to death. So, they take classes slower, they waste summers, and they work during college to lengthen and fund their college (carefree) lifestyles. Most students know that graduation means no more money from mom and dad, so they procrastinate, change majors multiple times, and just waste time to prolong the inevitable.

Make Lemonade and Sell it for Profit!

Professionals in the consulting arena can sometimes suffer from a fear of finishing. Why? Because, especially on longer well-funded projects, consultants get comfortable with the client, the environment, the plane trips, the nice hotels, and the frequent project dinners. Many other projects with shorter timelines and tighter budgets are not nearly as appealing. And the last thing the consultant wants to do is go back to sitting at the home office "unstaffed" or "unbillable". For this reason, some consultants intentionally attempt to make themselves indispensable to the client (even at the sake of alienating fellow team members), just to secure their spot on the project for as long as the client will pay for it.

With each of these cases, it's important to realize that we live in three tenses - the past, the present, and the future. These three scenarios are perfect examples of present-tense people. They can't get their eyes off of the present, to see themselves even better in their future. They are stuck in their present levels of comfort, forgetting that the only truly consistent thing in life is change itself. Things must and always do change, so we must, as my late Great Aunt Mae would say, "Be like a Ball, and keep on rolling!" Times change, seasons change, projects change, and the job market changes. You have to pull yourself up and realize that you are a uniquely gifted individual who is educated and prepared to roll with the best and the worst that life has to offer. Faith your fear to death, and GO FOR IT!

Delatorro L. McNeal II

Make Lemonade and Sell it for Profit!

3. Fear of too much Responsibility. This is a more general fear that gets us all at some point. This fear can manifest itself in our failure to apply for a better paying job, run for a political office, or become president of an organization that we believe in. Many times this fear stops gifted and talented people right in their tracks. It doesn't say, "I am not good enough", rather, it says, "This is probably too much for me to handle by myself". And you know what? That's right! A leadership role is too much for one person to handle by himself. That's why all great leaders have a staff of people who support and believe in them. It's called the Art of Delegation.

Don't let the fear of too much responsibility stop you from taking a leadership role that could help a company turn around, help a club gain prominent status, help a neighborhood get rid of drugs, or help a church reach lost souls. Take your rightful place.

And as Winston Churchill would say, "The price of greatness is responsibility!"

Remember, to whom much is given, much is required. **And as Winston Churchill would say, "The price of greatness is responsibility!"** Faith your fear to death, and GO FOR IT!

4. Fear of Change. This one gets us all. It is the fear that things will never be the same and that the current way of doing things will alter in some way. This fear

Make Lemonade and Sell it for Profit!

manifests itself in corporate America, in academia, in the faith-based community, government - you name it. We all deal with the fear of change. The fear of **change is dangerous and destructive because it keeps old outdated policies and procedures in place. It keeps outdated thinking in place. It keeps unqualified people in positions that produce bad results.** It keeps married couples together, but not really in love anymore because of the fear of spicing up the bedroom.

"The significant problems that we face today cannot be solved at the same level of thinking in which they were created!"
~ *Albert Einstein*

The amazing thing is that the same people who say that they "hate change" come into work day after day and **their outfit has changed, their hairstyle has changed, their mood has changed, their bagged lunch has changed, and even their cologne or perfume has changed.** The reality is, my friend, that we change ALL the time! We must change if we really want to grow and develop. Albert Einstein said something that really impacted my life. He said, **"The significant problems that we face today cannot be solved at the same level of thinking in which they were created!"** My goodness! What that means is that we must change our thinking to change our circumstances. So, my challenge to you is to be proactive and create the change that you want for yourself and this world. Faith your fear to death, and GO FOR IT!

Make Lemonade and Sell it for Profit!

5. Fear of Task-Complexity. This one keeps books from being written. It keeps businesses from being started. It keeps companies from re-organizing and re-structuring. It keeps old technology in buildings where new technology is needed. It keeps marriages ending in divorce instead of allowing families to work problems out. It keeps houses dirty and it keeps garages from ever getting cleaned and organized. It keeps people overweight for way too long because they don't know where to start, and because results are not seen overnight. On a spiritual note, it keeps most people from ever reading the bible cover-to-cover. It keeps college students from graduating in one major because they start one, and when it gets hard, they change. This becomes a cycle. **The fear of task-complexity is one of the worst fears.**

Studies show that one of the causes for habitual procrastination is fear of task-complexity. The job, task, assignment, or goal is so large that most people run because they don't know where and how to start to tackle that sucker! And understandably so. There are some tasks out there that can seem like Mission Impossible. But, if I can borrow a phrase from my dear friend and fellow speaker Tony McGee, **"Always remember that you are not on Mission Impossible, but rather you're on Mission I'm Possible!"** I love that!

> *"Always remember that you are not on Mission Impossible, but rather you're on Mission I'm Possible!"*
> ~ *Tony McGee*

Make Lemonade and Sell it for Profit!

I want to tell you a very powerful story that I think will help you learn how to overcome the fear of task-complexity. There once were two men fishing in a boat on a lake. One man was old in years. The other man was younger. They were fishing from opposite sides of the boat, not paying close attention to what each other was doing. The older man was catching little fish and big fish and securing them on ice in his creel. **The young man was catching little fish and big fish, but he kept throwing the big fish back.** They did this for hours and hours, until a storm approached. They stopped fishing and rowed back to shore. As they landed on shore, the wife of the younger man asked, *"Baby, I was watching you fishing out there, and I noticed something really odd. You were catching little fish and big fish, but you kept throwing the big fish back. I don't understand why you were doing that."* The young fisherman was silent for a moment. Then he replied, **"I hate doing that honey. But I've got to throw the big fish back because we've only got a little frying pan!"** The wife burst into laughter at her husband as they walked back to the cabin. She said, **"I know, that's why I bought us a bigger one earlier this morning!"**

My friend, the moral of this story is so powerful! First, let me explain a few things from the story, then I will talk about what this story means to you and I. You see, the entire time the young man was fishing, he was catching little opportunities and big opportunities. **But, because of his limited perception of what he**

Make Lemonade and Sell it for Profit!

could handle, he threw back the big opportunities and settled for the small ones. He got back to shore only to realize that his wife had solved the problem by purchasing a larger pan. But, by that time, it was **too late.** He had already thrown back his big opportunities for food.

Well, you and I are in that same boat. We are often given the big dream, the big goal, the big creative idea, the big vision, and the big opportunity. **But, we throw back the big things, because of our little resources, our little** environment, our little finances, and our little support. Even if the wife had not bought the bigger pan, he could easily have come home, and cut the big fish into smaller cookable pieces and froze the rest for another day. We have got to get to the point where we don't let the size of our dreams intimidate us. There will be times when you will sink your teeth into something that is too big for you. But when that happens, first ask for help carrying it. Second, if you can't get any help – DRAG THAT SUCKER until you get it to a place where you can manage it. That's what ants do. **Take your dream (the whole thing) and cut it up into phases, years, quarters, months, weeks, days, and hours until you can manage it - without it choking you.** Remember, life is hard by the yard, but if you take it by the inch, you will find out that life

> *We have got to get to the point where we don't let the size of our dreams intimidate us.*

Make Lemonade and Sell it for Profit!

> *Remember, life is hard by the yard, but if you take it by the inch, you will find out that life is a cinch.*

is a cinch. Another thing you will discover is that if you can catch the little opportunities and the big ones (despite your limitations), other people will help you out in ways that you know not of, to the extent that you can seize the entire thing and not have to store any of it for another day. Faith your fear to death, and GO FOR IT!

6. Fear of Success. This one shocked me when I first learned of it. Many people have a fear of becoming a success in their chosen field of expertise. I thought that everyone welcomed success, but then I learned that many shun it. **In fact, many people sabotage their own success, just to stay at an average level.** My friend and fellow speaker Joseph Washington calls the solution to this, "Overthrowing the Spirit of Average". Because of what the media has taught us about the way successful people's private lives are open to public scrutiny and tabloid slander, many people choose to not aim as high in life out of fear that their private business will become public. In addition, many people feel like the higher they climb, the harder they will fall. So they use excuses to justify aiming low in life.

My friend, the reality is that good people and not-so-good people become famous and successful. I told you in the last chapter that it's not so much the

Make Lemonade and Sell it for Profit!

achievement of the goal, as who you become in the process. Well, some people achieve the goal of being famous, but they don't become a person of integrity, character, and valor in the process. They make major public

Let life catch you pursuing greatness, not running from it.

and private mistakes that the media have a field day with. **We are all entitled to make mistakes. Whether you are well-known or not, mistakes are a part of life. No one is perfect.** But let life catch you pursuing greatness, not running from it. **As Nelson Mandela so eloquently states, "Your playing small does not serve this world!"** Let life find you working to make the dream come true, not working hard to make sure it doesn't. Face it - there are enough obstacles in life by itself. We don't have to add ourselves to the mix to confuse the issue. Help yourself, don't hurt yourself. Feel the fear and do it anyway. Faith your fear to death, and GO FOR IT!

7. Fear of Downtime. This one helped me to understand my wife better. People who have a fear of downtime hate going anyplace early. To avoid downtime, they would rather over compensate by being late! People who say that they like to arrive fashionably late often fear downtime, and thus prefer to arrive after an engagement has begun. They like to arrive on time or late so they don't have to wait for festivities to begin.

Make Lemonade and Sell it for Profit!

Remember, the people with whom you network will ultimately determine your net worth!

This one is a little less serious than some of the others, but it is still worth mentioning. It can and does have a very negative bearing on a person's image and the way they are viewed by their peers. Listen, stop that getting to places late stuff! **Learn how to network, how to work a room, how to mingle, how to have small talk, and how to take advantage of small communication opportunities.** See how you can help the event planner make the event even more special with your input. People that fear downtime miss out on golden networking opportunities. Remember, the people with whom you network will ultimately determine your net worth! Faith your fear to death, and GO FOR IT!

8. Fear of the Unknown. Les Brown says something I like. He says, "Most people prefer known hells rather than unknown heavens." I believe that this is true. This fear is what keeps many people from walking in faith and reaping the benefits of seeing what's on the other side. Many abused and mistreated women stay in bad relationships because they are afraid that if they leave, no one else will love them or want them. So they prefer known abuse, known infidelity, and known mistreatment rather then unknown abundance, unknown pampering, and unknown dream mates. How sad! But this happens in so many other areas of life.

Make Lemonade and Sell it for Profit!

Many people prefer the known hell of a stale job, rather than the unknown heavens of a new career opportunity. Many people prefer the known hells of a poor diet and a non-existent exercise routine, rather than the unknown heavens of total body wellness – mind, body, and soul. Many people prefer known hell, rather then unknown heaven. Granted, some of the unknown may be bad, that's why you investigate, do your research, get wisdom around your decision and then pursue. Faith your fear to death, and GO FOR IT!

My friend, I hope that by exposing the cause of many of these fears, you are motivated to go for it. You must go out on a limb, because that's where all the fruit is. **You have to take a step because your journey can't start without one.** You must be willing to leap, and grow your wings on the way down. In *Indiana Jones and the Last Crusade*, Indiana's final challenge was a faith challenge. He had come to a place where there was a big gap between where he was, and where he wanted to be. Using his own natural sight, he could not see the bridge to get across - but it was a test of faith. He clutched his chest, mustered up the faith, **and took the step (onto what appeared to be NOTHING), only to land successfully on an invisible narrow bridge that was paved all the way to the other side for him.** Imagine the number of explorers who probably got to the same point

You have to take a step because your journey can't start without one.

Make Lemonade and Sell it for Profit!

that Indiana did, but preferred known hells to unknown heavens. They were too afraid to take the step. Don't let that be you! Your victory is waiting for you on the other side of your "step of faith".

> *My friend, your breakthrough is hidden behind the door of an uncommon step of faith towards your dream.*

My friend, you have to take the step. You must go for it. On the other side of your step of faith you will find prosperity and abundant life. I want you to read a book that I just love to death. It's <u>Failing Forward</u>, by John C. Maxwell. It teaches you all about some of the most successful people in the world and how they overcame tremendous odds and took crazy steps of faith, but landed on unknown and blissful heavens! **My friend, your breakthrough is hidden behind the door of an uncommon step of faith towards your dream.** Faith your fear to death, and GO FOR IT!

The Four Types of Obstacles

I have learned that there are 4 types of obstacles. Fear creates many of the obstacles that we encounter, but one of the things that I have really learned from life is that each obstacle is an opportunity to understand and to grow. I believe that in all of our getting, acquiring, and seeking in life, we should get understanding. Ultimately, we should be able to

Make Lemonade and Sell it for Profit!

answer the question, "*Why*?" Many people go through things far longer than they need to, not because their obstacles last long, but because they don't find the purpose of the obstacle. Even after the challenge is gone, they still replay it in their minds. So it's important that we understand that each obstacle that comes into our lives will fall into 1 of these 4 types. I am willing to bet you that each of your obstacles will fall somewhere in the next few pages. Smiles! Let's go.

1. Anticipated / Learned – The first type of obstacle is one that was anticipated or expected (you knew it was coming) and you learned something from it. Many **times, these types of obstacles can manifest in the things that we ignore for a season, hoping that they will go away or get better.** However, after a period of time, the ignored issue festers and metastasizes to the point that it turns into an obstacle in your life. Allow me to give you an example. Once, the electric company forgot to send me a bill. When I noticed this, I said to myself, "Well they must have forgotten, or something. Maybe our house got skipped this month!" You know how silly we can get when we try to rationalize stuff. So, the next month, the bill came and it was twice the amount it normally is. I am so grateful that we were not in a big financial bind that month because we would have been in bad shape. **The reality was that the financial obstacle of the BIG electric bill was one that I really did expect or anticipate, but I tried to ignore it.** However, I learned from that experience. Now when that happens with

Make Lemonade and Sell it for Profit!

any of my bills, I call and request a statement. So as I explained earlier, it was an obstacle that I anticipated. However, I learned from it. What about you? In the space below, give me an example of a time when you encountered an obstacle that you knew was coming, but you ignored it anyway. Tell me how you ultimately dealt with it, and what life lesson you learned from it.

Here are just a few examples to get you started!

Examples: Anticipated Break Up because of communication issues you've known about for months.

Anticipated Car Trouble due to that engine light that you ignored for weeks.

Anticipated Poor Performance on a Test you should have studied for.

Anticipated Financial Loss due to an overly risky investment decision.

Anticipated Customer Complaint from a client that you know you should have treated better.

Anticipated Credit Score drops due to that Creditor whose calls you failed to return.

Make Lemonade and Sell it for Profit!

Your Example:

_____

_____

_____

_____

2. Unanticipated / Learned - The second type of obstacle is one that was unanticipated or unexpected (you were blindsided by it) and you still learned something from it. *Well Del, there have been things that I ignored, and then unexpectedly they came up out of nowhere. Don't these classify as type 1 obstacles*? GREAT QUESTION! No, they don't. Because even through the manifestation of the obstacle came at a time that you did not expect, deep within your heart of hearts, you knew that it would come back to haunt you later on. You ignored it, so that's why I call it an obstacle that you really and truly anticipated.

The unanticipated obstacle is one that you totally did not see coming. I mean you were maintaining your goals well, and all of a sudden, out of the clear blue sky, this obstacle comes and gives you a blow. These obstacles can be very frustrating because when your mind asks you *why*, you initially can't answer. **These obstacles manifest themselves in unexpected friendships dissolving almost overnight, and seemingly without reason. Or maybe you over-**

Make Lemonade and Sell it for Profit!

drafted on an account that you thought you were maintaining well, but by some accident, things got mixed up. Maybe you went to an evening dinner and you tried a new entrée. The next day you had a bad reaction to the food, causing your stomach to get very upset. You did not expect it, but I guarantee that you learned a thing or two about the right foods for your body type.

One thing that I have learned is that when unexpected obstacles come, they come to really test our character and integrity. They come to see what we are really made of. They come to remove the wrong people from our lives, and place the right people in our lives. They come to pull out of you things you did not realize you have. I remember the first time I got a flat tire on the highway while traveling to college. When I began my trip, my tires were in great shape. But something in the road must of have punctured my tire because, out of the blue, I was on the side of the interstate, upset, and worried. Well, after about 30 seconds of asking disempowering questions like, "Why me?" and "What did I do to deserve this?" I thanked God that it was not worse, and started working on the solution. I did the whole spare tire thing and got back on my way. *Did I like the flat tire issue? Did I ask for it?*

> *One thing that I have learned is that when unexpected obstacles come, they come to really test our character and integrity.*

Make Lemonade and Sell it for Profit!

Did I detour in my timetable? No, but did I learn something? Yes, I sure did. I learned that I could fix a flat all by myself. I learned that most people would never stop to help. I learned that the grass in the median of a highway is a lot taller than it appears at 70mph. Smiles! But out of that incident, I learned that Del could do something that he did not realize that he could do. So that when it happened to someone else in the future, I could be of some assistance. What about you?

The power to take lemons, make lemonade, and sell it for profit lies in your ability to LEARN FROM EACH OF YOUR LEMONS! Like Iyanla Vanzant says, "There is VALUE IN THE VALLEY!"

> *The power to take lemons, make lemonade, and sell it for profit lies in your ability to learn from each of your lemons!*

Other Examples:

Unanticipated Power Outage due to inclement weather

Unanticipated Illness due to an allergic reaction

Unanticipated Defeat in a competition

Unanticipated Diagnosis with a disease that other doctors did not detect

Unanticipated Car Accident due to the poor driving of another

Make Lemonade and Sell it for Profit!

Unanticipated Financial Loss due to corporate scandal or fraudulent behavior

Your Examples:

Notice that for the last two types of obstacles we are about to cover, the common denominator is that life lessons are not being learned. That's why these have the greatest impact on your psyche.

3. Unanticipated / Unlearned - The third type of obstacle is one that was unanticipated or unexpected (so it blindsided you) and you never figured out what you are supposed to learn from that thing! Before I go any further, **I need you to get real with me, my friend. I know that there have been times in your life when something happened to you unexpectedly, and you still are trying to ascertain what in the world you were supposed to get out of it.** Smiles! These are some of the most challenging obstacles because they don't make sense in our minds. We can't make heads or tails of why things did not work out. For example, I can remember putting a proposal together for a corporate client. The proposal was perfect. The local office loved it. The regional office

Make Lemonade and Sell it for Profit!

loved it. The proposal was for a speaking contract worth about $10,000. It got all the way to the national headquarters and was accepted by all but one person. Therefore, the contract fell through. I was crushed. "That

So when in the natural you can't make heads or tails of the lessons that life is trying to teach you, you must TRUST that God has your best interest at heart.

contract would have really helped my business", I thought. I did not, and still to this day do not, understand why things did not work out. So that was an unexpected business set back that I did not learn from. And even now, if you were to ask me what lesson I learned from it in terms of how to make my proposal better, I could not tell you. Why? Because I never got feedback. **So when in the natural you can't make heads or tails of the lessons that life is trying to teach you, you must TRUST that God has your best interest at heart** and that all things are going to ultimately work together for your benefit.

In lieu of giving you more of my examples, I really want you think of some examples from your life. Not learning from an obstacle keeps you from Robbing the Grave, and I don't want anything to hinder you from pulling every ounce of Greatness from the Grave that you can imagine.

Make Lemonade and Sell it for Profit!

Your Examples:

_____

_____

_____

_____

4. Anticipated / Unlearned – This type of obstacle can be tricky. But to be honest, only the unwise fall into this type. Think about it. **It's an obstacle that you see coming, and when it comes you still don't learn from it. That is unwise.** That's like smoking all your life, then getting lung cancer, and continuing to smoke. That is unwise. You encountered an obstacle that you expected, but your actions illustrate that you have not learned from your mistake. Let's talk about relationships. You are dating someone and you know that they are not treating you with love and respect. You put up with it for years until the situation gets violent, and then you leave. But you immediately go back to the same mistreatment. That was a problem that you expected, but your actions indicate that you have not learned that this person is not going to change. So you stay in that abusive relationship, settling for less then you deserve. Dealing with anticipated obstacles is bad enough, but adding the fact that you don't learn anything from the ordeal makes it much worse.

Make Lemonade and Sell it for Profit!

Put it like this. **The life lesson from any obstacle is the <u>sugar</u>. The time that passes after the obstacle takes place is the <u>water</u>. The obstacle itself is the <u>lemon</u>.** So, if you just have the sour lemon of your situation mixed with flowing water of time, you still have a very sour drink. No one wants to buy that! No one benefits from that either. **However, if you add the sweet taste of a life lesson that teaches you ways to avoid that mistake in the future, you now have a nice pitcher of sweet lemonade that others will buy from you.** People will pay money to sit in seminars and listen to people tell them how to avoid major mistakes in business, finance, real estate, college, companies, churches, and teams. I hope that you have very few examples of stuff that you knowingly went through, and still have not learned from. That is simply unwise, my friend. Remember, **every action you take in life is producing a result. Learning from that result is what makes people good. Helping others learn from that result is what makes people GREAT!**

2 Truths about Obstacles

1. No obstacle is meant to stop you permanently. The only reason why some people have allowed certain obstacles in life to stop them is because the obstacle came at a time when they had NO MOMENTUM. Momentum, as I already taught you, is critical for success. **Any illness, disease, accident,**

Make Lemonade and Sell it for Profit!

Don't let the small speed bumps of life stop you dead in your tracks. K eep on fighting, keep on striving, keep on working.

or calamity short of death is **NOT meant to stop you permanently.** It's only meant to slow you down. But, if you don't have the momentum of your other goals in life to keep you moving forward, you will be stopped dead in your tracks by things that are minor.

For example, if your car is going 3 miles per hour and you come to a speed bump, your car won't make it over the speed bump. Is it because the speed bump is too big? No. Is it because the car this too weak? No. **The only reason that tiny speed bump can stop that big car is because the car did not have enough momentum.** A speed bump encountered at 3 miles per hour, versus one encountered at 30 miles per hour has totally different impacts on the driver's ability to go forward. One stops the car; the other simply jolts the car. Don't let the small speed bumps of life stop you dead in your tracks. Keep on fighting, keep on striving, keep on living, keep on dreaming, and keep on working.

2. Most obstacles that you deal with have little to do with you. One of the things that I learned about 2 years ago was that most of the issues in my life were not even related to me. **They were funneled through my life experience to bless someone else.** The years of 2000 – 2002 were some of the hardest, trouble-

Make Lemonade and Sell it for Profit!

filled, character-building years of my life. My entire life has been a tremendous story of overcoming obstacles and setbacks. Many of the things that I went through, while beneficial to my life and my wisdom, have been for other people. **As soon as you go through something major in your life, you will encounter someone who is in a similar situation.** Now, think of it. You would not be of any help to that person had you not gone through the things that you went through prior.

For example, let's say that you work in sales. And let's say that you had a really bad 1st quarter. You bounce back during the 2nd and 3rd quarters. Then, in the 4th quarter, a fellow employee comes to you for advice because they are having a bad 4th quarter. What makes you qualified to counsel, advise, or mentor them? **Your previous pain! So it would be safe to say, that at least a part of the purpose or reason for your 1st quarter setback was to give you coaching material to use to help someone else through their tough times.** So I am a firm believer that many things that I endure and GROW THROUGH are not just about me. They almost always are about someone else who will enter my life and need my testimony of success to motivate them to victory as well.

One day, while working out at the gym with personal trainer and World Kickboxing Champion James Sisco, I got a powerful revelation about the two weight

Make Lemonade and Sell it for Profit!

classes of trouble. I believe that there is a direct relationship between working out your muscles, and working out your problems in life.

Check it out!

Heavy Trouble
Purpose: To build the muscles of your character. When God is trying to make you much stronger he will give you heavier troubles, but fewer of them.

Light Trouble
Purpose: To cut or define the muscles of your character. When God is trying to make you much more defined, he will give you lighter troubles, but more of them. This defines, refines, and shapes the character muscles that you already have. **You don't necessarily need to get stronger. You just need to be more defined, more focused, more committed, more centralized, and more grounded.** Consistent repetitions of light trouble will create this in your life. You know what I mean. Little stuff adds up over a long period of time. And sometimes little stuff can feel like it weighs tons because of the number of times you have to press it. But keep on pushing, you've come too far now. Don't let ANYBODY TURN YOU AROUND!

Make Lemonade and Sell it for Profit!

5 Changes that will Guarantee Successful Lemonade

1. Change Your OUTLOOK – Recognize that this is not a personal thing. Don't take obstacles as personal attacks. I know that it is hard to do. But to think that you bring obstacles onto yourself is very self-defeating and demotivating. Change your perception of your situation by looking at the totality of your past, present, and future and seeing how this present challenge fits into the grand scheme of the overall positive direction and impact of your life. Zig Ziglar says, *"When the outlook does not look good, try the Uplook. It is always much better!"*

2. Change Your QUESTIONS – Ask yourself empowering questions when trouble comes. Stop asking the types of questions that only frustrate you or lead you to believe that life is "out to get you"! The reality is that each obstacle is trying to teach you something, so ask better questions. Ask questions that seek a greater, deeper, or more empowering purpose behind your pain. I used to ask myself why I had to deal with credit card debt. Then I learned that it was because I was going to have to deal with people who had it, so I would need to be able to relate to them in order to show them how to get out and stay out. Remember these three empowering questions I always ask myself.

Make Lemonade and Sell it for Profit!

- What am I supposed to learn from this challenge?
- How could someone else benefit from my mistakes?
- How many lives would be impacted if I sold this lemonade?

3. Change Your FOCUS – There are 4 types of people.
- **Past Tense People** are those who always talk about what they used to do, who they used to know, and how life used to be. They are stuck in the past.

- **Present Tense People** are those who always talk only about their current situation. They can only see what is going on today, and are stuck in today - which is very temporary.

- **Future Tense People** are those who always talk about what they are going to do, going to be, and going to have. They are stuck in the future. Notice how the issue with each of these types of people is a <u>limited and narrow focus</u>. This is very dangerous and self-destructive. That's why you want to be a Total Tense Person.

- **A Total Tense Person** (or TTP) is one who uses the knowledge of their past and hope for their future to give them power and passion to work through their present. Remember, focus 20% of your time and energy on analyzing the problem and spend 80% of your time solving it and learning from it!

A Total Tense Person (or TTP) is one who uses the knowledge of their past and hope for their future to give them power and passion to work through their present.

Make Lemonade and Sell it for Profit!

4. Change Your ACTION – Get Up & Move. Get off of the nail, my friend. Take consistent assertive action steps towards altering your situation. Don't wait for others to get behind you. If you try one way and it does not work, then try another. Be creative. **Create multiple income streams, multiple mentors, and multiple moments of success in your daily routine.** Also, know when a method you are using is or is not working. Be flexible enough to adjust to technology and the latest methods and best practices for success. Remember, action creates reaction. Motion dictates emotion. You must create the change you seek.

5. Change Your ASSOCIATES – If you were sinking in quicksand, would you seek help from someone who was also sinking in the quicksand? Or, would you reach for someone who was standing on solid ground? Well, of course the correct answer would be to reach for someone who was already on a solid foundation. **Many times when we encounter obstacles, we seek advice from people who are just as messed up as we are, thinking that their sympathy will be a remedy to our situation.** The blind cannot lead the blind. In order to fight your obstacles and whip your mountain, maintain strong relationships with mentors and coaches who believe in your success. They will throw out a lifeline to you, while others will try to make

> *In order to fight your obstacles and whip your mountain, maintain strong relationships with mentors and coaches who believe in your success.*

Make Lemonade and Sell it for Profit!

you sink to save themselves. Purposely put yourself around people who are solution-oriented. Seek individuals who have vision, and who are Total Tense Oriented. These are the people that will not allow you to stay in your storm any longer than necessary.

Use these five simple steps to begin to dictate to your obstacle, instead of allowing your obstacle to dictate to you. You have so many spiritual, personal, professional, emotional, and motivational resources to use to fight your storms. **There are people right now, sitting on the sidelines of your storm waiting for you to simply admit that you need help, and reach out for them.**

Spiritual Sidebar: For those of you who do not have a spiritual life, you can skip this sidebar. However, for those of you who do, one additional weapon that you can use to fight the obstacles in your life is the PUSH method.

Pray	**P**raise	**P**lant Seed
Until	**U**ntil	**U**ntil
Something	**S**omething	**S**omething
Happens	**H**appens	**H**appens

Make Lemonade and Sell it for Profit!

Commercial Break

Do you realize how BAD you are? Do you understand how blessed and favored you are? Do you really get how powerful you are? You are an extremely precious, powerful, and resilient individual. You have bounced back from some of the best shots that life gave you, and guess what? YOU ARE STILL STANDING!

- Maybe you have **lost a job**, but you're **still standing!**
- Maybe you've **been through a divorce**, but you're **still standing!**
- Maybe you were **abused as a child**, but you're **still standing!**
- Maybe you got **fired or laid off unexpectedly**, but you're **still standing!**
- Maybe you **lost all of your money** in the stock market, but guess what? You're **still standing!**
- Maybe you **tried to start a business and failed** a few times, but you're **still standing!**
- Maybe you've been **lied on, mistreated, and discouraged** by your own family, but guess what? You're **still standing!**
- Maybe you changed **majors in college** like you changed underwear. That's okay because **you're still standing!**
- Maybe you're **up to your eyeballs in debt** and you don't see it ever coming down. Just a reminder - you're **still standing!**

Make Lemonade and Sell it for Profit!

- Maybe you have **not found a church home** that makes you feel welcomed. Guess what? You're **still standing!**
- Maybe doctors have told you for years that **you've only got 6 months to live**. Guess what? You're **still standing!**
- Maybe you've been in a **major accident, and you can't use a certain body part anymore.** That's okay too, because inside you're **still standing!**
- Maybe you are **looking for Mr. or Mrs. Right**, because all you have dated was the Wrong family. Well that's also okay because at least you are **still standing!**

My friend, it is important that you remember how BAD you are! Remember how special and blessed you are. You are a Champion and you may not even know it. If you were not a champion, you would not be reading this book. Over the many years of your life, you have overcome some of the biggest challenges that life has to offer, right? You may not have even expected to make it through some. However, each challenge made you stronger, wiser, faster, more resilient, and more focused. It's important that you understand that no matter what has come your way, **you are still standing.** You have come from many years of hardship to get to this book. I know, understand, and appreciate that about you. Know that you are a Champion, because the only way that someone can become a Champion is by defeating some of the best in the

Make Lemonade and Sell it for Profit!

industry. **You have taken life's best punches, now life better get ready for YOURS!**

In order to make lemonade and sell it for profit, you've got to remember how many lemons you have already encountered and overcome. Remember, lemons are symbolic of obstacles and struggle in your life. In the space provided, I want you to list some of the most challenging things that you personally, professionally, and spiritually have overcome. I want you be very honest and list at least 10 major things that you have overcome in your life. If you share yours with me, I will share mine with you! I promise. Smiles.

1.

2.

3.

4.

5.

6.

7.

8.

9.

10.

Make Lemonade and Sell it for Profit!

If it didn't kill you, **it was meant to craft you!**
If it didn't take you out,
it was meant to take you up!
If it didn't take you under,
it was meant to carry you over!
If it didn't cause you to die,
it was meant to help *you survive!*
If it didn't mutilate you,
it was meant to motivate you!
- Delatorro

Now, for each of the 10 lemons that you just listed, I want you to list a corresponding life lesson that you learned from that obstacle. In other words, I want you to tell me the sugar or honey (the sweet thing) that came out of your sour experience. **Wisdom is not only the principle thing; it's also the sweetest byproduct of pain, failure, calamity, tragedy, shame, embarrassment, obstacles, and hardships.** Again, for each of the 10 lemons (obstacles) you just listed, list at least one thing that you can consider as the sugar (life lesson) that came from it.

1. _____

2. _____

3. _____

4. _____

Make Lemonade and Sell it for Profit!

5. _____

6. _____

7. _____

8. _____

9. _____

10. _____

Fantastic, I am very proud of you. Now, there is one critical thing that you MUST be able to decree and declare after looking at the totality of your life's ups and downs. You must be able to not only say this, but also let this be your motivational

> *IT WAS WORTH IT!*
> *This is the only statement that harmonizes the totality of your trouble and still allows you be on top.*

anthem. You must affirm this within yourself everyday. It's four simple little words with unparalleled power and significance. Now that you have squeezed the lemons out of your obstacles, added the water of time, and stirred in the sweetness of your life lessons, you must be able to pour some of your lemonade into a tall glass with ice, drink it, wipe your mouth and say, " **IT WAS WORTH IT!**"

Make Lemonade and Sell it for Profit!

This is the only statement that harmonizes the totality of your trouble and still allows you be on top. **This is the only statement that makes sense of everything that you have been through, sacrificed, and endured. You must be able to weigh all of your good days, and all of your bad days and still say, "It was worth it!"** You must be able to look at your bank account, your goals and dreams, your family, your success, your painful past, your challenging present, and your glorious future and say, **"IT WAS WORTH IT!"**

- The **person** you **are** today makes it **worth it!**
- The **goals** that you have **achieved** make it **worth it!**
- The **wisdom** that you have **attained** makes it **worth it!**
- The **negative people** that you have **cut off** make it **worth it!**
- The **degrees** you have **earned** and the **lessons** you have **learned** make it **worth it!**
- The **children** you have **raised**, and the **lives** you have **saved** make it **worth it!**
- The **smiles** you **create** and the **dreams** you **initiate** make it **worth it!**
- The **prayers** you have **prayed** and the **foundations** you have **laid** make it **worth it!**
- The **tears** you have **cried** and the **mountains** you have **climbed** make it worth it!
- The **hope** you have **restored** and the **love** you have **poured** out make **it all WORTH IT!**

Make Lemonade and Sell it for Profit!

When you GROW through, what you go through, your brain is going to ask you one simple question – "Was it all worth it?" With enthusiasm, power, conviction, courage, tenacity, and sincerity you must reply, **"YES, IT WAS WORTH IT!"**

Thomas Edison failed at his masterpiece 2000 times, but the perfected light bulb invention on the 2001st try made it **WORTH IT!**

Baby Ruth struck out thousands of time in baseball, but his countless homeruns made it **WORTH IT!**

Martin Luther King Jr. was beaten, imprisoned, mistreated, ostracized, misquoted, and hated by many during his lifetime. But his Legacy of "I Have a Dream" and Non-Violent protests made it **WORTH IT!**

Truett Cathy lost both of his brothers in a plane crash, lost one of his restaurants to a fire, and underwent 2 colon surgeries. However, founding the billion-dollar Chick-fil-A company made it **WORTH IT!**

Albert Einstein was told by a Munich schoolmaster that he would "never amount to much". However, he became one of the greatest thinkers of our time. He would say that it was **WORTH IT!**

Bill Gates dropped out of college to pursue his dream of creating a technology empire that you and I now

Make Lemonade and Sell it for Profit!

know as the Microsoft Corporation. He would say that it was **WORTH IT!**

Mary Kay Ash invested her last $5,000 dollars to pursue her dream of becoming the CEO of one of the largest cosmetic companies in the world. A month before her business was to launch, her business partner and husband died! Today, you and I know her dream as the billion-dollar corporation of Mary Kay Cosmetics. Millions would agree that it was **WORTH IT!**

Bishop T.D Jakes invested his entire savings account into the self-publishing of his first book. He purchased 1000 copies, and sold out in 2 weeks. You and I know that book as <u>Woman Thou Art Loosed</u>! It created one of the largest Annual Christian Women's Conferences in the world today. Millions would agree that it was **WORTH IT!**

Willie Jolley, International Motivational Speaker, Singer, and Author started out as a jazz and jingle singer. One night, after a great show at a local club, he was fired and replaced with a karaoke machine. He is now the CEO of the million-dollar empire, Willie Jolley Worldwide and speaks to audiences all across the world from his mantra that, "A Setback is a Setup for a Comeback". I am proud to call him one of my mentors and dear friends. If you ask Willie, he will affirm that it was all **WORTH IT!**

Make Lemonade and Sell it for Profit!

My pastors, Drs. Randy and Paula White, moved to Tampa, Florida over 11 years ago with nothing but a big dream, a big God, and a big promise. With an army of 5 people, they started South Tampa Christian Center and, within 11 years, they have come to pastor the internationally respected ministry of Without Walls International Church (WWIC), one of the fastest growing churches in the country. WWIC & PWM has a potential viewership of over 4 Billion people. Drs Randy and Paula White, along with millions of Christians worldwide, will confirm that it was **WORTH IT!**

Don't Celebrate the Glory, until you know the Story!

In Chapter 3: Maximizing Your Human Potential, I used an iceberg as an example of your potential. I would like to use the iceberg again, but this time to illustrate a different point. I believe that it's critical that you educate people about everything that you endured to become successful. People cannot think that your success was created without failure and hardship. That would be like advertising lemonade made without lemons. Pastor Paula White says something I live by. She says, *"Don't celebrate my glory, until you know my story."* She talks about how she does not want people to only look at her million-dollar ministry, her million dollar home, and her million-dollar products, conferences, and contracts (her glory) without appreciating her story. She started out as a poor Mississippi girl who was sexually and physically

Make Lemonade and Sell it for Profit!

There is no such thing as an overnight success, and there's no such thing as painless success.

abused, whose father committed suicide when she was young, and who was written off by many as trailer trash. She wants you to appreciate that she and Pastor Randy know what it's like to eat government cheese, to be at the bottom financially, and still, through the grace and power of God, to comeback from all those setbacks and create a multi-million-dollar ministry empire that has won over 1 million people to Christ.

You can't appreciate someone's glory until you know their story. I would like to challenge you, my friend. Always learn all you can about how someone went from rags to riches, instead of just looking at their riches. Appreciate and celebrate their process. There is no such thing as an overnight success, and there's no such thing as painless success. Goodness is free, but Greatness will cost you! You have already paid a price for the level of greatness that you have attained. However, to go to the next level in greatness, there is a cost of admission. In the iceberg illustration, the waterline represents average, nominal, ordinary, and goodness. The tip of the iceberg represents above average, phenomenal, extraordinary, and greatness. Now here is the deal. Most people will sit in a boat on the waterline of average and look up at someone who has achieved greatness and say, "They think they are all that. They think that they are so special, and that they have

Make Lemonade and Sell it for Profit!

arrived!" **Well, the reality is that the degree that these high achieving people stick out of water is small compared to everything that they GREW through in order to be successful.**

Dr. Randy White, says, *"Don't ever be jealous of someone's harvest because, many times, you have no clue the seed that they have sown, and the price they have paid to reap that type of harvest in their life."* It's easy to see someone successful and think that it "just happened" for them. GARBAGE! They worked their butts off for it. Well, at least most of them did. And the ones who did not work hard and smart for their success will not be able to maintain it for any length of time because they did not go through the process of becoming the right person in the process of success to maintain what they attained.

Last point - make sure that you only surround yourself with people who know your story. People that know the struggle, trials, hardships, troubles, and storms that you have been through are the only ones who will REALLY appreciate your time, talents, and treasures. They are the only ones who will not take your gifting for granted. They are the only ones who will guard and protect your success, your empire, your goals, your dreams, your anointing, your ideas, your creativity, and your fruit.

> *Last point - make sure that you only surround yourself with people who know your story.*

Make Lemonade and Sell it for Profit!

Realize that you will Fail Your Way to Success!

Willie Jolley says, "A Success is nothing but a Failure who got MAD!"

My friend, I am a living breathing example that failure is a critical part of success. As promised, since you shared some of your lemons with me a few pages back, I will share some of mine with you. These are a few areas of my life that I failed in along the way to becoming who I am divinely designed to be. The following list is only a fraction of the justification for why I say that, "Goodness is free, but Greatness will cost you! The question is, are you ready to pay the price?" I have paid, am paying, and will continue to pay a tremendous price to enter into new levels of greatness daily and Rob the Grave of all of my stuff, and if you're not careful, some of yours too! Smiles. **WARNING! Some of these failures may not sound like a big deal to you, but remember to NEVER COMPARE PAIN! That is unwise and self-destructive. One man's floor is another man's ceiling. Pain is pain regardless of the form, fashion, or degree.** It all hurts and challenges us to go to a new level. So this is not a list of things for you to compare with and rank my life as more or less painful than yours or anyone else's. This is simply me sharing a little of my story, so that you appreciate my glory - a piece of which you are holding in your hands right now!

Delatorro L. McNeal II

Make Lemonade and Sell it for Profit!

Here are a few of the lemons that make up my Lemonade!

1. Prior to my birth, doctors said that I was a **medical impossibility** because my mother's birth canal was too narrow to bear a child. Also, because my father was paralyzed from a war injury, he could not move his body from the waist down.

2. Two years after I was born, **my parents got divorced**. So, for many years of my childhood, I longed for my father, but could not be close to him.

3. My mother remarried, and much to her surprise and mine, her new husband became **very abusive - both emotionally and physically**.

4. I can remember nights in my childhood when my mom sneaked my brother and I out of the house while my step-dad was asleep so that we could **escape his violence and mistreatment.**

5. I can remember **sitting outside our house and listening to my mother being beaten** by my stepfather when I was around 7 or 8 years old. I learned **about facades at a very early age** because the man that was abusive at home, was a deacon in the local church.

6. I can remember looking in the mirror as a little boy **and imagining myself** with a goatee and a mustache because that would mean that **I was a man**, and I

Make Lemonade and Sell it for Profit!

could have done something about the abuse in our home.

7. In the 5th grade **I was labeled an "at risk youth"**. In the sixth grade, I was placed in a special class of students who were labeled "at risk". I can remember being mocked by some of my peers because I was not as smart as them. However, as a result of some serious academic coaching from my mom and my 6th grade teacher Ms. Diane Williams, I went from being "at risk" to being "at promise"!

8. Early in grade school, I had a **major academic weakness for reading.** I hated reading out loud because I was so bad at it. I stumbled over words so other students laughed at me. But, out of that challenge, I learned how to memorize information and speak.

9. In high school, I **tried out for the varsity football team, and failed** because I was too small.

10. In high school, I **applied for a full scholarship to college and was rejected.**

11. In college, I **tried to pledge a fraternity and was rejected, outcast, and talked about.** I was **lied on and embarrassed** in ways I can't communicate.

12. In college, I tried to get grants and fellowships from graduate school and I was told that because I was graduating early, **there was no money for me.**

Make Lemonade and Sell it for Profit!

13. In college, I made some promises to God to live my life in certain ways, **and a many times I failed Him.**

14. I got married fresh out of college to my "college sweetheart". I was hardheaded and stupid and did not use divine wisdom in that decision. **We ended up filing for divorce 6 months later.** That was a major failure in my life. I **felt like a dented can at 23 years old.**

15. In corporate America, **I tried to fit into the "mainstream"** way of doing things, and failed.

16. In corporate America, I **tried to fit my dream into my corporate environment** and it did not work.

17. I started building my first home in Tampa in September of 2000. By May of 2001, I closed on the house. In July of 2001 **I got laid off**.

18. I went from **$50,000 per year to nothing in literally one day!**

19. For four months, I actively sought employment, to no avail. During that time, **I sent out 400 resumes and got no responses.**

20. I had great degrees and awards on my walls but **nothing in my bank account.**

Make Lemonade and Sell it for Profit!

21. God put the right woman in my life. We wanted to get married and have a big ceremony, but we had **no money** because she was **laid off** around the same time I was.

22. I **watched my credit score quickly drop from a 715 to a 560** because I had hit a financially dry season in my life.

23. I watched as my new house in Tampa was being **threatened with foreclosure proceedings** that **never took place**, because I could not afford the house anymore.

24. I was **forced to sell** the nice new townhouse in Tampa prior to my 24th birthday and move myself and my new wife (The Queen) into a small apartment.

25. I competed for Toastmaster's International Speech Competition, won at the first 3 levels, **but lost at the 4th level**. Many audience members felt I was robbed.

26. I went into my first major business venture with a trusted friend, money got in the way, he bailed out, and we have not talked since. That was a major unexpected obstacle in my life. **I trusted someone who did not return that trust and loyalty.**

27. During the time that I was unemployed, I tried to buy out my lease on my old car and **got turned down by 5 banks.**

Make Lemonade and Sell it for Profit!

28. I hosted monthly public seminars that made great impacts on people's lives **but financially cost me several thousand dollars in the hole.**

29. I attempted to get major success events covered by the news media and **many rejected or ignored my press releases.**

30. I have attempted to unite members of my family, but it was **to no avail** in some cases.

31. I entered a competition to win a $20,000 business grant for my company, and **my business plan did not win.**

32. For every 5 engagements that I book, **I get 10 rejections** for engagements.

33. I attempted to get my first book picked up by a major publisher, and **it got rejected** at that time.

My friend, you will FAIL YOUR WAY TO SUCCESS!

Each item that I shared, even though it was a negative incident, came at a new level in my life. I wanted to show you some of my iceberg that is under the waterline that most people don't see. **Now, I have had tremendous success in my life, my family, and my business, but it has come at a high price. I felt like giving up HUNDREDS of times, but because I did not and because I trusted my dream and my God, I can stand**

Make Lemonade and Sell it for Profit!

here today to tell you that I am on the track to becoming a self-made millionaire by the time I am 30 years old. Now, because of the lemons I have had, and because of my passion for learning from each lemon, I am selling my lemonade all across the country and it's doing very well. Now that you see a little bit of where I have been, hopefully you can appreciate where I am, and where I am going.

I have the following things to show for my success process, and the party has not even started yet.

- I have a beautiful family with my lovely wife Nova (The Queen).
- I authored 2 books under my belt prior to my 26th birthday.
- I produced 4 CD projects prior to my 26th birthday.
- My wife and I have a beautiful home that is TWICE the size of the one we sold in 2002.
- My family is 100% credit card debt free.
- My business is 100% credit card debt free.
- My company will earn over $150,000 in revenue in 2003.
- I have millionaire mentors that are helping me to achieve my goal of millionaire status by age 30.
- My company just started a new scholarship program for college students.
- I mentor several youth and young adults that are launching businesses and companies.

Make Lemonade and Sell it for Profit!

- I am a dedicated, devoted, Christian Businessman. I am a tither and a giver! I believe in financing the Kingdom (giving to the church).

I don't share any of these great things with you to impress you, because they don't impress me. I only share these things with you to **impress upon you the fact that you can only climb as high as the ladder that you select.** Pick a tall one and just keep climbing. I am about 20% where I want to ultimately be in my life. But, my friend, I am in hot pursuit of my destiny each day. I have come too far to let anybody or anything turn me around. SO HAVE YOU!

Don't allow money (or the lack thereof) to stop you from pursuing your dream. Get started with the little that you have, and watch the rest come your way. Here is a short list of a few things that I did with absolutely no money during the 4 months that I was transitioning from corporate America to my dream of being a full time professional Motivational Speaker, Author, Consultant, and Success Coach.

What I did while FLAT BROKE!

- Conceptually rebuilt my Business
- Recorded 13-tracks for my 1st Motivational CD Project
- Wrote the content for my 1st Book
- Sent out over 400 resumes

Make Lemonade and Sell it for Profit!

· Designed, Built, and Published my own Website
· Increased my ministry commitment at Church
· Got Married
· Read 15 Books

Zig Ziglar says, **"When you do more than you're paid to do, soon the day will come when you are paid more for what you do!"** Success is no respecter of persons, and neither is God. Greatness can happen for anyone who seeks it. I believe that because I was faithful over my dry season in life, that God rewarded me and will continue to reward me many times over. That's why my business is exploding in ways that I could have never thought possible. **You don't have to be great to get started,** but you do have to get started to be great! GO AFTER YOUR DREAM. SNATCH YOUR STUFF BACK.

Okay Del, I think I get it. I know how to make lemonade out of my life story. But once I have done that, how do I "Sell it for Profit?" GREAT QUESTION!

Success is no respecter of persons, and neither is God.

Trust me, my friend. There is a **market** for your **misery**, a **consumer** for your **calamity**, and a **patron** for you **pain**. There is a **client** for your **catastrophe**, and a **patient** for your **problems**. Think about it. One of the biggest

Make Lemonade and Sell it for Profit!

reasons why people drink lemonade is because they are thirsty. They want something in their lives to be quenched. Your story, with all of its up and downs, AND twists and turns - quenches someone's thirst for a successful solution.

> *There are people out there who need to hear how low you went, and how high you have risen as a result.*

There are people out there who need to hear how low you went, and how high you have risen as a result. **My challenge to you is simple** - At least go as high as you went low. As I have mentioned before, engineers say that when the building is going to go really high, they have to dig really low. Many of us have been dug low by life, but please understand this point. **The depth of your past is nothing but an indication of the height of your future.** So what does all of this mean?

If there is a book inside of you, **WRITE IT**. Someone will **buy it**!

If there is a song inside of you, **SING IT**. Someone will **listen to it**!

If there is a company inside of you, **START IT**. Someone will **work for you**!

If there is an invention inside of you, **PATENT IT**. Someone will **use it**!

Make Lemonade and Sell it for Profit!

If there is a movie inside of you, **DIRECT IT**.
Someone will **watch it**!

If there is a role inside of you, **ACT IT**.
Someone will **applaud you**!

If there is a sermon inside of you, **PREACH IT**.
Someone's soul will be **saved because of it**!

If there is an idea inside of you, **WORK IT**.
Someone will **run with it**!

If there is a recipe inside of you, **COOK IT**.
Someone will **eat it**!

If there is a restaurant inside of you, **BUILD IT**!
Someone will **make reservations**!

If there is a course inside of you, **DESIGN IT**!
Someone will **teach it or be taught by it**.

If there is a romantic inside you, **BE IT**!
Someone will be **swept off their feet because of it**!

If there is a piece of real estate inside if you, **BUY IT**!
Someone will want to **buy it from you later**!

If there is a dream life inside you, **LIVE IT**!
Someone will be **touched beyond measure by it**.

Have Mercy!!!!!

Delatorro L. McNeal II

Make Lemonade and Sell it for Profit!

<u>8 Quick Review Points for a New Beginning in your Quest!</u>

1. Take life's lemons, make lemonade, and sell it for profit.

2. **There were only 2 fears credited to your account when you were deposited onto this earth.** They are the fear of falling, and the fear of a loud sound. Every other fear is a learned behavior. If you can learn fear, you can learn faith. So, get up and FAITH YOUR fears to death.

3. Don't throw back the big things in life because of your little resources. **Chop up your big dreams into small pieces and take consistent daily action to see them come true.**

4. Learning is the sugar that provides the sweetness for your lemonade. Whatever you GROW through, learn from it. **Don't dare go through anything without becoming BETTER in the process!**

5. Most obstacles have little to do with you personally, **but have much to do with someone else's success.**

6. **Don't allow others to celebrate your glory (the things you have earned), until they know your story (the things you have learned).**

Make Lemonade and Sell it for Profit!

7. Looking over the totality of your life experiences, you must be able to calculate your successes and failures and resolve that, "IT WAS **WORTH IT!** "

8. There is a market for your misery, a patron for your pain, and a customer for your calamity. Take life's lemons, make your lemonade, and sell it for profit!

Notes:

_____

_____

_____

_____

_____

_____

_____

_____

_____

_____

_____

Make Lemonade and Sell it for Profit!

One of my Favorite Poems
THE ROAD TO SUCCESS
Author Unknown

THE ROAD TO SUCCESS IS NOT STRAIGHT.

THERE IS A CURVE CALLED FAILURE....

A LOOP CALLED CONFUSION...

SPEED BUMPS CALLED FRIENDS...

RED LIGHTS CALLED ENEMIES...

CAUTION LIGHTS CALLED FAMILY.

YOU WILL HAVE FLATS CALLED JOBS, BUT

IF YOU HAVE A SPARE CALLED DETERMINATION...

AN ENGINE CALLED PERSEVERANCE...

INSURANCE CALLED FAITH...

AND

A DRIVER CALLED JESUS...

YOU WILL MAKE IT TO A PLACE CALLED

SUCCESS!

Delatorro L. McNeal II

Notes

Chapter 8

Creating & Seizing Opportunity!

Creating and Seizing Opportunity

Meditate on this quote about greatness. It will bless your life tremendously when you begin to apply it.

"It's a great thing to recognize greatness before greatness is greatly recognized."

~ By Nicole West

Creating and Seizing Opportunity

My friend, we are coming to the end of our journey together. In this final chapter I want to challenge you on one final topic. **I want to make you fully aware of the fact that you have the power to create your future.** Now, that statement sounds very simple on the surface, but it has a tremendous amount of depth in it. Allow me to explain why! You see, many people believe that life is 100% predestined and that everything in life is already planned out; that we are simply walking out steps that have already been laid. In fact, many people of faith believe that God predestined all of life. "And if that is the case", they wonder, "what would be the reward for obedience?" Believing that life is already predetermined for you is a theory that Dr. Mike Murdock says, "Destroys Motivation and Annihilates Ambition." I believe that God predestines the consequences of our choices, but our choices are still up to us.

Everyday, we arise out of bed with Power. This is power to change tomorrow - today. **It is power to do something today that literally changes the way tomorrow looks.** The days of the 1-900 psychics and the mystery behind success

My friend, you possess the Power to Create your Destiny.

and achievement are over. My friend, you possess the Power to Create your Destiny. You have the power to change your life. **You have the power to make tomorrow different from today by doing something**

Delatorro L. McNeal II

Creating and Seizing Opportunity

different today than you did yesterday. TODAY is the middleman between your past and your future. And yesterday will never equal tomorrow as long as today is better than yesterday. In other words, your past will never equal your future as long as your present is greater than your past. Some people have been duped into believing that because they started wrong, they will finish wrong. **I totally disagree because it's not about how you start; it's about HOW YOU FINISH!** And as a result of this book, I want you to finish STRONG!

How do you finish strong? You create and seize every opportunity you can. Everyday, you are blessed with 86,400 opportunities. From a chronological standpoint, we call them seconds. However, each one carries a weight of its own. Think of the many opportunities that come and go each day, such as:

The opportunity to **give**
The opportunity to **receive**

The opportunity **to love**
The opportunity **to dislike**

The opportunity **to choose**
The opportunity **to select**

The opportunity to **go forward**
The opportunity to **go backward**

Creating and Seizing Opportunity

The opportunity to **make A's**
The opportunity to **make F's**

The opportunity to **live**
The opportunity to **die**

The opportunity to **create wealth**
The opportunity to **deplete wealth**

The opportunity to **save**
The opportunity to **spend**

The opportunity to **please customers**
The opportunity to **sell new products**

The opportunity to **increase revenues**
The opportunity to **decrease market share**

The opportunity to **smile**
The opportunity to **frown**

The opportunity to **cook**
The opportunity to **go out to eat**

As you can see, opportunity is all around us every single day. So what separates the good from the great? **It's the ability to not only have opportunities, but to seize the ones you have, CREATE the ones you don't have, and then seize those too!** This one thing is what separates the Men from the Boys, and the Daughters from the Divas.

Creating and Seizing Opportunity

When you die, there will be at least 3 things on your tombstone. The date you were born, a dash, and the date you died. That little dash between your beginning and your ending dates represents 100% opportunity. **So as long as you have breath in your body, you have opportunity. It's just a matter of recognizing it when it exists, and creating it when it does not!**

Opportunity loves to be seized. It loves hugs and it loves work. It hates being ignored. Opportunity is very selfish and picky.

Many people say, "When opportunity knocks, you better be ready!" And I agree with that. But I would like to take that statement a little further because, for many people, the "right opportunity" has not yet come their way. In my opinion, when opportunity is not knocking on your door, it may be because you have not given it an invitation. Invite opportunity over to your house for dinner, and see if it doesn't show up. You see, opportunity loves to be seized. It loves hugs and it loves work. It hates being ignored. **Opportunity is very selfish and picky.** If it does not get the attention it deserves, it will go somewhere else to get it. As John C. Maxwell says, "Opportunity always takes NOW for an answer!" So in truth, my friend, if you don't Rob the Grave of Its Greatness, either the grave will take your stuff or someone else will.

Commercial Break: One of the best movies I have ever seen in my life is *Men of Honor*. In this movie,

Creating and Seizing Opportunity

Cuba Gooding Jr. plays the part of Carl Brashear, a deep-sea navy diver. Against some of the most insurmountable odds, he takes situations that most would consider impossible, and he does the only thing he knows to do. He creates his own opportunities. Watch this movie and it will change your life.

There are two lines in this movie that stir me to tears every time I watch it. The first is when Carl Brashear is approaching a library attendant to tutor him for his diving school exams. After telling her that he only has a 7th grade education, she rudely rejects him by telling him that he will fail regardless of his persistence. He immediately replies by saying that he can't fail and he won't quit. She asks him a simple question - "Why do you want this so badly?" He replies, **"Because they said I couldn't have it!"**

My friend, let me ask you a question. What successful, positive, and empowering dream do you have that others have said you can't have?

Whatever your dream is, my friend, you can achieve it if you want it badly enough!

Delatorre L. McNeal II

Creating and Seizing Opportunity

The second line that I love in the movie is when Carl encounters Master Chief Billie Sunday (played by Robert De Niro) in his sleeping quarters after a successful day of training. Master Chief Sunday informs Brashear that regardless of how well he does on his exams, the captain of the Diving School will not graduate a "colored diver". Brashear and Sunday have a strong-willed disagreement, and Sunday throws Brashear's favorite radio to the ground, smashing it into hundreds of pieces. Then, in a fit of anger, Sunday reaches for something else to throw - Brashear's only picture of his deceased father. Brashear interrupts with a violent scream. Sunday looks at the picture, then back at Brashear, back and forth several times. Finally, he asks a powerful question, "What did he say to you to make you try so hard?" Brashear replied with conviction and passion, **"Be the Best!" Sunday concurred, "Well, you are!"**

Allow me to ask you a second question, "What inspiring words has someone spoken into your life that keep you pressing towards your best in spite of life's lemons?"

_____

_____

_____

The reason that person spoke those words into your life is because they believe in you and they want you

Creating and Seizing Opportunity

to succeed. *Well Del, what if no one has spoken positive words into my life?* GREAT QUESTION. Over the last 8 chapters and including this one, I have been speaking greatness into your life. So if you have never had anyone speak motivational blessings into your life, I am honored to be the first. Now you have no excuse. Be the BEST!

Opportunity Defined

So far, we have talked a great deal about that little word called "opportunity", but we have not yet defined it. I like the way that the American Heritage Dictionary defines opportunity. It defines it as a *set of circumstances providing a chance or possibility*. Let's explore this definition a little closer.

A Set – Opportunities always come as a series of moments to maximize. Opportunity is never a one-hit wonder. Life gives you chance after chance to take advantage of opportunity. So, when looking for opportunity, don't just look at one isolated incident. **Look for a series or set of events in a process that create an open door.**

Of Circumstances – Review this section very carefully because this is where I have created my philosophy on opportunity. You see, most people think that opportunities have to be given by someone or something else. Many people think that opportunity

Creating and Seizing Opportunity

must be showered upon them by a person willing to create a moment in the spotlight for them. Well, this may be one way that opportunity manifests itself, but it's not the only way. Notice that the definition does not say "a set of circumstances created by **someone else**, providing a ...." No, it simply says, "a set of circumstances".

Circumstance is defined as *a condition that determines a course of action*. This means that circumstances can be imposed on a person, or **created by a person** for the ultimate purpose of creating a sequence of action. This does not refer to thought or decision - but ACTION!

Providing a Chance or Possibility – Do you realize that all you need is the right person to see you doing the right thing at the right time for the right reason, and it's all over? But, until that "right person" sees you doing the right thing, watch yourself do the right thing, for the right reasons, and soon you will end up creating a chance or possibility for yourself. Ultimately, my own personal belief system reassures me that **my gift will make room, make space, carve a location for me, and place me before the greatest of the land.** I personally believe that God is the author of all opportunity. I can't put myself in the right place at the right time, without His wisdom, insight, strength, grace, mercy, and divine navigation. So ultimately, Delatorro's help comes from above. But you better believe, I don't wait on others to make me. I make myself. I don't wait for others to celebrate me. celebrate myself. I don't wait for other to speak into my life. I speak over myself. I don't wait for other to accept me, I accept myself. Not because I am independent, but because I understand that there is greatness inside me. **If others see it or not, I SEE IT! If others celebrate it or not, I CELEBRATE IT!**

Again, let's revisit the definition of Opportunity. It is a set of circumstances providing a chance or possibility. I like the way the Chinese define Crisis. In the US, we define crisis as a dangerous opportunity for intense BAD. **However in China, they define Crisis as a dangerous opportunity for intense GOOD or BAD. So, in that definition, crisis can be a positive thing.** Because, many times the greatest businesses were started because someone hit rock bottom, had a dangerous opportunity for intense bad, got tired of being sick and tired, changed their perception of the definition of crisis, and began **to look at their setback as a dangerous opportunity for INTENSE GOOD!** However, regardless of how nice my or American Heritage's definition for opportunity is, the true definition of opportunity in your life is the meaning that you associate with it.

Creating and Seizing Opportunity

<u>Your Opportunity Listing!</u>

In the space below, list the top 10 opportunities that you would want if God granted you any Opportunity Blessing you could imagine.

1._____

2._____

3._____

4._____

5._____

6._____

7._____

8._____

9._____

10._____

If man can't do it, then it must be a God Job!

I am willing to bet that each of the opportunities that you just listed will fall into one of 3 categories. These opportunities will be:

1. Created by God – This means that no one in this world has the power to create the type of supernatural opportunity that you are seeking. **If man can't do it, then it must be a God Job!** It helps to know when an

Creating and Seizing Opportunity

opportunity is 100% out of your direct control because it allows you to focus your energies on things you can control until God answers your prayer. Additional footnote: Once God opens a door, no man can shut it, and once He closes a door, no man can open it. Ultimately, in my opinion, God has the final say when it comes to all three of these categories of opportunities. But, again, it's up to you to take action.

2. Created by Others – This means that someone of influence or affluence has the power to create the opportunity for you. This is very important because now you know what types of mentors and coaches you need to have in your life. Once you have identified an opportunity that another person can help you create, your energy is focused on getting yourself exposed to them, so that they can make a decision to open a door for you. **This is why endorsements, letters of recommendation, testimonials, and references are so important.** These people pinch hit for you and get you into the right circles so that you can begin to grow and develop.

3. Created by You – You have the power to create this opportunity for yourself. This is critical for success. If you want it bad enough, you will make the calls, send the emails, create the website, post the resume, pass out the

God won't ever do for you what you can do for yourself.

Creating and Seizing Opportunity

business cards, network, research, and purposefully place yourself in the right place at the right time. **God won't ever do for you what you can do for yourself.** His job ends at giving you strength, wisdom, and mentors. **Beyond that, it's up to you to MAKE IT HAPPEN! So, if you want to network with successful businessmen and businesswomen, create that opportunity yourself by looking for the next Chamber of Commerce meeting in the local newspaper and attending the meeting as a visitor.** Don't underestimate the power you have to put yourself in the right places on purpose.

7 Quick Truths about The Opportunities you Seek

1. The opportunities you request reveal the gifts you want others to see.
2. The opportunities you request reveal to whom you wish to be assigned.
3. The opportunities you request reveal the motive of your heart.
4. The opportunities you request reveal the unspoken goals you wish to achieve.
5. The opportunities you request reveal the people that need to be in your life.
6. The opportunities you request reveal the type of person you long to become.
7. The opportunities you request reveal the problem you wish to solve for others.

Creating and Seizing Opportunity

The Power of ASKing

Willie Jolley says, ***"Most people ask not, seek not, knock not, and then wonder why not!"*** I love that one. My friend, there is incredible power in asking for the things that you want and need to be successful. You know, a famous person once said, "You have not because you ask not!" We must begin to open our mouths about the things that we really desire in our lives. When you ASK for anything, I believe that you are:

Actively – engaged in hot pursuit
Seeking – looking, researching, requesting
Knowledge – insight, wisdom, truth, and revelation

Many people get disappointed when they don't have the opportunities that other people seem to get. But their action is not consistent with their words. That's why I classify people as three types of bones:

1. Wish Bones – Those who just think about it, want about it, wonder about it, and dream about it.
2. Jaw Bones – Those who just talk about it, converse about it, and gossip about it.
3. Back Bones – Those who get up and DO it. They have enough grit, determination, and fortitude to make things happen for themselves and others.

Which one are you?

Creating and Seizing Opportunity

You've got to be a person of action. In order to Rob the Grave of Its Greatness and be a professional Grave Robber, you must be a person of action. Not just action, but intelligent action.

There are two reasons why people fail.

1. They plan without acting. These people get stuck in the paralysis of analysis. They can never get past planning to pursuing and practicing. **They never get past decision.** Many people think that decision is the end. Mentally it may be, but from a physical standpoint, it's just the beginning. For many years, I planned on making it to the gym three times a week, but it was 2003 when I actually acted consistently with my plan.

2. They act without a plan. These people never take the time to consider their actions or the consequences of them. They just live life by the seat of their pants. This is very dangerous. I am a living witness. I have made many mistakes because I acted without a plan.

Action creates Reaction. So, if you are not experiencing people reacting to you, maybe you should check your action towards those individuals. Determine if you have gotten their attention. Many times, we let our own ignorance get in the way of asking destiny-unlocking questions. Many people say that the dumbest question is the one that you never ask. **Well, I have found one even dumber. It's the question of why you didn't ask the question that you did not**

Creating and Seizing Opportunity

ask! Call me when you figure that one out. Smiles!

Here are seven questions that you should ask yourself anytime you attempt to ask someone for an opportunity that you desire.

1. Does this person really know and understand my interest or desire? Do I understand the role they play in my success?

2. What is the worst that could happen if they say "No"?

3. What is the best that could happen if they say "Yes"?

4. Am I ready to run with the opportunity that this person may give me, if they say yes?

5. How could my life be different if this person blessed me with an opportunity to showcase my gifting?

6. Who is coming up behind me that I could bless with an opportunity once I have gotten on my feet with my dreams?

7. Who else do I need in my life to hold me accountable for maintaining the success that this opportunity will create in my life?

Creating and Seizing Opportunity

Seizing Your Moments!

Having an opportunity is on 50% of the battle!

I want you to give some thought to how you will create and seize the opportunities that you have identified for yourself. What will be your action plan for creating the opportunity and what will be your action plan for seizing the opportunity? You do know the difference, right?

Having an opportunity is only 50% of the battle. Once you get the opportunity, you must be able to maximize, optimize, capitalize, and seize the opportunity that you just got. Many people seek opportunities without doing the internal preparation necessary to maintain what they attain. What a shame. **That's why they say that it's better to be prepared and not have an opportunity, than to have an opportunity and not be prepared.** The reason why this is such a popular phrase is because it stresses the importance of character development. When you are prepared for an opportunity and it does not come when you expect it, it develops your character. And you know that your character creates your destiny. So it's important that you not only pursue opportunity, but also create a plan to master that opportunity once you get it.

Creating and Seizing Opportunity

For example, what a tragedy it would be to work so hard to get your big break (let's say American Idol), only to get in front of millions of people and sound horrible.

For example, what a tragedy to win the lottery – a once in a lifetime financial opportunity - only to be a poor steward of your money and go bankrupt in 3 to 5 years.

Don't be like these people. Prepare! Prepare! Prepare for Greatness! **Prepare for your next level BEFORE you get there.** Don't wait for the ship to be sinking before you create an emergency escape plan. Think ahead of your present situation.

In the space provided, create your action plans for at least 3 major opportunities that you want.

Prepare for your next level BEFORE you get there.

Opportunity #1 _____

Action Steps

1. _____

2. _____

3. _____

Creating and Seizing Opportunity

Opportunity #2 _____

Action Steps

1. _____

2. _____

3. _____

Opportunity #3 _____

Action Steps

1. _____

2. _____

3. _____

> *One of the biggest lessons I have learned is that it DOES NOT MATTER HOW TALENTED YOU ARE.*

TIPS for Seizing Your Opportunity

1. Market Yourself. One of the biggest lessons I have learned is that it DOES NOT MATTER HOW TALENTED YOU ARE. If nobody knows that you are talented, you won't get the exposure necessary to get the opportunities you desire. As I taught you in Chapter 6, get business

Creating and Seizing Opportunity

cards that communicate who you are, not what you do. Make your business cards speak in your absence. Be confident in public by handing your card to each person that you meet. You never know who knows somebody who could BLESS YOUR SOCKS OFF. Therefore, market yourself and tell the world who you are. **Don't assume that your talent alone will get you there. There are people more talented than you and I in prison somewhere! Really! It's true. Talent-for-Talent, there are people living under a bridge someplace who could out speak me, out sing me, and out write me.** However, I can't focus on that. All I can do, and you do the same, is focus on becoming the best that we can be, and playing with the cards that we were dealt. **There is always someone out there more gifted than you, but it's you using your special gift and getting the right person to see it (and support it) that really counts.** Start with business cards and build from there.

2. Be Persistent! This is one of the HARDEST and most humbling tips I can give you. Some people are just naturally gifted with the ability to be persistent. Others, like myself, have to work at it. I know people who won't give up no matter how much abuse they take. Persistence is a very tricky tactic. **There is a fine line between being persistent and being out of season and timing.** There is a spiritual principle that says that there is a time and a season for everything under the Son. And it's important to understand that even though we may want things really badly, being

Creating and Seizing Opportunity

persistent is not always the right weapon to use. Sometimes, being wise about discerning the season that you are in is a better weapon.

Let me give you an example. In the late part of 2002, I was wanted to buy a new laptop for my business. The one I wanted had a price tag of about $2,500. I really wanted and needed it for my business, so I applied for credit to finance it, but I was declined. I could not figure out why. So as I left the store, I told God, "Okay Lord, you know I need a laptop, so if you won't let me finance it, create a way for me to pay for it 100% cash!" About 2 weeks later, I did an event that generated exactly $2,500 dollars to invest into my new laptop. I was very excited about buying the laptop cash, until I talked with two of my millionaire mentors. They both reminded me that I had exactly $2,500 in credit card debt left to pay off in order for myself and my family to be 100% credit card debt free. They encouraged me to put the whole thing towards that debt because that was the SEASON I was in at the time - a debt elimination season. And they were right! Did I hate it? YES! Was I a little disappointed? YES! But I am so glad I waited, and did not use the weapon of persistence in that instance! Why? Because I used the first $2,500 to pay off that debt, and then within a week of me doing that, a door opened up for me to buy the laptop, cheaper than the original price point and with more features! I paid for it in FULL with CASH. Now, that may not be a big deal to you, but for me that was huge!

Creating and Seizing Opportunity

Persistence has its place. I can tell you a story about how I got $3,500 for a speaking engagement that I only got because I was persistent. Had I not been, people would have mislead me with tricky policies and I would have missed out on $3,500. But because I knew that I was being taken advantage of, I pulled out all the guns and got the right people fighting for me, and got PAID! *Men of Honor* is a true movie about a man with an Uncommon Gift of Persistence. You can learn a great deal from it. Add this movie to your motivational DVD collection. **So in short, go after what you deserve, be sensitive and obedient to the seasons of your life, and when the right time comes, push the envelope until you get what you deserve.** Don't allow others to run you over. Most people have to say NO, 7 times before they say YES! Keep going after your dream, using ANY POSITIVE MEANS NECESSARY. The key word is positive. **Persistence is a powerful weapon, but so is patience! Use both in proper season and you will be massively successful.**

3. Be Very Proactive! Think ahead. Think beyond today. Work today, but envision tomorrow. Action will take place whether you want it to or not. Either life will act on you, or you can act on life. **I prefer to act on life, and make life react to my action. I don't want to be on the short, "reacting" end of the stick.** Why? Because that puts me on the defensive instead of the offensive. If you are going to be a professional Grave Robber you must learn to be proactive. Start

Creating and Seizing Opportunity

taking your stuff back NOW! I don't care how young you are, and I don't care how old you are either - NONE OF US is promised tomorrow. Each day we are blessed to live is ONLY because our Creator thought enough of us to bless us with a piece of the Future, and deposit it into our chronological bank account called the Present. That's why they call it the present, because it's a gift! USE YOUR STUFF. Remember action creates reaction. I remember hearing of a businesswoman who complained about the fact that she was not getting any phone calls about her business. A speaker friend of mine asked her a simple question, "Do you have a listing in the phone book?" She said no! She was not proactive with her marketing, therefore her business suffered. Think ahead of the game, think ahead of your customer, think ahead of your professor, think ahead of your spouse, and think ahead of your family and friends. Not to be cocky or show how much you think you know, but to set up opportunities to bless people with your creativity and thoughtfulness.

4. Create Your 30-second Commercial! Your first impression is critical. Small talk can create HUGE opportunities. For this reason, you need to create and utilize your 30-second commercial. This is exactly what it sounds like. It is a statement of introduction of yourself to anyone you meet. Within 30 seconds you need to be able to let people know who you are, why you are, and how knowing you will bless their lives at some point in the future. You need to make it simple, yet impactful. It needs to be 100% real and from the

Creating and Seizing Opportunity

heart. It needs to be accompanied by a firm handshake, a business card exchange, a big smile, and engaging eye contact. You should practice this commercial in front of your family, friends, mentors, and trusted colleagues. Once you perfect it, start attending networking functions to try it out. Tweak it as necessary. Most of all, create a common way of introducing yourself to people so that you can make a powerful lasting impression. Never judge how powerful someone is based upon how they are dressed. **I know millionaires who dress like bums, and I know people who look like a million dollars, but are as broke as a joke.** So don't be over impressed with people, but be inspired and motivated to allow your connections with people to be divine setups for greatness to be born.

5. Hold Your Tongue until the Right Time! Reduce the number of enemies you will face by shutting up about your larger and more profitable opportunities until they come to pass. When you announce your success too early, you allow enemies to form and if they do so strong enough, they can attempt to stop you from moving forward. **I am a strong believer that the only major people that need to know about your dreams and big opportunities are those who deserve access to that information because they have proven faithful and committed to your success.**

True success leaves footprints.

Delatorro L. McNeal II

Creating and Seizing Opportunity

Divine connections come through your willingness to serve.

I am also a strong believer that once your success has reached a level where it is unstoppable, you should shout it from the rooftops. You need to let everyone know how blessed you are. Why? Because people need to hear about your success so that they too can become successes. **True success leaves footprints.** Don't cover yours up trying to throw people off the path of following your success. That is selfish and stingy. Leave your tracks in the sand, and help people take the steps you have taken. But again, be very careful who you open your mouth to. Make sure that those you tell will build your dream, and not try to destroy it.

6. Invest in Other's Visions! Some of my biggest mentorship relationships have developed out of me placing myself in the position of a servant. I met Les Brown because I was willing to serve him and his staff when he came to town 2 years ago. I met Willie Jolley because, again, I was willing to serve him and his staff when they came to town. I met Steven Covey, Bishop T.D Jakes, Zig Ziglar, Fred Hammond, Maya Angelou, and several others because I put myself in a position to serve these people when they came into my hometown or college town. I met the greatest mentors of my college career, Dr. Lee Jones and Dr. Naim Akbar because of my willingness to serve their visions. I am telling you the truth. Divine connections come through your willingness to serve. I believe in a powerful principle that says that what you make happen for others, God will make happen for you. So, when I help other people with conferences, I am setting myself up for other people to help me with my conferences. **When I sell someone else's books and products, I am creating an opportunity for someone to sell my stuff in the future.** It's the same powerful boomerang principle that I shared with you in Chapter 6. We always hear the motivational phrase, "Make it Happen!" Well, with this action step, I want you to **"Make it Happen...For Someone Else!"** It seems kind of odd, but you will be amazed at what happens and what you learn when you serve someone else's vision.

Don't half bake your dreams and goals, trying to live DOWN to other people's low expectations of what they think you should produce with your life.

7. Be Radical! Think outside the box! Dream like a fool, and go for the big stuff. You don't have time for the little stuff. Be a little outrageous - it's okay. As my mentor Pastor Scott Thomas would say, **"LIVE LIFE LOUD!"** What he means by this is simple. So many people go through life soft spoken, soft visioned, soft willed, soft communicated, and soft activated. The problem with this approach is that nobody can hear them. Some people need to turn up the volume. Maybe you do! **Let people hear you living this thing called life. If you are going to go for it, then stop sticking your toes in the water, because**

Creating and Seizing Opportunity

that is not living life loud. Go ahead, and jump in with both feet. If you are going to put your heart into something, put it in all the way. Don't half-do life. Don't half bake your dreams and goals, trying to live DOWN to other people's low expectations of what they think you should produce with your life. GARBAGE! Turn up the volume of your **dreams**, the volume of **your smiles**, the volume of **your pursuit of the things you want**, the volume of **your willingness to pay the price**, and the volume of your **focus and commitment** to seeing a task all the way through to completion. Sometimes the best opportunities come to those who are radical enough to take a step out on what "appears" to be nothing, only to land on everything that they need to be successful. Wow!

8. Be Prepared! Get READY! Get SET! Practice! Use every small opportunity that you can to get prepared. **Preparation is what I call the lonely work.** It's the stuff that the world never sees. It's the stuff that makes men and women great. Prepare yourself for greatness. **Prepare your heart.** Make sure that your motives for why you do what you do are clear and pure. **Prepare your mind.** Make sure you delete any negative self-running programs that keep you feeling self-defeated, and that you reinstall new software that empowers you to prosper and succeed. **Prepare your wallet.** Work on

Remember, preparation is the lonely work towards an opportunity that you currently do not have.

Creating and Seizing Opportunity

eliminating high amounts of unsecured and revolving debt. It's a financial slave institution. Set up bank accounts for the opportunities that you want. You will need money to fund your vision. Use every opportunity to practice your gifting because opportunities come in two forms -**Expected and Unexpected.** Sometimes they call and tell you that they are coming over for dinner. Other times they just show up, and if you can't accommodate them, they go to someone else's house to eat.

Before you go opening your mouth asking for opportunities, make sure that you are **ready to seize them once you get them.** Remember, preparation is the lonely work towards an opportunity that you currently do not have. I prepared for you to read this book, this chapter, this page, and this sentence far before I ever met you. I am so glad that I did! You are a special, destined, and unique individual and I am committed to providing motivational products, events, and media that will empower you to possess the land that you have already been given.

9. Create Your Day Each Day! Again, this is one of the most powerful concepts you should have down to a science by now. It's your ability to create the day that you want, each and every day of your life. Use each day, each

Nobody can make you feel less than you're worth without your permission.

Creating and Seizing Opportunity

hour, and each minute to seize your opportunity for greatness. **Don't let these daily moments pass you by because of your false assumption that you are on direct deposit and your days are promised to you, because they are not.** My friend, you have the power to determine how your day goes. No, you will not be able to control 100% of the things that happen to you, but you can control the way you react and respond to the things that happen to you. Nobody can make you feel less than you're worth without your permission. So take your stuff back. Take back your joy and happiness throughout the day. Get off of that stupid bandwagon that says that Mondays are bad! Garbage! Create a new association that says that each day is awesome regardless of the weather, because if you keep sunshine in your heart, the outside weather can do you no harm. **Create the type of meetings you want, create the type of car ride you want, create type of work environment you want, create the type of screensavers you want, and create the types of conversations you want to have.** When I want to create a spiritual environment, I know who to call. When I want to create a business environment, I know who to call. When I want to create a humorous environment, I know who to call.

Create your world and take it with you, but PLEASE make it Positive. **Chose to be happy, chose to have joy, chose to have peace, chose to keep a prayerful heart, chose to do random acts of kindness, chose to email people back in a timely manner, and chose**

Creating and Seizing Opportunity

to be polite to telemarketers that are just doing their job. You have the power of choice. Chose wisely, and the opportunities you seek will soon seek you!

8 Quick Review Points for a New Beginning in your Quest!

1. Remember, it is a great thing to celebrate greatness before greatness is greatly celebrated. **Always take the time to encourage the greatness in others.** You can't shower this type of appreciation on others without getting some on yourself.

2. Opportunity is defined as a set of circumstances providing a chance or possibility. **Many times, you have to create the circumstances you want, because life will not just hand them to you.**

3. There are 3 types of Opportunities - **those created by God, those created by Others, and those created by You.** Maximize each one, and use them all as allies to help you Rob the Grave of all your stuff.

4. Never be afraid to ask. When you A.S.K., you are Actively Seeking Knowledge. **But remember, knowledge alone is NOT power! Applied knowledge is power!**

5. Having an opportunity is only 50% of the battle. Seizing the opportunity and using that as a seed for

Creating and Seizing Opportunity

future opportunities is the other 50% of the battle. But you can do it!

6. Preparation is the lonely work towards an opportunity that currently does not exist. **Be prepared, because opportunity shows up only at two times - when you expect it, and when you don't.**

7. **You will miss 100% of the opportunities that you don't take.** So step out of the boat, think out of the box, and LIVE LIFE LOUD! Go for it!

8. Be sensitive to the timings and the seasons of your life. **Turbo-charge your destiny through servanthood.** The opportunity you help create for another, will soon be made available for you!

Notes:

_____

_____

_____

_____

_____

_____

_____

Creating and Seizing Opportunity

One of my Favorite Poems
The Race – by D. H. Groberg

"Quit! Give up! You're beaten!"
They shout at me and plead.
"There's just too much against you now.
This time you can't succeed!"

And as I start to hang my head
In front of failure's face
My downward fall is broken by
The memory of a race.

And here refills my weakened will
As I recall that scene
For just the thought of that short race
Rejuvenates my being.

A children's race: Young boys, young men
How I remember well.
Excitement, sure! But also fear.
It wasn't hard to tell.

They all lined up so full of hope
Each thought to win that race.
Or tie for first, or if not that
At least take second place.

And fathers watched from off the side
Each cheering for his son
And each boy hoped to show his dad

Creating and Seizing Opportunity

That he would be the one.

The whistle blew and off they went
Their hearts and hopes afire.
To win and be the hero there
Was each young boy's desire.

And one boy in particular
whose dad was in the crowd
Was running near the lead and thought:
"My dad will be so proud."

But as they speeded down the field
Across a shallow dip
The little boy who thought to win
Lost his step and slipped.
Trying hard to catch himself
His hand flew out to brace
And 'mid the laughter of the crowd
He fell flat on his face.

So down he fell and with him hope
— He couldn't win it now —
Embarrassed, sad, he only wished
To disappear somehow.

But as he fell his dad stood up
And showed his anxious face
Which to the boy so clearly said:
"Get up and win the race."

He quickly rose, no damage done.

Creating and Seizing Opportunity

— Behind a bit that's all —
And ran with all his mind and might
To make up for his fall.

So anxious to restore himself
— To catch up and to win —
His mind went faster than his legs:
He slipped and fell again!

He wished then he had quit before
With only one disgrace
"I'm hopeless as a runner, now;
I shouldn't try to race."

But in the laughing crowd he searched
And found his father's face.
That steady look which said again:
"Get up and win the race."

So up he jumped to try again
— Ten yards behind the last —
"If I'm to gain those yards," he thought
"I've got to move real fast."

Exerting everything he had
He regained eight of ten
But trying so hard to catch the lead
He slipped and fell again!

Defeat! He lay there silently
— A tear dropped form his eye —
"There's no sense in running anymore"

Creating and Seizing Opportunity

"Three strikes; I'm out; Why try?"

The will to rise had disappeared
All hope had fled away
So far behind; so error prone
A loser all the way.

"I've lost, so what's the use," he thought
"I'll live with my disgrace"
But then he thought about his dad
Who soon he'd have to face.

"Get up" an echo sounded low
"Get up and take your place,
You were not meant for failure here
Get up and win the race."

"With borrowed will get up," it said
"You haven't lost at all
For winning is no more than this:
To rise each time you fall."

So up he rose to run once more
And with a new commit
He resolved that win or lose
At least he wouldn't quit.

So far behind the others now
— The most he'd ever been —
Still he gave it all he had
And ran as though to win.

Delatorro L. McNeal II

Creating and Seizing Opportunity

Three times he's fallen, stumbling,
Three times he rose again
Too far behind to hope to win
He still ran to the end

They cheered the winning runner
As he crossed the line first place
Head high, and proud, and happy
No falling; no disgrace.

But when the fallen youngster
Crossed the line last place
The crowd gave him the greater cheer
For finishing the race.

And even though he came in last
With head bowed low, unproud,
You would have thought he won the race
To listen to the crowd.

And to his dad he sadly said
"I didn't do so well,"
"To me, you won," his father said
"You rose each time you fell."

And now when things seem dark and hard
And difficult to face
The memory of that little boy
Helps me in my race.

For all of life is like that race
With ups and downs and all

Creating and Seizing Opportunity

And all you have to do to win
Is rise each time you fall.

"Quit! Give up! You're beaten!"
They still shout in my face.
But another voice within me says:
"Get up and win the race!"

Creating and Seizing Opportunity

The Official License to Rob!

On _____(date) of _____(year),
A Noval Idea, Inc. would like to officially bestow
the honor of Graduate Par Excellence to
_____(your name) for completing
this book *Robbing the Grave of Its Greatness*! You
are now hereby armed with the tools necessary to
take daily consistent action steps towards
committing the greatest, most positive, most
empowering, most life-changing, nation-shaking,
territory-gaining, legacy-leaving, paradigm-shifting
crime of the century.

You my friend are now an
Officially Licensed GRAVE ROBBER!

Now, move beyond just reading this book. Use this
book as your secret weapon to snatch everything
that belongs to you and yours from the grips of the
Grave that wants to keep them.
Your mission, if you choose to accept it.....

LIVE FULL & DIE COMPLETELY EMPTY!
IT'S ALL OR NOTHING...
GIVE YOUR EVERYTHING!
Goodness is free, but Greatness will cost you!
YOU ARE NOW READY TO PAY THE PRICE!

Jabez Blessings Upon You!
The Greatness Guy

Creating and Seizing Opportunity

Empowered Closing Thoughts!

My friend, this is not the end. It is simply the beginning. Thank you for taking this journey with me. It has been my honor to escort you down the corridors of my heart, mind, and soul over the past few moments that you have read this book. I want you to know something special. **This book is a dream come true for me.** Birthing it was like giving birth to a real child. Many nights, I went to bed extra late, with my fingers and forearms killing me from typing. But, I want you to know something. I wrote this book for you. I typed every word. Not a ghostwriter, not a transcriber. There's nothing wrong with those methods, but I think that there is something very special about you getting the best of me. I believe that there is something special about me penning each word that entered your heart and mind. **This book is beyond me. I believe that it is bestseller quality. Whether the world ever recognizes that or not, I recognize it for myself.**

I want to personally thank you for walking with me through this journey and I pray that God blesses your life beyond belief with all of the things that you will begin to implement as a result of reading this book. I thank you for your greatness. Even though I know that God has more for me to do, if He were to take me now, I would be satisfied that I robbed the grave of my stuff before it got my body! Smiles. **You reading this book is good, but you living this book is GREAT. It will cost you, but pay the toll and enter the**

Delatorro L. McNeal II

Creating and Seizing Opportunity

abundant life of GREATNESS! You deserve the very best. Why Settle?

SNATCHING MY STUFF DAILY,

Delatorro C. McNeal, II
Professional Grave Robber

Notes:

_____

_____

_____

_____

_____

_____

_____

_____

_____

_____

Notes

About the Author

Delatorro L. McNeal, II is the CEO and Founder of A Noval Idea, Inc. and a professional Motivational Speaker, Author, Performance Consultant, and Success Coach. Affectionately known as "The Greatness Guy" he takes audiences across the country by storm with this powerful, practical, and prolific keynotes and seminars centered around is mantra, "Goodness is free, but Greatness will cost you! Are you ready to pay the price?"

In his travels Delatorro speaks to corporations, colleges, professional associations, churches, schools, conferences, and conventions. He empowers professionals, entrepreneurs, students, staff, administrators, and youth to become all that they were divinely-designed to be.

An honor graduate with B.S. and M.S. degrees from Florida State University, Delatorro resides in Tampa, Florida with his lovely wife Nova.